Group Processes
and
Intergroup
Relations

REVIEW OF PERSONALITY AND SOCIAL PSYCHOLOGY

Editor: Clyde Hendrick, *Texas Tech University*

Associate Editors:
Susan T. Fiske, *University of Massachusetts*
John H. Harvey, *University of Iowa*
Richard P. McGlynn, *Texas Tech University*
Walter G. Stephan, *New Mexico State University*

Editorial Board

Group Processes and Intergroup Relations

Editor
CLYDE HENDRICK

9
REVIEW of PERSONALITY and SOCIAL PSYCHOLOGY

Published in cooperation with the Society for Personality and Social Psychology
(Division 8 of the American Psychological Association)

SAGE PUBLICATIONS
The Publishers of Professional Social Science
Newbury Park   Beverly Hills   London   New Delhi

For information address:

SAGE Publications, Inc.
2111 West Hillcrest Drive
Newbury Park, California 91320

SAGE Publications Inc.	SAGE Publications Ltd.
275 South Beverly Drive	28 Banner Street
Beverly Hills	London EC1Y 8QE
California 90212	England

SAGE PUBLICATIONS India Pvt. Ltd.
M-32 Market
Greater Kailash I
New Delhi 110 048 India

Printed in the United States of America

International Standard Book Number 0-8039-3090-9
0-8039-3091-7 (pbk.)

International Standard Series Number 0270-1987

FIRST PRINTING

CONTENTS

Editor's Introduction

GROUP PROCESSES AND INTERGROUP RELATIONS

CLYDE HENDRICK

Clyde Hendrick is Professor of Psychology and Dean of the Graduate School at Texas Tech University. He was previously Chairperson of Psychology, University of Miami. His scholarly interests include close relationships, sex roles, and philosophy of science. He has served as Editor for *Personality and Social Psychology Bulletin* and as Acting Editor for *Journal of Personality and Social Psychology.*

Whatever happened to the group in social psychology? Ivan Steiner (1974) posed this question within the context of describing changes in research traditions within social psychology. Several other commentators also noted that the strong emphasis on group research in the 1940s and 1950s had given way to research on individual attitudes, motives, and cognitions in the 1960s. In general, the study of group processes was largely replaced by the study of individual processes. The 1970s saw the full flowering of the "cognitive revolution," and, if anything, the focus on individual processes became even more extreme.

Steiner predicted that the group would rise again, probably in the late 1970s. The prediction, though perhaps delayed by about five years, appears to be in the process of validation. The study of group processes is experiencing a strong resurgence of interest, coming to clear public fruition in the current duo of volumes of the Review (Vols. 8 and 9).

The call for chapter proposals for Volume 8 was advertised broadly. Over forty proposals were received. It was clear that at least two fine volumes could be produced. After hurried consultation among the Editor, members of the Publications Committee of Division 8, and the

EDITOR'S NOTE: In addition to members of the Editorial Board who reviewed chapters, I am indebted to the following individuals for their reviews of one or more chapters: Jeanne M. Brett, Stuart Cook, Howard S. Friedman, Connie Gersick, J. Richard Hackman, Stephen G. Harkins, David Johnson, Marianne LaFrance, Norman Miller, Brian Mullen, David Myers, Jerrold M. Post, Alan Sillars, Abraham Wandersman, David A. Wilder, and Jane Winer. I am also grateful to Charles T. Hendrix, Executive Editor of Sage Publications, for his friendly cooperation in making possible two volumes on group processes and intergroup relations.

Executive Editor of Sage, the decision was made to go forward with the two-volume set. The result was twenty chapters, forming Volumes 8 and 9. A great variety of topics is covered in these volumes. From the perspective of an editor, group processes as a field of endeavor now shows amazing vitality after being moribund for a quarter-century. A large measure of credit for this revitalization must go to our European colleagues, especially Tajfel, Moscovici, and their respective collaborators.

The rationale for allocation of the twenty chapters into the volumes resulted from the chapters' contents and the Editor's intuition. An attempt at justification could be made, but it is expected that each volume will stand on its own merits, thereby foreclosing the need for such justification.

OVERVIEW OF CHAPTERS: VOLUME 9

Of the 20 chapters constituting Volumes 8 and 9, only 2 are concerned with intergroup relations in ongoing social life. Chapter 1, by Walter Stephan, provides an excellent historical review of the contact hypothesis in intergroup relations. He shows that the original hypothesis focused solely on attitude (or prejudice) as a function of situational factors and initial attitude. Stephan reconceptualizes the contact hypothesis so that person, situational, and societal antecedents are included, and traces the effects of this broad set of variables on individuals and (ultimately) society. Stephan makes the valuable point that so much effort has been expended on variables that can affect the outcomes of contact, that researchers have neglected the (unknown) few factors that may be critically important for contact to improve intergroup relations. This integrative chapter should stimulate further research on the effects of intergroup contact.

Chapter 2, by Miller and Davidson-Podgorny, deals with a specific aspect of intergroup contact, the effects of cooperative learning teams in desegregated school settings. Several strategies have been used in school settings to reduce ethnic prejudice, and the authors discuss several team learning interventions that have been attempted. Three conceptual approaches to intergroup relations, called the expectation state, ignorance, and social categorization models, are compared and implications drawn for structuring cooperative interactions. Empirical consequences of these implications are assessed by a meta-analysis of 21 published studies with respect to six variables. This chapter is a nice example of conceptual analysis and empirical exploration of the effects of group contact in learning situations.

The remainder of the chapters cover a wide variety of topics in the realm of group processes. Chapter 3, by Paulus and Nagar, considers the effects of the environment on social interaction and group development. The chapter is a good review of environmental psychology as it relates to social interaction. The authors note that environmental variables can promote group cohesion and sense of community, as well as negative group interactions and social avoidance. The authors propose a transactional model of the individual/environment that they consider more useful than an interactive model. The transactional model stimulates several interesting questions. How do individuals self-select environments? How do individuals interact with and change their environments? How does changing an environment affect and possibly change the individual? Why do some individuals stay in a given environment while others exit from it? These questions represent only a sample, but they are sufficient to indicate the fertility of the transactional perspective in suggesting significant research.

The important area of personality is represented in Chapter 4, by Driskell, Hogan, and Salas, who deal with the intersection of individual personality with group performance. The general problem is practically important, namely, whether the mix of individuals in a group matters with respect to group productivity. The authors review previous research and note problems with it. They then specify a general model for group performance and define six broad dimensions of personality. Next, a scheme for task classification is adopted. Finally, the six dimensions are cross-classified with the classification of tasks, suggesting a personality profile for each task type. Several hypotheses are proposed concerning the effectiveness of personality dimensions for task types. The chapter is interesting and will hopefully stimulate detailed empirical work.

Chapter 5, by Tickle-Degnen and Rosenthal, is at first glance out of place in a volume on group processes. The authors analyze the concept of rapport and develop its usefulness for group interactions. In fact, the chapter is most valuable as a different way of viewing group processes. The authors describe the various meanings of rapport and link the concept to nonverbal behavior. The argument is developed that nonverbal behavior may be viewed as a determinant, indicator, and consequence of the level of rapport within an interaction. There are several methodological suggestions for future research, especially for issues of direct experience versus observation of rapport, and for temporal aspects of rapport via nonverbal behavior. This chapter is a valuable beginning.

Chapter 6, by Bodenhausen, Gaelick, and Wyer, develops a model of communication processes for love and hostility. The model was developed for dyadic communication in heterosexual couples. Conceptual elements in the model include intent of the sender, receiver's perception/reaction to sender's intent, sender's expectancy concerning receiver's reaction, and perception of how the receiver actually reacted. These elements are combined in a simple mathematical model that is quite powerful in predicting the effects of different kinds of sequences of affective communications. Of particular interest for this volume is the fact that the authors extrapolate the dyadic model to larger aggregations. In particular, the model is applied to interactions between nations. The model certainly has the capability to stimulate much research.

Chapters 7 and 8 deal with topics that several years ago would have been collectively gathered under the rubric of "social facilitation." Chapter 7, by Harkins and Szymanski, compares two areas of research usually treated separately, social facilitation and social loafing. Social facilitation research suggests that coaction will enhance performance, relative to individuals' performances. Social loafing research suggests that the group will produce a performance decrement, relative to individuals' performances. The authors argue that these two research traditions are actually complementary. In loafing research, subjects' efforts are pooled; in coaction research, individual subjects' efforts remain knowable. The possibility of linking evaluation of performance to the individual may be a critical variable. While it is clear that evaluation is a critical variable, their review of the facilitation and loafing literatures suggests that there is considerable ambiguity concerning which of the potential sources of evaluation available in these settings (the experimenter, the coparticipant, the self) mediate(s) these effects. The authors then go on to describe research on the effects of the potential for self-evaluation that demonstrates one way to attack problems posed by previous research in which the effects of these sources have been confounded.

Chapter 8, by Mullen and Baumeister, takes a different approach via self-attention theory. The mechanism of the Other-Total ratio is presumed to vary degree of self-attention, in analogy to figure-ground in perception. Loafing, facilitation, and impairment are explained in terms of the interaction of self-attention caused by group composition and a family of moderator variables. Three types of impairment are described: diving, withdrawing, and choking. The authors consider the implications of the self-attention perspective for social applications. Chapters 7 and 8 combined suggest a strong renewed interest in an old area of research.

Chapter 9, by Ancona, provides a valuable perspective on group processes from the vantage point of an organizational theorist. Traditional research on groups focuses inward on the ongoing dynamics of the group. An external perspective includes the transactions of a group with its wider environment. The level of analysis of this approach is the group per se, usually within the context of a larger organization, and especially the group's adaptation to environmental constraints. The external perspective borrows concepts from areas such as population ecology. This approach also provides a possible new avenue to issues of group processes, such as group development and decision making. A group must evolve not only in terms of internal problems of authority and intimacy, but also in terms of external pressures and resources. The external perspective provides a means to force us to enlarge our conceptual net for group processes. Ultimately, we may develop more effective theories and research programs for small groups by using such encompassing perspectives from organizational research. This chapter should therefore be of value for all small group researchers.

Chapter 10, by McCauley and Segal, provides an excellent analysis of terrorism from a social psychological perspective. Data reviewed indicate that terrorism is not a function of individual psychopathology. Terrorism appears to be the outcome of traditional vehicles of group dynamics. The operation of terrorist groups is very difficult to study directly. The authors provide parallels to terrorist group socialization through analysis of religious cults, the group opinion extremity shift, and obedience to authority. These analogues provide a beginning basis for understanding an important and growing phenomenon of the modern world. This timely chapter makes fascinating reading.

CONCLUSIONS

The chapters in this volume are in some respects more varied in topical coverage than the chapters in Volume 8. However, both volumes touch upon nearly all issues in group processes that are of current research interest. It seems clear that Steiner's prediction that the group would rise again has come true.

REFERENCE

Steiner, I. D. (1974). Whatever happened to the group in social psychology? *Journal of Experimental Social Psychology, 10,* 94-108.

1

The Contact Hypothesis in Intergroup Relations

WALTER G. STEPHAN

Walter G. Stephan is Professor of Psychology at New Mexico State University. He specializes in the study of intergroup relations. He has published a chapter on this topic in the *Handbook of Social Psychology* and he is coauthor with Cookie Stephan of *Two Social Psychologies,* a text integrating the sociological and psychological approaches to social psychology.

Under certain circumstances desegregation . . . has been observed to lead to the emergence of more favorable attitudes and friendlier relations between the races. . . . There is less likelihood of unfriendly relations when change is simultaneously introduced into all units of a social institution. . . . The available evidence also suggests the importance of consistent and firm enforcement of the new policy by those in authority. It indicates also the importance of such factors as: the absence of competition. . . the possibility of contacts which permit individuals to learn about one another as individuals; and the possibility of equivalence of positions and funcitons among all the participants. (F. H. Allport and 35 cosigners, 1953, pp. 437-438)

Prejudice (unless deeply rooted in the character structure of the individual) may be reduced by equal status contact between majority and minority groups in the pursuit of common goals. The effect is greatly enhanced if this contact is sanctioned by institutional supports (i.e., by law, custom, or local atmosphere), and if it is of the sort that leads to the perception of common interests and common humanity between the members of the two groups. (G. W. Allport, 1954, p. 267)

When social scientists turned their thoughts homeward after World War II, they confronted one of the major domestic issues of our times— the relations between the races. From the attention devoted to this issue, the contact hypothesis was born. The initial versions, such as those of

AUTHOR'S NOTE: The author wishes to thank Cookie Stephan, Clyde Hendrick, Susan Hendrick, and Norman Miller for their comments on earlier versions of this article.

Gordon Allport (1954), Robin Williams, Jr. (1947), Goodwin Watson (1947), and the framers of the social science brief in the *Brown* (1954) desegregation case (F. H. Allport et al., 1953), focused primarily on the effects of factors within the contact situation on subsequent prejudice.

Prejudice was regarded as irrational and morally wrong, and the task of social scientists was to design means of eliminating it (Harding, Kutner, Proshansky, & Chein, 1954). The emphasis on prejudice in the original contact models was most likely due to the belief that attitudes cause behavior. Thus changing prejudice was expected to change relevant behaviors. The contact hypothesis was oriented toward the future. It was relatively unconcerned with the historical causes of poor intergroup relations. The problem-solving orientation of the researchers led them to be interested in variables that could be controlled. They were less concerned with societal and person factors not subject to situational control. Also, they were less concerned with the person factors that mediated improvements than with the situational factors that would bring about improved intergroup relations. Further, the contact hypothesis was more oriented toward changing the prejudices of individuals in small group settings, such as might occur in schools, neighborhoods, or workplaces, than in improving relations between groups as entities.

One of my goals in this chapter is to trace the growth of the contact hypothesis during the last 40 years. I will present the underlying conceptual models that have guided the contact hypothesis over the years. I will also outline the gaps in our knowledge of the causes and consequences of contact and I will highlight some of the specific problem areas where further research would be beneficial.

CONCEPTUAL MODELS UNDERLYING THE CONTACT HYPOTHESIS

The situational variables central to the early formulations of the contact hypothesis included equal status among the participants (Riordan, 1978; Robinson & Preston, 1976), cooperative interaction (Johnson, Johnson, & Maruyama, 1984; Worchel, 1986), institutional support for the contact (Adlerfer, 1982; Cohen, 1980; Williams, 1977), and relatively high levels of intimacy (Amir, 1976; Brown & Turner, 1981). Both Williams and Allport stated that factors within the person play a role in influencing the outcomes of contact, but the only person factor explicitly mentioned in these discussion was the initial intergroup attitudes of the participants.

The initial conceptual model of the contact hypothesis was similar to the classic Lewinian model in which behavior was thought to be a function of the person and the environment (B equals f(P + E)). However, early statements of the contact hypothesis focused on attitudes (A), rather than behavior. Also, the only person variable included was the initial attitudes (A'). Thus the model for the original contact hypothesis was:

$$A = f(A' + E).$$

In the robustness of its youth, the contact hypothesis aspired to the role of dragon slayer. The Amicus brief in the *Brown* case (1954) concluded with the version of the contact hypothesis quoted above (F. H. Allport et al., 1953). The impact of this brief on the Supreme Court's decision is still being debated, most recently by Harold Gerard and Stuart Cook (Cook, 1978, 1984, 1985; Gerard, 1983). Gerard argued that the social scientists misled the Court and should have foreseen that desegregation would require means such as busing and that it would occur in places where favorable conditions for contact did not exist (e.g., the North). Cook replied that the social scientists were not asked to address the outcomes of contact under circumstances in which busing might be required and that when the conditions favorable to positive outcomes exist, race relations do improve. I will return to this issue later.

What is not an issue for debate is that the contact hypothesis languished after its turbulent youth until the 1960s, when Stuart Cook added several new situational factors (Cook, 1962), including stereotyping disconfirmation, close physical proximity, and high similarity among the participants (on demographic characteristics, values, and personality traits). Cook also added a new factor not easily categorized in terms of either the situation or the person. He suggested that the norms and attitudes held by other in-group members toward intergroup contact would also affect the outcomes of contact. In referring to the larger context in which the contact occurs, Cook was dealing with a new domain of variables, societal factors.

Also in the 1960s, Secord and Backman (1964) discussed another societal factor, the role relationships between the participants in an intergroup interaction. They cited studies indicating that when minority group members occupied roles that created expectancies and behavior incompatible with their minority status, prejudice decreased (e.g., Harding & Hogrefe, 1952; Minard, 1952). Consistent with Cook's suggestion regarding the importance of the norms and attitudes of in-group members, Secord and Backman argued that when the central values of the society favored intergroup contact, positive intergroup relations tended to prevail (see also, Williams, 1964).

The revised model that emerged from a consideration of these social factors suggests that intergroup attitudes are a function of three factors—the person, the environment, and the societal context:

$$A = f(P + E + S).$$

At this point the focus continued to be on the effects of these factors on intergroup attitudes, usually the prejudice of Whites toward Blacks.

In the 1970s the contact hypothesis achieved a measure of maturity due to three significant developments. First, there was an increasing interest in behavioral and affective dependent variables, including intergroup helping and aggression (e.g., Donnerstein & Donnerstein, 1972, 1973; Geartner, 1975), participation in future interactions (Rokeach, 1971), participation in group decisions (Cohen & Roper, 1972), and the anxiety elicited in intergroup interactions (Hendricks & Bootzin, 1976; Randolph, Landis, & Tzeng, 1977). Due to this focus on behavior during the 1970s, the contact hypothesis became a more conceptually complete, if not fully integrated, model of the effects of intergroup contact:

$$B = f(P + E + S).$$

Second, during the 1960s and 1970s considerable new research was undertaken, a good portion of it in the laboratory (for reviews, see Amir, 1976; Ashmore, 1970; Cook, 1969; Williams, 1977). This research yielded a number of new situational variables that affect the outcomes of contact, although it did not change the underlying model. The situational factors included positive outcomes of the interaction (Blanchard, Adelman, & Cook, 1975), and the potential for attitude changes to generalize to other situations (Amir, 1976; Brewer & Miller, 1984). Research also indicated that, in small groups, balanced ratios of in-group to out-group members were the most beneficial (Amir, 1976; Gonzales, 1979). In contrast, in large group settings such as schools and government agencies, balanced ratios of in-group and out-group members may lead to perceptions of threat and may have negative effects on intergroup relations (Hallinan & Smith, 1985; Hoffman, 1985; Longshore, 1982).

New person factors included demographic variables (positive change most likely with younger, better educated, and higher social class individuals, Williams, 1964); personality traits, such as high self-esteem, adherence to the Protestant ethic, and low authoritarianism (Katz, Wackenhut, & Glass, 1986; Stephan & Rosenfield, 1978a, 1978b; Wagner & Schonbach, 1984; Weigel & Howes, 1985); and high competence in task relevant skills (Blanchard & Cook, 1976; Cohen & Roper, 1972; Rosenfield, Stephan, & Lucker, 1981). Additional societal variables included favorable prior relations between the participating groups (Brislin & Pedersen, 1976; Tajfel, 1978; Williams, 1977), and a high degree of acculturation of minority groups (Eshel & Peres, 1973).

At this stage in its development, the contact hypothesis resembled a bag lady who is so encumbered with excess baggage she can hardly move. The contact hypothesis seemed to be arriving at that stage in the life of a paradigm where the working assumptions become so complex that the paradigm begins to die. Fortunately, the contact hypothesis was revitalized in the 1970s by a third development, a growing concern with the processes that mediate changes in intergroup behaviors and cognitions.

Ashmore (1970) mentioned a variety of mediating processes that might account for the effects of contact on behavior, including stereotype destruction, unlearning assumed incongruence in beliefs, cognitive consistency, and stimulus generalization. To this list other investigators contributed discussions of the mediating effects of acquiring knowledge about the subjective culture of the other group (Brislin, Cushner, Cherrie, & Yong, 1986; Triandis, 1972), instrumental conditioning of positive attitudes and behaviors (Hauserman, Welen, & Behling, 1973), classical conditioning of positive affect and extinction of negative affect (Parrish & Fleetwood, 1975; Sappington, 1976), and imitation of nonprejudiced attitudes and behavior (Williams, 1977). Unlike the person variables that had been emphasized earlier, these mediators did not refer to personality traits, but to cognitive and affective processes occurring within the person.

CURRENT RESEARCH

Research in the late 1970s and early 1980s has added a few new variables to each of the categories of factors affecting the outcomes of contact, but the primary focus has been on cognitive variables that mediate the effects of contact. I will review these variables in somewhat more detail than those presented previously because they are less widely known among traditional intergroup relations researchers.

Unlike the earlier approaches, the more recent cognitive approaches are concerned with how the information available in contact situations is processed. For the most part, the additions made to contact theory by the cognitive approach consist of explanations of ways in which biases enter into the processing of intergroup information. Biases may enter at all stages in the process: attention, encoding, and retrieval.

Among the attentional biases is the tendency to attribute causation to salient social stimuli. In intergroup interactions, the behavior of out-group members is often the focus of attention (Taylor, Fiske, Etcoff, & Ruderman, 1978) and may lead to an overemphasis on dispositional factors to explain their behaviors (Duncan, 1976; Sager & Schofield, 1980). Out-group members are particularly likely to be attended to if they are in the minority or if they behave in negative or deviant ways (Langer, Fiske, Taylor, & Chanowitz, 1976). Thus one reason it may be valuable to have an equal balance of in-group and out-group members in intergroup contact situations is to avoid undue focus on the minority group.

The saliency/attribution bias helps in understanding why positive outcomes are so important in intergroup contact situations. If the outcomes are negative, out-group members are likely to be blamed, particularly if the out-group is initially disliked (McArthur & Soloman, 1978; Pettigrew, 1979). Even when the out-group is not disliked, the complexity-extremity effect (extreme evaluations are made for members of out-groups that are perceived in relatively simple terms) may cause out-group members to be evaluated more negatively than in-group members in situations where the outcomes are negative (Linville, 1982; Linville & Jones, 1980). The complexity-extremity effect is most likely to occur when in-group members are not committed to their attitudes toward the out-group and when the dimensions of the out-group stereotype are not closely related to one another (Millar & Tessor, 1986).

One encoding bias that affects the processing of intergroup information is the expectancy-confirmation bias. There is a tendency to seek out and prefer information about members of other groups that confirms preconceptions concerning their traits (Bodenhausen & Wyer, 1985; Skov & Sherman, 1986; Sndyer & Swann, 1978a). Also, expectancies based on stereotypes, beliefs, assumed or actual dissimilarities, roles, or situational factors may be perceived as having been confirmed, even when confirming evidence is absent (Bodenhausen & Wyer, 1985;

Cantor & Mischel, 1977; Rothbart, Evans, & Fulero, 1979). In addition, people may behave in ways that increase the chances that their expectancies will be confirmed (Snyder & Swann, 1978b; Snyder, Tanke, & Berscheid, 1977; Word, Zanna, & Cooper, 1974). These expectancy-confirmation biases help to understand why out-group members must behave in nonstereotyped ways if stereotypes are to be altered.

Rothbart and John (1986) argue that disconfirmations will only modify stereotypes if the behavior clearly disconfirms the expectancy, occurs repeatedly, occurs in a variety of settings, the group members engaging in the disconfirming behaviors are perceived as otherwise prototypical group members, and if the disconfirmation is associated with the group label (see Weber & Crocker, 1982). A problem with stereotype-disconfirming behavior is the existence of a countervailing tendency to negatively evaluate others who violate category-based expectancies (Costrich, Feinstein, Kidder, Maracek, & Pascale, 1975). Thus stereotype-disconforming behaviors that lead to changes in stereotypes may not lead to corresponding changes in prejudice (in fact, prejudice and stereotyping are often uncorrelated or evidence only small correlations, e.g., Rogers, Hennigan, Bowman, & Miller, 1984).

Assimilation and contrast effects during encoding undermine the formation of differentiated perceptions of out-group members (Quattrone, 1986; Wilder, 1978, 1986). For this reason, Miller, Brewer, and Edwards (1985) argue that it is important for information concerning out-group members to be processed on an individual level, instead of in terms of social categories. Information about individuals must then be integrated into the perceiver's beliefs about the out-group, if the perceptions of that group are to change.

Another encoding bias that may affect subsequent judgments of the out-group is that individuating information tends to be overemphasized in forming impressions of groups (Hamill, Wilson, & Nisbett, 1980). The result may be that negative individual behaviors are used as a basis for making negative inferences about the group as a whole. As Rothbart (1981) has suggested, "Our perceptions of groups may be disproportionately influenced by the characteristics of the group's most memorable constituents" (p. 36). This bias may be particularly disadvantageous to minority groups, given that negative behaviors tend to be salient and that distinctive negative behaviors are easily associated with members of a group that is in the minority (Hamilton & Gifford, 1976; Hamilton, Dugan, & Troiler, 1985).

During encoding, social comparisons between groups often lead to effects similar to contrast effects (Hinkle & Schopler, 1986). In-group performances are generally evaluated more favorably than out-group performances, and in-group members typically favor the in-group over the out-group in the allocation of rewards for performance, even in minimal social situations (Tajfel, 1978). This in-group/out-group bias is especially pronounced when social categories are salient (Doise, 1978), when the out-group is dissimilar to the in-group (Billig & Tajfel, 1973), when the in-group is cohesive (Ferguson & Kelley, 1964), and among members of the comparatively more successful group (Hinkle & Schopler, 1986). When out-groups are internally differentiated by creating crosscutting social categories, less discrimination occurs (Doise, 1969). Negative social comparisons may account for some of the adverse outcomes of competitive intergroup contact. Because competitive contact heightens the salience of social categories and increases in-group cohesion, it may facilitate in-group/out-group bias (Kahn & Ryen, 1972).

Taken together, this set of encoding biases suggests that exposure to multiple members of the out-group who repeatedly behave in vivid, nonuniform ways that disconfirm prevailing views of the out-group may be necessary if intergroup contact is to result in more differentiated perceptions of out-group members. The value of creating such perceptions is that differentiated perceptions of out-group members have been found to reduce discrimination against members of the out-group (Caspi, 1984; Katz, 1973; Katz & Zalk, 1978; Langer, Bashner, & Chanowitz, 1985; Wilder, 1978). The studies of encoding biases also indicate why nonsuperficial contact may be important to improving intergroup relations. Superficial contact is likely to be encoded categorically (Higgins, Rholes, & Jones, 1977; Rose, 1981).

One retrieval bias indicates that category-inconsistent and individuating information tends to be lost over time (Lingle, Geva, Ostrom, Leippe, & Baumgardner, 1979; Ostrom, Lingle, Pryor, & Geva, 1980). There is also a bias toward the recall of information that is affectively consistent with one's prior judgments (Dutta, Kanungo, & Freibergs, 1972; Higgins & Rholes, 1978). These retrieval biases reinforce the importance of creating positive individualized contact over relatively long periods of time with multiple out-group members who engage in numerous, vivid, counterstereotypical behaviors.

Another advance in the 1970s and 1980s has been an increased interest in the interactions among the factors included in previous models, particularly those concerning the conditions under which cooperation leads to improved intergroup relations (Johnson et al., 1983). It has been found that cooperation is most effective when it is successful (Blanchard, Adelman, & Cook, 1975), when measures are taken to avoid the negative effects of different levels of task ability (Cohen, 1980, 1984; Slavin, 1978), when the in-group and out-group are similar in attitudes (Brown & Abrams, 1986), when the in-group and out-group are numerically balanced (Gonzales, 1979), when assignment to groups does not make social categories salient (Miller et al., 1985), when both in-group and out-group members are well represented among the authority figures sanctioning the conduct (Cohen, 1980), and when the interaction is socially oriented rather than task oriented (Miller et al., 1985).

A RECONCEPTUALIZED CONTACT MODEL

It is readily apparent that the contact hypothesis needs a new set of clothes, for the earlier ones seem to be bursting at the seams. In an effort to move in this direction, I will reformulate the earlier conceptual models into one that more adequately captures the complexity of our knowledge about intergroup contact. This model uses the same categories of factors used in earlier models, but it incorporates several additional factors and makes some causal assumptions.

As Figure 1.1 indicates, this model postulates that societal factors influence situation and person factors. The situation and person factors are presented as interacting with one another. Further, the model explicitly notes that there are factors that mediate the effects of the person and situation variables on subsequent behavior, cognitions, and affect. Finally, the model indicates that changes in people can ultimately bring about changes in society (Bochner, 1982).

Although the model was developed on the basis of a consideration of the previous literature on the contact hypothesis, it appears to be more generally applicable within social psychology. Social psychologists have traditionally been most interested in the stream of events that runs from situational factors through the mediating variables to the person consequences, but this model also encompasses our interest in the interaction between person and situation factors and in the societal antecedents and consequences of the variables we study.

The model has implications for both empirical and applied research on intergroup contact. Empirically, the model makes explicit the

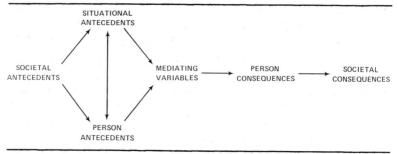

Figure 1.1 Revised Model of the Contact Hypothesis

interactive and causal nature of the variables affecting the outcomes of contact. It suggests an array of variables within each category that may have an impact in any study of the effects of intergroup contact. From the applied perspective, the model indicates the domains of factors that should be considered in attempts to improve intergroup relations through contact. The model may be especially useful in diagnosing problems in unsuccessful contact situations. The use of the model in an applied setting can be illustrated by considering the outcomes of school desegregation.

A recent review of the effects of desegregation indicates that, in the first year or two after desegregation, intergroup relations improved in only about one-quarter of the cases studied (Stephan, 1986). Cook (1979, 1984) has used an earlier version of the contact hypothesis to explain why school desegregation has not been more successful in changing intergroup relations. He suggests that the contact in desegregated schools is frequently competitive, unequal in terms of ethnic balance and status within the school, nonintimate, and it is often opposed by authority figures. The current model would suggest, in addition, that we examine the societal context in which school desegregation takes place, the characteristics of the participants, additional situational factors, the mediators of change, and the long-term effects of contact.

An examination of societal factors indicates that the historical relations between Blacks and Caucasians have much to do with the short-term lack of success of school desegregation. The two groups have historically been segregated, a trend that continues today (Farley, 1975). This segregation means that each group is, to some extent, ignorant of the subjective culture of the other group and has norms and values that are not supportive of intergroup contact. The two groups are of disproportionate size and power in our society, which means that the two groups bring unequal statuses to contact situations. In addition, prior intergroup conflict has led many members of both groups to be anxious about intergroup contact in the schools.

With respect to person factors, many of the participants enter the school situation with negative attitudes and other personal characteristics unlikely to lead to favorable outcomes (e.g., ethnocentrism, low self-esteem, authoritarianism). Also, there are situational factors other than those mentioned by Cook that may work against improved intergroup relations in the schools. The outcomes of contact often are not positive, stereotype-confirming behaviors may occur, and the contact is nonvoluntary.

A consideration of some of the mediators of favorable changes indicates further problems. The conditions of contact in desegregated schools may lead to categorical processing and other information processing biases that work against the learning of the subjective culture of the other group and the unlearning of stereotypes and assumed dissimilarities. Further, people who serve as models of positive intergroup contact are usually absent, as are rewards for positive contacts.

In addition to focusing on the antecedents of intergroup contact in the schools, the model suggests that the long-term societal effects of desegregation should be examined. Cook's (1979) and Gerard's (1983) relatively negative assessments of the effects of desegregation were based exclusively on studies of the short-term effects of desegregation. Until recently, little attention has been paid to the long-term effects of desegregation. The evidence suggests that these effects have been more positive than the short-term effects (Braddock, 1985; Greenblatt & Willie, 1980; Stephan, 1986). Recent longitudinal studies indicate that desegregation increases the chances that Blacks will subsequently work in integrated settings and that Blacks and Whites will live in integrated neighborhoods. It has also been found that desegregation increases college attendance among Northern Blacks and increases the matriculation of Southern Blacks at previously all-White schools (see Braddock, 1985, and Stephan, 1986, for reviews).

THE UNFINISHED BUSINESS

A causal model provides a blueprint indicating the relationships among the specified sets of variables. In the case of the contact

TABLE 1.1
Variables Included in the Contact Hypothesis

SITUATIONAL ANTECEDENTS

Setting
  social and physical
Nature of interaction
  purpose
  real/vicarious contact
  superficial/intimate
  formal/informal
  structured/unstructured
  voluntary/coerced
  individualized/impersonal
  stereotyped/non-stereotyped
  authority support
  means interdependence
  duration
  frequency
Group composition
  specific groups involved
  ingroup/outgroup ratio
  relative statuses
  similarity of participants
  diversity of group members
  group size
Task
  content
  goals interdependence
  outcomes

SOCIETAL ANTECEDENTS
Social structure
  social stratification
Historical relations
  prior contact
  degree of conflict
  social norms and roles
  group size
Current relations
  recent events
  government policies
  Socialization practices

PERSON ANTECEDENTS
Demographic characteristics
Behavior
  personality traits
  task abilities
  prior contact
Cognitions
  ingroup schemata
  outgroup schemata
  prejudice
  stereotypes
  expectancies
  scripts
  values
Affect

MEDIATORS
Behavioral
  modeling
  reinforcements/punishments
Cognitive
  attention
  encoding
  retrieval
Affective
  classical conditioning

PERSON CONSEQUENCES
Behavior
  positive/negative
  short/long-term
Cognitions
  outgroup schemata
  prejudice
  stereotypes
  expectancies
  scripts
Affective states
  labeled emotions

hypothesis some of the causal relationships have already been closely examined, but there are a number of relationships that have been only superficially studied and some have hardly been studied at all. In order to simplify my discussion of the unfinished business on the contact hypothesis, I will use the model presented in Figure 1.1 as a basis for categorizing all of the variables that have been previously discussed (see Table 1.1).

Societal antecedents. Among the categories of societal context variables that seem important are (1) the structure of the society, especially its stratification into social groups, (2) the historical relations between the groups that are in contact with one another, (3) the current relations between these groups, and (4) the groups' socialization practices.

Situational antecedents. The variables that comprise the situational context in which the contact takes place can be categorized as follows: (1) the setting in which the contact occurs, (2) the nature of the interaction, (3) the composition of the groups, and (4) the task in which the participants are involved.

Person antecedents. The person antecedents are made up of (1) demographic characteristics, (2) behaviors, (3) cognitions, and (4) affect.

Mediators. The proposed mediators of the effects of contact include (1) behavioral, (2) cognitive, and (3) affective processes.

Person consequences. The principal consequences include (1) behaviors, (2) cognitions, and (3) affective reactions.

My discussion of the gaps in our knowledge will follow the causal flow of the model from antecedents to consequences. There is very little information on the ways in which societal level variables shape the situational contexts in which contact occurs. It would be valuable to understand these background factors because such an understanding would provide information on where and why intergroup contact occurs in a society. From a social policy perspective, this knowledge would make it easier to choose where and how to intervene in the social system to have the greatest impact on intergroup relations.

For example, the lawyers for the National Association for the Advancement of Colored People (NAACP) who brought the desegregation cases to trial are an example of the successful use of this type of background information in formulating a strategy to modify intergroup relations. They were pursuing a purposeful strategy to bring about greater racial equality by attacking a vulnerable institution where the legal strategy promised to have the greatest possible impact (Kluger,

1976). It should be added that an appreciation of social background factors suggests that programs that are effective for some groups may not succeed with other groups whose historical relations, positions in the social hierarchy, and socialization practices differ.

We have considerable knowledge about the effects of societal antecedents of some of the person antecedents that affect the outcomes of contact. For example, socialization and some aspects of social stratification (e.g., social class) as antecedents of prejudice, authoritarianism, ethnocentrism, and self-esteem have received extensive study (Adorno, Frenkel-Brusnwik, Levinson, & Sanford, 1950; Bachman, 1970; Coppersmith, 1967). Other aspects of the relationships between societal antecedents and person antecedents—for instance, how ethnic group differences in socialization practices affect the preceding traits and other traits, values, and cognitions—have been little studied. Knowledge of these relationships might be useful in advising parents and educators on techniques of educating or socializing children that improve intergroup relations.

Our knowledge of the effects of person antecedents on the consequences of contact is very limited. We know that demographic characteristics, such as age and education, are related to prejudice (Campbell, 1971; St. John, 1975; Williams, 1964), but we know little of the effects of demographic characteristics on other cognitive consequences of contact (e.g., schemata, expectancies, prototypes), or on behavioral or affective outcomes of contact. Similarly, we know something about the effects of individual differences in precontact prejudice on postcontact prejudice and behavior (Stephan, 1985). However, we know little of the effects of individual differences in intergroup cognitions (other than prejudice) on behavior or affect. Knowing more about the effects of person variables might enable us to target change programs toward those people who are most likely to benefit from them.

We know more about the relationship between situational antecedents and the short-term consequences of contact than about any other set of relationships in the model. However, there is one large gap in our knowledge: We know very little about the relationship between situational antecedents and the affective or emotional consequences of contact (e.g., anxiety, anger, relief, disgust, happiness). We also have only limited information on the effects of interactions among situational antecedents on the outcomes of contact (an exception is our knowledge of the conditions under which cooperation is most effective).

Another substantial knowledge gap exists for the interaction of person and situation antecedents. This gap is important because all intergroup contacts involve a variety of person and situation variables. Although isolated studies suggest that such interaction effects occur (e.g., studies of individual task competence under cooperative and competitive conditions, Cohen & Roper, 1972; Rosenfield et al., 1981), we know surprisingly little about the characteristics of the people whose attitudes and behaviors change most during different types of contact.

We have little or no information concerning most of the proposed mediators of changes in behavior, cognitions, or affect in actual intergroup contact situations. One exception to this pattern concerns studies of knowledge of the other group, where a substantial literature concerning the effects of cross-cultural training programs exists (Brislin & Pedersen, 1976; Stephan & Stephan, 1984).

Finally, only a limited range of the potential effects of intergroup contact has been investigated. Although behaviors such as aggression, helping, discrimination, and contributions to group decisions have been investigated, other behaviors, particularly those of a more normative nature, have scarcely been examined in contact situations. The cognitive approach to intergroup relations invites us to consider broader categories of intergroup perceptions than the prejudices and stereotypes that have been the stock and trade of earlier studies. Concepts such as scripts, schemata, prototypes, and subjective culture offer new opportunities to examine a wide range of intergroup cognitions. The emotional and affective outcomes of contact have rarely been studied, but it would be valuable to understand when contact leads to fear, resentment, relief, joy, guilt, and disgust, and not just to positive or negative evaluations.

TOPICS FOR FUTURE RESEARCH

In the creation of a new wardrobe for the contact hypothesis, some aspects of the unfinished business seem more important than others.

(1) Disputes remain concerning the variables included in the traditional contact hypothesis. There is considerable confusion about whether there should be equal-status on person factors external to the situation, treatments to offset such inequalities, equal-status only within the contact situation, or even whether equal-status is important in improving intergroup relations (Cohen & Roper, 1972; Norvel & Worchel, 1981; Pettigrew, 1971; Robinson & Preston, 1976; Riordan, 1978). It is unclear whether group differences should be made salient in

intergroup contact so that stereotypes can be disconfirmed (Rothbart & John, 1986), or whether the salience of groups should be minimized (Miller & Brewer, 1984). Likewise, it is unclear whether cooperation can be beneficial even when accompanied by intergroup competition (Slavin, 1985), or whether intergroup competition should be avoided (Miller et al., 1985). Does individuating out-group members reduce the tendency to stereotype them (Locksley, Borgida, Brekke, & Hepburn, 1980), or does this effect depend on the nature of the groups or the traits associated with the group (Brown, 1986; Grant & Holmes, 1981)?

(2) Traditionally, contact theory has been concerned with the conditions under which contact improved intergroup relations, but in many instances a reduction in intergroup conflict is sought. The past emphasis on improving relations means that we know little about the situational contexts in which contact has negative effects on intergroup relations. Under what conditions does contact lead to conflict (Donnerstein & Donnerstein, 1976)? How can intergroup conflict be reduced? Are the processes that mediate reductions in conflict the same as those involved in improving relations between groups that are not in conflict?

(3) We need to know more about the degree to which laboratory findings generalize to other contexts within our society. Our knowledge of the conditions under which contact is most effective comes primarily from laboratory studies where the independent variables are carefully manipulated. In field settings, independent variables related to contact tend to be clumped together, and it is impossible to determine which variables are most important (Riordan, 1978). The result is that we know too little about the specific variables that generalize from the laboratory to applied settings.

(4) We need to understand more about the specific behaviors, cognitions, and emotional reactions that occur during intergroup contact. Most studies manipulate independent variables and examine their effects on dependent measures such as prejudice or discrimination, but the ongoing behavior of the participants during the interaction is rarely studied (for exceptions, see Erickson, 1979; Ickes, 1984). It would be valuable to do content analyses of intergroup interactions to determine the ways in which they differ from within-group interactions.

(5) Too little is known about the mediating roles of the affective states experienced during contact and their subsequent effects on behavior, cognitions, and emotions (Stephan & Stephan, 1985; Wilder, 1986). We also need to begin studying the factors that mediate changes in intergroup behavior and cognitions in real interaction settings. How can

knowledge of the cognitive processes underlying intergroup cognitions be applied to improving intergroup relations? Studying the cognitive and affective mediators of the effects of contact may be the only way of reducing the conceptual complexity of the contact hypothesis. If we could identify the mediators common to sets of situational variables, it could greatly simplify the contact hypothesis.

It might be reasonable to apply a broad theory, like social learning theory (Bandura, 1986), to the behavioral mediators. Effects of situational factors such as the rewards and self-efficacy generated by success, the mutual reinforcements created by cooperation, the modeling by and reinforcement from authority figures, and the rewards of interacting with similar others could all be explained in terms of reinforcement principles (Guthrie, 1975). Similarly, the information processing approach could be applied to many of the cognitive mediators of change. The role of stereotype disconfirmation, and individuated, informal, and voluntary contact could be understood within this framework (e.g., Rothbart & John, 1985). The classical conditioning approach could be applied to affective mediators. Classical conditioning may explain the effects of frequency and variety of contacts, as well as the effects of success, intimacy, and similarity (which should all elicit positive affect on the basis of prior conditioning).

(6) We should continue to broaden the nature of the groups that are studied. Much of the early work on intergroup relations concentrated on Blacks and Whites or on anti-semitism. We could benefit from more work on relations among Hispanics, Oriental-Americans, and other ethnic groups. Recently, there has been an increasing interest in sexism, age discrimination, and discrimination against the handicapped (Jones, Farina, Hastorf, Markus, Miller, & Scott, 1984), which suggests that there is a movement toward broadening the base of knowledge about the groups that come in contact in our society.

(7) We could also benefit from an integration of the literature on cross-cultural contact with the traditional intergroup contact literature. Studies of international contact indicate that knowledge of intergroup differences is important in improving communications and relations. Attempts to improve relations often rely on educational programs and vicarious contact simulations such as role playing (for reviews, see Brislin & Pedersen, 1976; Brislin et al., 1986; Stenning, 1979; Stephan & Stephan, 1984). Also, these programs often attempt to deal with the anxiety and ethnocentrism elicited by intergroup contact, in some cases through the use of social skills training (Argyle, 1979; Furhman &

Bochner, 1982). An underlying premise of these approaches is that there are real differences between cultural groups and that people must understand the cultural system of the other group before they can effectively interact with individuals from that group. This emphasis on cultural differences contrasts sharply with the emphasis on group similarities in most domestic intergroup contact training programs (for exceptions, see Katz, 1978; Landis, Day, McGrew, Thomas, & Miller, 1976; Landis, Brislin, Swanner, Tseng, & Thomas, 1985; Weldon, Carlston, Rissman, Slobodin, & Triandis, 1975). What is the proper balance between information on group differences and information on group similarities, and how does this balance relate to the nature of the two groups involved?

(8) Finally, I would like to end by discussing a seeming paradox. Nothing should be clearer than the fact that, like the bag lady's packages, the list of conditions considered important in creating contact situations that have positive outcomes continues to grow and grow. Implicitly, each of these conditions also carries information on factors that can lead to negative consequences. Taken together, this long list of factors suggests that improving intergroup relations is extremely difficult and that there are many ways in which contact can lead to negative consequences. If this were actually the case, most intergroup contacts in our society would be expected to have negative or, at best, neutral consequences. How, then, are we to explain the fact that intergroup relations in this country have improved enormously during the postwar period (Crosby, Bromley, & Saxe, 1980)? Most observers agree that we live in a much less racist, sexist, and anti-semitic society today than we did 40 years ago (Feagin & Feagin, 1978; Taylor, Sheatsley, & Greeley, 1978; Wilson, 1980). How can we explain this paradox?

One explanation may be that by focusing on so many factors that can affect the outcomes of contact, we have failed to isolate the few factors that are critically important for contact to improve intergroup relations. Past research has rarely compared the relative strength of different factors on the outcomes of contact. It may be that most of the factors that have been investigated are not necessary for contact to have positive effects. Another problem is that most studies only concern themselves with short-term effects of contact and not with long-term changes that occur gradually. It may be that factors other than those that have been studied influence the outcomes of long-term contact. Perhaps many factors influence short-term contact, but very few have lasting effects.

Thus if the factors influential in the long run are present, then long-term changes could take place, even though the contact situation seems unfavorable in the short term.

Research on the contact hypothesis has not been much concerned with naturally occurring contact. Such contacts are rarely characterized by the optimal conditions for positive outcomes. They tend to involve superficial contact and unequal statuses, do not involve cooperation, lack support by authority figures, involve unequal representation of the groups, etc. Nonetheless, these superficial norm- and role-governed interactions may have cumulative positive effects over time. Studies of naturally occurring contact typically find that informal voluntary contact is moderately correlated with favorable out-group attitudes (Carter, DeTine, Spero, & Benson, 1975; Stephan & Rosenfield, 1978b; Stephan & Stephan, 1984; Webster, 1961). We need to know more about the long-term consequences of naturally occurring contact. Where does such contact occur and under what conditions? What changes take place during naturally occurring contact and what mediates these changes? Two types of naturally occurring contact that could benefit from additional study are intergroup friendships (Blumberg & Roye, 1980; Hallinan & Smith, 1985; Hansell, 1984; Maruyama, Miller, & Holtz, 1986) and intergroup marriages, but the causes and consequences of more casual contact are also of interest.

It is also possible that studies of the short-term effects of contact have focused on the wrong dependent measures. Instead of studying changes in prejudice and stereotypes, perhaps we should be studying changes in the behaviors and norms associated with mutual accommodation. Over time, intergroup contact may lead to the gradual acquisition of interaction skills that reduce fear and ignorance concerning the out-group (Argyle, 1979).

Vicarious intergroup contact and social policy also have played a role in the postwar changes in race relations. With increasing exposure to other groups through the mass media, people may gradually change their attitudes toward the depicted groups, particularly if members of the group are presented frequently (Cantor, 1972; Perlman & Oskamp, 1971; Zajonc, 1980), positively, or in individuating ways (Katz, 1973; Katz & Zalk, 1978; Wilder, 1978; for reviews, see Stephan, 1985; Williams, 1947). Social policy, beginning with President Truman's decision to integrate the armed forces and running through the school desegregation cases, has until recently favored improved relations between the races. These social policies have undoubtedly contributed to a climate in which positive normative and attitudinal changes could take place (Greenblatt & Willie, 1980).

CONCLUSION

Over the years, the contact hypothesis has lost the exuberance of youth, been shorn of some of its illusions, become overburdened, and yet still managed to yield a measure of wisdom. I hope that the new clothes in which I have cloaked it will prove to be less ephemeral than the emperor's.

REFERENCES

Adlerfer, C. P. (1982). Problems of changing white males' behavior and beliefs concerning race relations. In P. Goodman & Associates (Eds.), *Change in organizations* (pp. 122-165). San Francisco: Jossey-Bass.

Adorno, T. W., Frenkel-Brunswik, E., Levinson, D. J., & Sanford, R. N. (1950). *The authoritarian personality.* New York: Harper.

Allport, F. H., et al. (1953). The effects of segregation and the consequences of desegregation: A social science statement. *Minnesota Law Review, 37,* 429-440.

Allport, G. W. (1954). *The nature of prejudice.* Cambridge, MA: Addison-Wesley.

Amir, Y. (1976). The role of intergroup contact in change of prejudice and race relations. In P. Katz (Ed.), *Towards the elimination of racism* (pp. 245-308). New York: Pergamon.

Argyle, M. (1979). New Developments in the analysis of social skills. In A. Wolfgang (Ed.), *Non-verbal behavior* (pp. 139-158). New York: Academic Press.

Ashmore, R. D. (1970). The problem of intergroup prejudice. In B. Collins, *Social Psychology* (pp. 247-297). Reading, MA: Addison-Wesley.

Bachman, J. G. (1970). *Youth in transition II: The impact of family background and intelligence on tenth-grade boys.* Ann Arbor, MI: Institute for Social Research.

Bandura, A. (1986). *Social foundations of thought & action.* Englewood Cliffs, NJ: Prentice-Hall.

Billig, M., and Tajfel, H. (1973). Social categorization and similarity of intergroup behavior. *European Journal of Social Psychology, 3,* 339-343.

Blanchard, F. A., Adelman, L., & Cook, S. W. (1975). Effect of group success and failure upon interpersonal attraction in cooperating interracial groups. *Journal of Personality and Social Psychology, 31,* 1020-1030.

Blanchard, F. A., & Cook, S. W. (1976). Effects of helping a less competent member of a cooperating interracial group on the development of interpersonal attraction. *Journal of Personality and Social Psychology, 34,* 1245-1255.

Blumberg, R. G., & Roye, W. J. (1980). *Interracial bonds.* New York: General Hall.

Bodenhausen, G., & Wyer, R. S., Jr. (1985). Effects of stereotypes on decision making and information-processing strategies. *Journal of Personality and Social Psychology, 48,* 267-282.

Bochner, S. (1982). The social psychology of cross-cultural relations. In S. Bochner (Ed.), *Cultures in contact* (pp. 5-44). New York: Pergamon.

Braddock, J. H., II (1985). School desegregation and Black assimilation. *Journal of Social Issues, 41* (3), 9-23.

Brewer, M. B., & Miller, N. (1984). Beyond the contact hypothesis: Theoretical perspectives on desegregation. In N. Miller & M. B. Brewer (Eds.), *Groups in contact: The psychology of desegregation* (pp. 281-302). New York: Academic Press.

Brislin, R. W., Cushner, K., Cherrie, C., & Yong, M. (1986). *Intercultural interactions: A practical guide.* Newbury Park, CA: Sage.

Brislin, R., & Pedersen, P. (1976). *Cross-cultural orientation programs.* New York: John Wiley/Halsted.

Brown, R. (1986). *Social psychology: The second edition.* New York: Free Press.

Brown, R., & Abrams, D. (1986). The effects of intergroup similarity and goal interdependence on intergroup attitudes and task performance. *Journal of Experimental Social Psychology, 22,* 78-92.

Brown, R. J., & Turner, J. C. (1981). Interpersonal and intergroup behavior. In J. Turner & H. Giles (Eds.), *Intergroup behavior* (pp. 33-65). Chicago: University of Chicago Press.

Campbell, A. (1971). *White attitudes toward black people.* Ann Arbor, MI: Institute for Social Research.

Cantor, G. N. (1972). Effects of familiarity on children's ratings of pictures of whites and blacks. *Child Development, 43,* 1219-1229.

Cantor, N., & Mischel, W. (1977). Traits and prototypes: Effects on recognition memory. *Journal of Personality and Social Psychology, 35,* 38-48.

Carter, D. E., Detine, S. L., Spero, J., & Benson, F. W. (1975). Peer acceptance and school related variables in an integrated junior high school. *Journal of Educational Psychology, 67,* 267-273.

Caspi, A. (1984). Contact hypothesis and inter-age attitudes: A field study of cross age contact. *Social Psychology Quarterly, 47,* 74-80.

Cohen, E. (1980). Design and redesign of the desegregated school: Problems of status, power, and conflict. In W. G. Stephan & J. Feagin (Eds.), *School desegregation* (pp. 251-280). New York: Plenum.

Cohen, E. (1984). The desegregated school: Problems of status and power and interethnic climate. In N. Miller & M. B. Brewer (Eds.), *Groups in contact* (pp. 77-96). New York: Academic Press.

Cohen, E., & Roper, S. (1972). Modification of interracial interaction disability: An application of status characteristic theory. *American Sociological Review, 37,* 643-657.

Cook, S. W. (1962). The systematic study of socially significant events: A strategy for social research. *Journal of Social Issues, 18* (2), 66-84.

Cook, S. W. (1969). Motives in a conceptual analysis of attitude-related behavior. In W. J. Arnold & D. Levine (Eds.), *Nebraska symposium on motivation* (Vol. 18, pp. 179-236). Lincoln, NE: University of Nebraska Press.

Cook, S. W. (1978). Interpersonal and attitudinal outcomes of cooperating interracial groups. *Journal of Research and Development Education, 12,* 97-113.

Cook, S. W. (1979). Social science and school desegregation: Did we mislead the Supreme Court? *Personality and Social Psychology Bulletin, 5,* 420-437.

Cook, S. W. (1984). The 1954 social science statement and school desegregation: A reply to Gerard. *American Psychologist, 39,* 819-832.

Cook, S. W. (1985). Experimenting on social issues: The case of school desegregation. *American Psychologist, 40,* 452-460.

Coppersmith, S. (1967). *The antecedents of self-esteem.* San Francisco: W. H. Freeman.

Costrick, N. J., Feinstein, J., Kidder, L., Maracek, J., & Pascale, L. (1975). When stereotypes hurt: Three studies of penalties for sex-role reversals. *Journal of Experimental Social Psychology, 11,* 520-530.

Crosby, F. S., Bromley, K., & Saxe, L. (1980). Recent unobtrusive studies of black and white discrimination and prejudice: A literature review. *Psychological Bulletin, 87,* 546-563.

Doise, W. (1969). Intergroup relations and polarization of individual and collective judgments. *Journal of Personality and Social Psychology, 12,* 136-143.

Doise, W. (1978). *Groups and individuals: Explanations in social psychology.* Cambridge: Cambridge University Press.

Donnerstein, E. M., & Donnerstein, M. (1972). White rewarding behavior as a function of Black retaliation. *Journal of Personality and Social Psychology, 24,* 327-333.

Donnerstein, E. M., & Donnerstein, M. (1973). Variable in interracial aggression: Potential ingroup censure. *Journal of Personality and Social Psychology, 27,* 143-150.

Donnerstein, M., & Donnerstein, E. (1976). Research in the control of interracial aggression. In R. G. Geen & E. G. O'Neal (Eds.), *Perspectives on aggression* (pp. 133-168). New York: Academic Press.

Duncan, B. L. (1976). Differential social perception and attribution of interracial violence: Testing the lower limits of stereotyping Blacks. *Journal of Personality and Social Psychology, 34,* 590-598.

Dutta, S., Kanungo, R. N., & Friebergs, V. (1972). Retention of affective material: Effects of intensity of affect on retrieval. *Journal of Personality and Social Psychology, 23,* 65-80.

Erickson, F. (1979). Talking down: Some sources of miscommunication of interracial interviews. In A. Wolfgang, (Ed.), *Non-verbal behavior* (pp. 99-126). New York: Academic Press.

Eshel, S., & Peres, Y. (1973). The integration of a minority group: A causal model. In Y. Amir (1976). The role of intergroup contact in change of prejudice and race relations. In P. Katz (Ed.), *Towards the elimination of racism* (pp. 245-308). New York: Pergamon.

Farley, R. (1975). Residential segregation and its implications for school integration. *Law and Contemporary Problems, 39,* 189-208.

Feagin, J. R., & Feagin, C. B. (1978). *Discrimination American style.* Englewood Cliffs, NJ: Spectrum.

Ferguson, C. K., & Kelley, H. H. (1964). Significant factors in overevaluation of own group's products. *Journal of Abnormal and Social Psychology, 69,* 223-228.

Furhman, A., & Bochner, S. (1982). Social difficulty in a foreign culture: An empirical analysis of culture shock. In S. Bochner (ed.), *Cultures in contact* (pp. 161-198). New York: Pergamon.

Geartner, S. L. (1975). The role of racial attitudes in helping behavior. *Journal of Social Psychology, 97,* 95-101.

Gerard, H. B. (1983). School desegregation: The social science role. *American Psychologist, 38,* 869-877.

Gibbons, F. X., Stephan, W. G., Stephenson, B., & Petty, C. R. (1981). Contact relevance and reactions to stigmatized others: Response amplification vs. sympathy. *Journal of Experimental Social Psychology, 16,* 591-605.

Gonzales, A. (1979). Classroom cooperation and ethnic balance. Paper presented at the annual convention of the American Psychological Association, New York.

Grant, P. R., & Holmes, J. G. (1981). The integration of implicit personality theory, schemas, and stereotype images. *Social Psychology Quarterly, 44,* 107-115.

Greenblatt, S. L., & Willie, C. V. (1980). The serendipitous effects of school desegregation. In W. G. Stephan and J. Feagin (Eds.), *School desegregation* (pp. 51-66). New York: Plenum.

Guthrie, G. M. (1975). A behavioral analysis of culture learning. In R. W. Brislin, S. Bochner, & W. Lonner (Eds.), *Cross-cultural perspectives on learning* (pp. 95-116). Newbury Park, CA: Sage.

Hallinan, M. T., & Smith, S. S. (1985). The effects of classroom racial composition on students' interracial friendliness. *Social Psychology Quarterly, 48,* 3-16.

Hamill, R. T., Wilson, T. D., & Nisbett, R. E. (1980). Insensitivity to sample bias: Generalizing from atypical cases. *Journal of Personality and Social Psychology, 39,* 578-589.

Hamilton, D. L., Dugan, P. M., & Troiler, T. K. (1985). The formation of stereotypic beliefs: Further evidence for distinctiveness-based illusory correlations. *Journal of Personality and Social Psychology, 48,* 5-17.

Hamilton, D., & Gifford, R. K. (1976). Illusory correlation in interpersonal perception: A cognitive bias in stereotyping. *Journal of Experimental Social Psychology, 12,* 392-407.

Hansell, S. (1984). Cooperative groups, weak ties, and the integration of peer friendships. *Social Psychology Quarterly, 47,* 316-328.

Harding, J., & Hogrefe, R. (1952). Attitudes of white department store employees toward Negro co-workers. *Journal of Social Issues, 8* (1), 8-28.

Harding, J., Kutner, B., Proshansky, N., & Chein, I. (1954). Prejudice and ethnic relations. In G. Lindzey (Ed.), *Handbook of social psychology* (Vol. 2, pp. 1021-1061). Cambridge, MA: Addison-Wesley.

Hauserman, N., Walen, S. R., & Behling, M. (1973). Reinforced racial integration in the first grade: A study of generalization. *Journal of Applied Behavioral Analysis, 6,* 193-200.

Hendricks, M., & Bootzin, R. (1976). Race and sex as stimuli for negative affect and physical avoidance. *Journal of Social Psychology, 98,* 111-120.

Higgins, E. T., & Rholes, W. S. (1978). "Saying is believing": Effects of message modification on memory and liking for the person described. *Journal of Experimental Social Psychology, 14,* 363-378.

Higgins, E. T., Rholes, W. S., & Jones, C. R. (1977). Category accessibility and impression formation. *Journal of Experimental Social Psychology, 13,* 141-154.

Hinkle, S., & Schopler, J. (1986). Bias in the evaluation of in-group and out-group performance. In S. Worchel & W. G. Austin (Eds.), *Psychology of intergroup relations* (pp. 196-212). Chicago: Nelson-Hall.

Hoffman, E. (1985). The effect of race-ratio composition on the frequency of organizational communication. *Social Psychology Quarterly, 48,* 17-26.

Ickes, W. (1984). Compositions in black and white: Determinants of interaction in interracial dyads. *Journal of Personality and Social Psychology, 47,* 330-341.

Jones, E. E., Farina, A., Hastorf, A. H., Markus, H., Miller, D. T., & Scott, R. A. (1984). *Social stigma*. New York: Freeman.

Johnson, D. W., Johnson, R., & Maruyama, G. (1983). Interdependence and interpersonal attraction among heterogeneous and homogeneous individuals: A theoretical formulation and a mata-analysis of the research. *Review of Educational Research, 53,* 5-54.

Johnson, D. W., Johnson, R., & Maruyama, G. (1984). Goal interdependence and interpersonal attraction in heterogeneous classrooms. In N. Miller & M. B. Brewer (Eds.), *Groups in contact* (pp. 187-213). New York: Academic Press.

Kahn, A., & Ryen, A. (1972). Factors influencing bias toward one's own group. *International Journal of Group Tensions, 2,* 33-50.

Katz, I., Wackenhut, J., & Glass, D. G. (1986). An ambivalence-amplification theory of behavior toward the stigmatized. In S. Worchel & W. G. Austin (Eds.), *Psychology of intergroup relations* (pp. 103-117). Chicago: Nelson-Hall.

Katz, J. (1978). *White awareness: Handbook for anti-racist training*. Norman, OK: University of Oklahoma Press.

Katz, P. A. (1973). Stimulus differentiation and modification of children's racial attitudes. *Child Development, 44,* 232-237.

Katz, P. A., & Zalk, S. R. (1978). Modification of children's racial attitudes. *Developmental Psychology, 14,* 447-461.

Kluger, R. (1976). *Simple justice*. New York: Knopf.

Landis, D., Brislin, R. W., Swanner, G. M., Tseng, O.C.S., & Thomas, J. A. (1985). Some effects of acculturative training: A field evaluation. *International Journal of Group Tensions, 15,* 68-91.

Landis, D., Day, H. R., McGrew, P. L., Thomas, J. A., & Miller, A. B. (1976). Can a Black "culture assimilator" increase racial understanding? *Journal of Social Issues, 32,* 169-183.

Langer, E. J., Bashner, R. S., & Chanowitz, B. (1985). Decreasing prejudice by increasing discrimination. *Journal of Personality and Social Psychology, 49,* 113-120.

Langer, E. J., Fiske, S. T., Taylor, S. E., & Chanowitz, B. (1976). Stigma, staring, and discomfort: A novel stimulus hypothesis. *Journal of Experimental Social Psychology, 12,* 451-463.

Lingle, J. H., Geva, T. M., Ostrom, T. M., Leippe, M. R., & Baumgardner, M. H. (1979). Thematic effects of person judgments on impression organization. *Journal of Personality and Social Psychology, 37,* 674-687.

Linville, P. W. (1982). The complexity-extremity effect and age-based stereotyping. *Journal of Personality and Social Psychology, 42,* 192-211.

Linville, P. W., & Jones, E. E. (1980). Polarized appraisals of outgroup members. *Journal of Personality and Social Psychology, 38,* 689-703.

Locksley, A., Borgida, E., Brekke, N., & Hepburn, C. A. (1980). Sex stereotypes and social judgment. *Journal of Personality and Social Psychology, 39,* 821-831.

Longshore, D. (1982). School racial composition and blacks' attitudes toward desegregation: The problem of control in desegregated schools. *Social Science Quarterly, 63,* 674-687.

Maruyama, G., Miller, N., & Holtz, R. (1986). The relation between popularity and achievement: A longitudinal test of the lateral transmission of value hypothesis. *Journal of Personality and Social Psychology, 51,* 730-742.

McArthur, L. Z., & Soloman, L. K. (1978). Perceptions of an aggressive encounter as a function of the victim's salience and the perceiver's arousal. *Journal of Personality and Social Psychology, 36,* 1278-1290.

Millar, M. G., & Tessor, A. (1986). Thought-induced attitude change: The effects of schema structure and commitment. *Journal of Personality and Social Psychology, 51,* 259-269.

Miller, N., & Brewer, M. B. (1984). Beyond the contact hypothesis: Theoretical perspectives on desegregation. In N. Miller & M. B. Brewer (Eds.), *Groups in contact* (pp. 281-302). New York: Academic Press.

Miller, N., Brewer, M. B., & Edwards, K. (1985). Cooperative interaction in desegregated settings: A laboratory analogue. *Journal of Social Issues, 41* (3), 63-81.

Minard, R. D. (1952). Race relations in the Pocahontas coal field. *Journal of Social Issues, 8,* 29-44.

Norvel, N., & Worchel, S. (1981). A re-examination of the relation between equal-status contact and intergroup attraction. *Journal of Personality and Social Psychology, 41,* 902-908.

Ostrom, T. M., Lingle, J. H., Pryor, J. B., & Geva, N. (1980). Cognitive organization of person impressions. In R. Hastie, T. Ostrom, E. Ebbeson, R. Wyer, D. Hamilton, & D. Carlston (Eds.), *Person memory: The cognitive basis of social perception* (pp. 55-88). Hillsdale, NJ: Lawrence Erlbaum.

Parrish, T. S., & Fleetwood, R. S. (1975). Amount of conditioning and subsequent change in racial attitudes of children. *Perceptual and Motor Skills, 40,* 79-86.

Perlman, D., & Oskamp, S. (1971). The effects of picture content and exposure frequency on evaluations of Negroes and Whites. *Journal of Experimental Social Psychology, 7,* 503-514.

Pettigrew, T. F. (1971). *Racially separate or together?* New York: McGraw-Hill.

Pettigrew, T. F. (1979). The ultimate attribution error: Extending Allport's cognitive analysis of prejudice. *Personality and Social Psychology Bulletin, 5,* 461-476.

Quattrone, G. A. (1986). On the perceptions of a group's variability. In S. Worchel & W. G. Austin (Eds.), *Social psychology of intergroup relations* (pp. 25-48). Chicago: Nelson-Hall.

Randolph, G., Landis, D., & Tzeng, O.C.S. (1977). The effects of time and practice upon cultural assimilator training. *International Journal of Intercultural Relations, 1,* 105-119.

Riordan, C. (1978). Equal-status interracial contact: A review and revision of the concept. *International Journal of Intercultural Relations, 2,* 161-185.

Robinson, J. W., Jr., & Preston, J. D. (1976). Equal-status contact and modification of racial prejudice: A re-examination of the contact hypothesis. *Social Forces, 54,* 911-924.

Rogers, M., Hennigan, K., Bowman, C., & Miller, N. (1984). Intergroup acceptance in classroom and playground settings. In N. Miller & M. B. Brewer (Eds.), *Groups in contact: The psychology of desegregation* (pp. 204-228). New York: Academic Press.

Rokeach, M. (1971). Long-range experimental modification of values, attitudes and behavior. *American Psychologist, 26,* 453-459.

Rosenfield, D., Stephan, W. G., & Lucker, G. W. (1981). Attraction to competent and incompetent members of cooperative and competitive groups. *Journal of Applied Social Psychology, 11,* 416-433.

Rose, T. (1981). Cognitive and dyadic processes in intergroup contact. In D. L. Hamilton (Ed.), *Cognitive processes in stereotyping and intergroup behavior* (pp. 259-302). Hillsdale, NJ: Lawrence Erlbaum.

Rothbart, M. (1981). Memory processes and social beliefs. In D. L. Hamilton (Ed.), *Cognitive processes in stereotyping and intergroup behavior* (pp, 145-191). Hillsdale, NJ : Lawrence Erlbaum.

Rothbart, M., Evans, M., & Fulero, S. (1979). Recall for confirming events: Memory processes and the maintenance of stereotypes. *Journal of Experimental Social Psychology, 15,* 343-356.

Rothbart, M., & John, O. (1986). Social categorization and behavioral episodes: A cognitive analysis of the effects of intergroup contact. *Journal of Social Issues, 41* (3), 81-103.

Sagar, A., & Schofield, J. W. (1980). Racial and behavioral cues in black and white children's perceptions of ambiguously aggressive acts. *Journal of Personality and Social Psychology, 39,* 590-598.

St. John, N. (1975). *School desegregation: Outcomes for children.* New York: John Wiley.

Sappington, A. A. (1976). Effects of desensitization of prejudices whites to blacks upon subjects' stereotypes of blacks. *Perceptual and Motor Skills, 43,* 938.

Secord, P. F., & Beckman, C. W. (1964). *Social psychology.* New York: McGraw-Hill.

Skov, R. B., & Sherman, S. J. (1986). Information-gathering processes: Diagnosticity, hypothesis-confirmatory strategies, and perceived hypothesis confirmation. *Journal of Experimental Social Psychology, 22,* 93-121.

Slavin, R. E. (1978). Student teams and achievement divisions. *Journal of Research and Development in Education, 12,* 381-387.

Slavin, R. E. (1985). Cooperative learning: Applying contact theory in desegregated schools. *Journal of Social Issues, 41* (3), 45-62.

Snyder, M., Tanke, E. D., & Berscheid, E. (1977). Social perception and interpersonal behavior: On the self-fulfilling nature of social stereotypes. *Journal of Personality and Social Psychology, 35,* 656-666.

Snyder, M., & Swann, W. B., Jr. (1978a). Hypothesis testing processes in social interaction. *Journal of Personality and Social Psychology, 36,* 1202-1212.

Snyder, M., & Swann, W. B., Jr. (1978b). Behavioral confirmation in social interaction: From social perception to social reality. *Journal of Experimental Social Psychology, 14,* 148-162.

Stenning, B. W. (1979). Problems in cross-cultural contact: A literature review. *International Journal of Intercultural Relations, 3,* 269-313.

Stephan, W. G. (1985). Intergroup relations. In G. Lindzey & E. Aronson (Eds.), *Handbook of social psychology* (Vol. 3, pp. 599-658). New York: Addison-Wesley.

Stephan, W. G. (1986). Effects of school desegregation: An evaluation 30 years after Brown. In L. Saxe & M. Saks (Eds.), *Advances in applied social psychology* (Vol. 4, pp. 181-206). New York: Academic Press.

Stephan, W. G., & Rosenfield, D. (1978a). The effects of desegregation on racial attitudes. *Journal of Personality and Social Psychology, 36,* 795-804.

Stephan, W. G., & Rosenfield, D. (1978b). The effects of desegregation on race relations and self-esteem. *Journal of Educational Psychology, 70,* 670-679.

Stephan, W. G., & Stephan, C. W. (1984). The role of ignorance in intergroup relations. In M. B. Brewer & N. Miller (Eds.), *Groups in contact: The psychology of desegregation* (pp. 229-257). New York: Academic Press.

Stephan, W. G., & Stephan, C. W. (1985). Intergroup anxiety. *Journal of Social Issues, 41* (3), 157-175.

Tajfel, H. (1978). *Differentiation between social groups.* London: Academic Press.

Taylor, D. C., Sheatsley, P. B., & Greeley, A. M. (1978). Attitudes toward racial integration. *Scientific American, 238,* 42-49.

Taylor, S. E., Fiske, S. T., Etcoff, N. L., & Ruderman, A. J. (1978). Categorical and contextual bases of person memory and stereotyping. *Journal of Personality and Social Psychology, 36,* 778-793.

Traindis, H. C. (1972). *The analysis of subjective culture.* New York: John Wiley.

Wagner, U., & Schonbach, P. (1984). Links between educational status and prejudice: Ethnic attitudes in West Germany. In M.B. Brewer & N. Miller (Eds.), *Groups in contact: The psychology of desegregation* (pp. 29-52). New York: Academic Press.

Watson, G. (1974). *Action for unity.* New York: Harper.

Weber, R., & Crocker, J. (1982). Cognitive processes in the revision of stereotypic beliefs. *Journal of Personality and Social Psychology, 45,* 961-977.

Webster, S. W. (1961). The influence of interracial contact on social acceptance in a newly desegregated school. *Journal of Educational Psychology, 52,* 292-296.

Weigel, R. H., & Howes, P. W. (1985). Conceptions of racial prejudice. *Journal of Social Issues,* 41(3), 117-138.

Weldon, D. W., Carlston, A., Rissman, A. K., Slobodin, L., & Triandis, H. C. (1975). A laboratory test of the effects of culture assimilator training. *Journal of Personality and Social Psychology, 32,* 300-310.

Wilder, D. A. (1978). Perceiving persons as a group: Effects on attributions of causality and beliefs. *Social Psychology, 41,* 13-23.

Wilder, D. A. (1986). Cognitive factors affecting the success of intergroup contact. In S. Worchel & W. G. Austin (Eds.), *Social psychology of intergroup relations* (pp. 49-66). Chicago: Nelson-Hall.

Williams, R. M., Jr. (1947). *The reduction of intergroup tensions.* New York: Social Science Research Council.

Williams. R. M., Jr. (1964). *Strangers next door.* Englewood Cliffs, NJ: Prentice-Hall.

Williams, R. M., Jr. (1977). *Mutual accommodation: Ethnic conflict and cooperation.* Minneapolis: University of Minnesota Press.

Wilson, W. J. (1980). *The declining significance of race.* Chicago: University of Chicago Press.

Worchel, S. (1986). The role of cooperation in reducing intergroup conflict. In S. Worchel & W. G. Austin (Eds.), *Psychology of intergroup relations.* Chicago: Nelson-Hall.

Word, C. O., Zanna, M. P., & Cooper, J. (1974). The non-verbal mediation of self-fulfilling prophecies in interracial interaction. *Journal of Experimental Social Psychology, 10,* 109-120.

Zajonc, R. B. (1980). Compresence. In P. B. Paulus (Ed.), *Psychology of group influence* (pp. 35-60). Hillsdale, NJ: Lawrence Erlbaum.

2

Theoretical Models of Intergroup Relations and the Use of Cooperative Teams as an Intervention for Desegregated Settings

NORMAN MILLER
GAYE DAVIDSON-PODGORNY

Norman Miller, Professor of Psychology at the University of Southern California, is interested in intergroup relations and, with Marilynn Brewer, has recently edited *Groups in Contact: The Psychology of Desegregation* (Academic Press). He is also interested in social projection and in the extension of meta-analysis procedures to test theoretical interpretations of social psychological phenomena.

Gaye Davidson-Podgorny is a Ph.D. candidate at the University of Southern California. Her research interests include intergroup relations and decision making.

Separation, hostility, conflict, and mutual rejection characterize intergroup relations, irrespective of whether or not most members of the groups in question are in direct contact. Though social science has long sought constructive approaches to these issues, simple solutions have not emerged. Undoubtedly, the complexity of real-world situations contributes to the difficulties. School desegregation, however, seemed to be a particularly appealing remedial approach for a number of reasons. Once the political problems in achieving it could be successfully overcome, it constituted a structural change at a macro social level that sends a normative message to all the racial/ethnic groups within the society. It signals an intent and policy not simply of fairness in the distribution of educational resources, but also one of social acceptance of the diverse groups within a pluralistic society. Additionally, however, by promoting contact between group members in whom social habits of

AUTHORS' NOTE: We thank Stuart Cook, Clyde Hendrick, David Johnson, Walter Stephan, and David Wilder for constructive criticism. Additionally, we thank the Social Science Research Institute for help in preparing the manuscript for publication.

rejection and hostility are presumably not as well practiced and entrenched as they are among adults, it seemed to have greater likelihood of success than did other structural changes. Moreover, by producing intergroup contact in a setting that rivals, if not exceeds, that of any other environment (including the home) in terms of the number of waking hours that the child spends in it, its cumulative impact could be expected to be considerable. Finally, a parallel but previous social experiment, the integration of the armed services, seemed to have met with some success (Stouffer, Lumsdaine, Lumsdaine, & Williams, 1949).

Though debate will always arise on matters of degree, many commentators feel that the promise of school desegregation anticipated in the social science statement appended to the plaintiff's case in the *Brown* decision has not been fulfilled (e.g., Hochschild, 1984; Miller, 1981; St. John, 1975). While communities, the courts, and school districts have in recent years backed away from initiating new desegregation plans, researchers and practitioners at the same time began to develop procedures and programs to promote academic mastery and intergroup acceptance in racially heterogeneous schools. One might argue that such efforts are foolhardy, given the change in social climate. In a pluralistic society, however, there will always be schools within neighborhoods of transition where distinct racial/ethnic groups occupy contiguous residential space. As minority groups increase in size and number, such naturally desegregated schools will also increase. Thus the practical problem of making such schools effective learning environments in which intergroup friction is not a disruptive force will remain, irrespective of the political decisions that frame the nature and direction in which national school desegregation policy moves. And for those interested in understanding intergroup relations, such schools provide a continuing laboratory for testing relevant principles and procedures.

By far, the most widespread intervention for schools that are heterogeneous in their racial/ethnic composition is the use of some form of cooperative team activity. Distinct procedures have been developed by researchers within education (DeVries & Edwards, 1974; Sharan & Sharan, 1976; Slavin, 1978a), social psychology (Aronson, Blaney, Stephan, Sikes, & Snapp, 1978; Johnson & Johnson, 1975; Miller, Rogers, & Hennigan, 1983), and sociology (Cohen & Roper, 1972). At the same time, other researchers have sought to develop basic social psychology theory about prejudice, some emphasizing cognitive factors and others attending primarily to perceptual or motivational factors (Brewer & Miller, 1984; Berger, Cohen, & Zelditch, 1972; Cook, 1984;

Katz, 1981; Rothbart & John, 1985; Stephan & Stephan, 1984; Tajfel, 1981). More often than not, work by the latter group has been conducted within university laboratory settings rather than in schools.

Although those in each research group have an awareness of those in other groups, this chapter seeks to strengthen the link between the theoretical and applied work. First, for illustrative purposes we describe important features of some of the most prominent of the cooperative team learning interventions developed for classroom use. We then select three theoretical models regarding intergroup acceptance, briefly describing each. Focusing primarily on the theoretical propositions that distinguish them from one another, we discuss implications regarding specific aspects of the way in which the classroom interventions are implemented. Then, to the degree possible with a relatively small set of published studies on the effects of the classroom interventions, we use meta-analytic procedures to examine some of the consequences of variations in the manner in which they are implemented. Within space constraints, we cannot be comprehensive. Instead, we hope to do three things: In general, we want to draw attention to the reciprocal bearing on one another of (a) field experimentation on intragroup cooperation within racially heterogeneous educational settings, and (b) aspects of mainstream social psychological intergroup theory and research. Second, by discussing the ambiguities in translating the ideas of existing theoretical models into practical procedures, we thereby hope to encourage theorists to give more attention to such concerns. Finally, in presenting some empirical data, our goal is not to evaluate the relative validity of the three models, but rather to suggest variables that may be important to a comprehensive theory of intergroup prejudice and to consider their relation to the three theoretical models.

Classroom Team Learning Interventions

This section describes and compares some of the cooperative team learning interventions in relatively wide use in educational settings.

In Teams Games Tournament (TGT), as developed by Edwards, DeVries, and Snyder (1972), students are assigned to four- or five-member learning teams. Typically, teams are constructed to be heterogeneous with respect to gender and racial/ethnic background. Each week the teacher introduces new material via lecture or discussion, but the major aspect of learning occurs when team members study worksheets and other material relevant to the week's lesson. The children may use a variety of procedures to master the material. Within each team they may take turns quizzing one another, tutoring each other, discussing the material as a group, and in general spending their allocated time on Monday through Thursday preparing one another for the interteam competition scheduled for Friday. In this latter phase, which is designed to assess the degree to which team members have mastered the material, a member of one team competes against members of two other teams at each of several separate tables in the classroom. At each table the selection of children for that competition is stratified (matched) on the basis of their respective performance levels the preceding week, thus roughly equating the achievement levels of the competitors. The children proceed by consecutively turning over cards from a stand in the center of the table, quizzing each other in rotation, and accumulating points for their team as they correctly answer each question or challenge answers given incorrectly. A class newsletter, often posted visibly, recognizes the highest scoring teams and tournament subdivision winners.

Other procedures are similar, but differ in important ways. Learning Together (Johnson & Johnson, 1975) and Jigsaw (Aronson et al., 1978) omit the interteam competition that characterizes TGT. On the other hand, whereas the Johnsons emphasize positive interdependence by using team scores to reward students at the team level, the Jigsaw procedure only includes individual testing. Moreover, in their own implementation of Jigsaw, Aronson et al. typically included some instruction and work designed to sensitize the children to issues about group process, directly dealing with motivational and communicative patterns that promote or disrupt group functioning. The Johnsons also instruct teachers to sensitize them to these concerns. In contrast, when Slavin (1980) implements the Jigsaw procedure in what he terms Jigsaw II, he omits these group process ingredients. Additionally, Jigsaw differs from other procedures in that it explicitly requires role specialization at the individual level. Prior to the team learning phase, each team member is assigned responsibility for a specific section of the lesson unit. The members of each team who are assigned responsibility for a common section of the unit meet together (as an expert group) to master that aspect of the material, and only then does each return to his or her own team to "assemble" the unit. Thus Jigsaw also contains interteam cooperation, as well as division of labor, as important structural features.

Student Teams Achievement Divisions (STAD) parallels TGT but omits its competitive game table (Slavin, 1978a). Instead, the outcomes of interteam competition are based on the improvement scores of team members when assessed against their past performance. As in TGT, team scores are publicized via a class newsletter. An important psychological feature of STAD may include its absence of face-to-face competitive interaction. Additionally, in its use of relative academic improvement (gain scores) as opposed to absolute performance scores, it masks group differences in achievement that may be correlated with race or ethnicity within a given school setting. TGT also achieves this effect, though in a different manner.

Three Theoretical Approaches
to Intergroup Relations

In this section we describe briefly each of three models concerned with intergroup relations. Probably none is intended to be sufficient or complete. More likely, each focuses on subsets of variables it deems important. For illustrative purposes, we choose expectation states theory (Cohen, 1982; Berger et al., 1972), the ignorance model of Stephan and Stephan (1984, 1985), and the social categorization model as developed by Brewer and Miller (1984). Clearly others could have been added and/or substituted, thus there is an arbitrariness in our selection. The authors of each, however, were familiar with cooperative learning interventions and, as a group, the three models have the feature of emphasizing cognitive, motivational, and perceptual variables respectively, although none is as pure as this simplified depiction suggests.

The expectation states model. Focusing on the effect of status on intergroup behavior, this approach argues that status differences between groups on any dimension are generalized inappropriately to new situations. Furthermore, intergroup contact will tend to reinforce prior differences in status unless explicit efforts are made to undermine them in the contact situation (Berger et al., 1972; Cohen, 1982; Humphreys & Berger, 1981).

A distinction is made between two kinds of status characteristics, diffuse and specific. A status characteristic is diffuse if it is evaluated by society in terms of honor, esteem, and desirability, and a set of general expectations for behavior, such as intelligence or competence, is associated with it. Race is an example of a diffuse characteristic, in that many Americans believe that whites are typically more competent than blacks. On the other hand, a status characteristic is specific if it is valued and if a distinct or specific expectation is associated with it. An example of a specific status characteristic is reading ability. A student who excels in reading may also be expected to excel in other related subjects, such as composition, but not necessarily in mathematics, chess, or sports.

Expectation states theory specifies certain conditions, called "scope conditions," in which the status-organizing process is likely to occur. A task elicits the status-organizing process when there is more than one participant involved in a collective effort that encourages the participants to evaluate each other's contributions, the group believes that the contribution of each member will affect the success or failure of the outcome, and group members are distinguishable on at least one status characteristic. The more salient the status characteristic, the more likely is the task to encourage status-organizing processes.

When a status-organizing process occurs, both specific and diffuse status characteristics combine to produce an expectation. Depending on the situation, some specific characteristics will contribute more or less than others. Given the unitary curriculum emphases on reading in the typical classroom, the specific status characteristic of reading ability will have much greater weight in its combination with the diffuse characteristic of race than would, for instance, the specific status characteristic of ability to play chess. The point, however, is that the two types of status characteristics combine to affect expectations and behavior with respect to activities other than those associated specifically with the status dimension. Moreover, position on a diffuse status dimension will carry over to create expectancies even in the absence of information on specific status dimensions.

From these propositions, Cohen (1984) derived a model that relates classroom peer interaction to competence expectations. Its basic hypothesis is that classroom social status influences the frequency of interaction with fellow classmates. Interaction patterns in the classroom will reflect expectations for competence and prior attitudes toward the out-group.

The ignorance model. Among the three, the ignorance model is the most elaborate. It emphasizes the role of knowledge about and familiarity with the out-group as a determinant of intergroup attitudes and behaviors (Stephan & Stephan, 1984). The main assertion, simply put, is that ignorance causes prejudice. Intergroup contact leading to increased knowledge about an out-group's culture will promote intergroup acceptance and reduce intergroup hostility.

A key variable believed to mediate the indirect effects of ignorance and other antecedent variables on prejudice is anxiety. Consequently, even though the model invokes cognitive and perceptual factors, we have characterized it as a motivational model. It argues that contact between distinct social groups often creates anxiety (Heiss & Nash, 1967; Hendricks & Bootzin, 1976; Rankin & Campbell, 1955), and that ignorance about the culture of out-groups is an important contributor to that anxiety, in that people tend to fear that which they do not understand and cannot predict. Although information about the differences between own and other groups can decrease prejudice, in accord with much other literature, the model also notes that perceived differences can augment prejudice. Thus assumed dissimilarity to the out-group can contribute to the anxiety that leads to negative intergroup relations by selectively focusing attention on comparisons that favor the in-group, promote discrimination in favor of the in-group, and foster a disliking of the out-group (Brewer, 1979; Byrne, 1961; Hensley & Duval, 1976). Presumably, the critical feature that determines a beneficial direction of effect is that information denoting differences must be presented as a positive attribute, perhaps by portraying it as reflecting an underlying need or goal common to both the in-group and the out-group. Finally, lacking sufficient information about the out-group, in-group members characterize them by relying on stereotypes that typically reflect ethnocentric biases and present the out-group negatively (Campbell, 1967).

To combat the roles of ignorance, perceived dissimilarities, stereotypes, and anxiety in creating intergroup hostility, group members need to learn more about the out-group. The contact environment should facilitate understanding about group differences as well as similarities. Although Stephan and Stephan (1984) cite studies showing that the biases inherent in stereotypes may sometimes be offset with specific information about out-group members (Fiske, 1982; Kahneman & Tversky, 1973; Nisbett & Borgida, 1975), it is their discussion of knowledge about the out-group as defined at the group level, rather than at the level of individual out-group members, that most clearly distinguishes their model from others. Therefore, our discussion often focuses on this feature.

The social categorization model. In an elegant review, Wilder (1986) comprehensively discusses the application of principles of social categorization to intergroup relations. The essential notion is the discernment of group boundaries. Campbell (1956) provided impetus to this view by emphasizing the bearing of Gestalt perceptual organizing processes on the definition of a group. The process of categorization, however, undoubtedly involves other types of cognitive processes as well. A key necessity in any categorization process is the existence of another category that does not exemplify the features of the first. In the case of social groups, their self-reflective nature, fluidity, and contribution to members' self-identities all act to differentiate them from other types of categories (Wilder, 1986). The latter feature in particular probably accounts for the fact that members of social groups also invoke special attributional patterns when depicting out-groups (Pettigrew, 1979).

Apart from whatever motivational and other psychological processes are induced when the categories in question are social groups, the sheer process of categorization leads to overestimation of similarity within categories and overestimation of distance between them (Campbell, 1956; Tajfel & Wilkes, 1963). Moreover, when the categories are social groups, an evaluative overlay is ubiquitously added to this picture (Campbell, 1967; Merton, 1948; Tajfel, 1970).

Social categorization theory, as applied to the improvement of intergroup relations, posits that anything that increases category salience is likely to have deleterious effects. Brewer and Miller (1984) argue that when features of the setting promote an interpersonal as opposed to a task focus and when the basis for assignment to roles, status, special functions, or subgroups is perceived to be category independent, social interactions between members of distinct groups are less likely to exhibit the otherwise pervasive bias (see Hinkle & Schopler, 1986) that characterizes intergroup evaluations. In addition, other general features of the setting, such as the numerical composition of the groups (Taylor, Fiske, Close, Anderson, & Ruderman, 1975), the presence of crosscutting categories (Levine & Campbell, 1972), the presence of external threat (Tajfel, 1978), and the valence of task outcomes (Kahn & Ryen, 1972; Zander, Stotland, & Wolfe, 1960) will affect category salience.

Implications of the Three Models
for Structuring Cooperative Interaction

There is little doubt that cooperative interaction improves intergroup relations. Slavin (1983) demonstrated this clearly in his review of studies that compare traditional teaching methods to TGT and STAD procedures, as did Sharan in an earlier review (1980). Johnson, Johnson, and Maruyama (1984) confirmed this outcome in their meta-analysis of studies that compare the use of competitive, individualistic, cooperative, and mixed-goal structures in racially heterogeneous classrooms. Nevertheless, "there is much work to be done to discover the critical components of cooperative learning for intergroup relations and to inform a model of how cooperative learning methods operate to affect intergroup relations" (Slavin, 1983, p. 88). Though functional interdependence to some degree characterizes any cooperative interaction, the theoretical models described above differ in the additional theoretical variables that they uniquely emphasize or see as most important in moderating the effect. In this section we discuss the bearing of these aspects of the three models on the classroom intervention procedures.

The expectation states model. The expectation states model stresses the destructive effects of information that confirms the expectations that high-status children have toward the low-status out-group children on their team. On first thought, a procedure like TGT, which groups the competitors at each game table in terms of their performance level of the previous week, appears sensitive to this concern. On the other hand, children quickly size up the academic meanings that are discernable in any given situation—for instance, who is smart and who is not (Hoffman & Cohen, 1972; Lippit & Gold, 1959). Additionally, in settings in which there is an average performance difference between blacks and whites, students at some game tables may be homogeneously white and others homogeneously black. The Johnsons's method, by eliminating both interteam competition and a high salience of individual scores, appears to eliminate important sources of potential stereotype confirmation. On the other hand, this entire discussion may be misleading in that attention to the nature and extent to test score feedback ignores the fact that the interaction with one's teammates in the mastery phase of the cooperative learning intervention inevitably provides one with information about the quality of the individual, and, implicitly, ethnic group performance. Thus, rather than emphasizing implementation procedures that may, but probably will not, succeed in masking such ethnic group differences as may exist in the particular school setting, it seems better to adopt a strategy of explicitly building in structural ingredients that will function to eliminate them. In this sense, one might expect the Jigsaw method to be superior to less structured procedures; the personal responsibility implicit in individual role assignments, along with the corresponding dependence of teammates on the quality of one another's preparation, is likely to provide strong impetus to improved performance. In the same vein, the competitive aspect of TGT might serve a similar function. In Slavin's analyses of team learning methods, however, he concludes that the key structural feature that augments academic achievement is the presence of group rewards based on individual achievement (Slavin, 1983, 1986), a feature absent in Jigsaw but present in TGT. Presumably, this feature also maximizes the closing of racial/ethnic achievement gaps and in this sense leads to reduced opportunity to confirm existing stereotypes.

The ignorance model. According to the ignorance model, knowledge about the out-group at the group level will be salutary. Although existing cooperative team learning procedures do not differ in the extent to which they provide such information, the principle might imply a statistical interaction between their use and the substantive content of the segment of the educational curriculum to which they are applied. Specifically, in comparison to use with science or mathematics, they might be more beneficial when used in conjunction with social studies segments concerned with racial/ethnic and national group history, cultures, and customs, especially when they are presented positively and concern the specific minority groups in the class.

Additionally, language in part comprises culture. Language arts components of the curriculum might draw attention to language differences and, consequently, result in increased knowledge about the subgroups in the class. In the context of mastering standard English, however, such differences implicitly may have pejorative implications for minority members, perhaps especially in the case of black speech. From this standpoint, the component of the ignorance model that sees perceived dissimilarities that are not put into a positive evaluative context as contributing to prejudice, suggests that effects obtained with language arts as compared to those with science and mathematics might be less, rather than more, positive.

Anxiety associated with interacting with out-group persons is another important ingredient. Highly structured activity tends to reduce intergroup anxiety (Stephan & Stephan, 1985). This implies that a procedure such as Jigsaw may be superior to others in that it is the one technique that clearly imposes individual role assignments. The resulting increase in within-team structure should reduce the tendency of interethnic interaction to arouse anxiety. Similarly, a strong task focus also provides structure to social interactions and might thereby reduce anxiety. From this standpoint, mixed reward structures (intrateam cooperation and interteam competition) as found in TGT and STAD, in contrast to the pure cooperative reward structure used in Jigsaw and Learning Together, should be more facilitative in that the interteam competition that they feature will augment a task focus which, in turn, structures activity. Additionally, Aronson's Jigsaw should be superior to Slavin's modification of it (Jigsaw II) because the latter eliminates group process work with the children on issues of communication, interpersonal relations, and facilitation of group goals. Developing children's capabilities to deal with the difficult aspects of social interaction should reduce social anxiety associated with interracial interaction.

We see the ignorance model as implicitly distinguishing between anxiety in general and anxiety that derives from (anticipated) interaction with out-group members. To the degree that general anxiety is critical, the Johnson procedure should stand above others as superior by virtue of its use of group-based rewards and deemphasis on intergroup or interindividual competition, conditions that should minimize many sources of anxiety.

The social categorization model. Turning to the social categorization model, concern centers on the aspects of interventions that increase category salience. As indicated, one such source is factors that promote a task as opposed to an interpersonal focus. Competition increases task focus (Miller, Brewer, & Edwards, 1985). To the degree that attention is focused on the task, information about the individual attributes of teammates is not processed. This leaves category distinctions, attendant stereotypes, and out-group prejudice intact. Thus, mixed goal structures (as found in TGT and STAD) should be less effective than pure cooperation, an outcome confirmed in a recent meta-analysis (Johnson et al., 1984).

As previously indicated, another feature that can decrease category salience is the perception that assignment to teams, roles, and subgroups within teams, is independent of category membership (Miller et al., 1985). None of the cooperative team procedures explicitly espouses rules for assignment to subgroups. Indeed, with the exception of Jigsaw and Group Investigation (Sharan & Sharan, 1976), which also uses individual role assignments, none employs any single or multiperson role specialization. On the other hand, guidelines for implementing TGT and STAD specify distribution of minority members to teams in a ratio that roughly approximates their proportion in the class as a whole. Although they too explicitly recommend diversity within teams, Jigsaw and Learning Together seem less direct on this point. At any rate, it is clear from talking with teachers and children in TGT classes that children are aware that racial identity is used as a basis for assignment to teams. This feature should function to enhance the salience of category membership in that the children see the teacher, a high-status role model, use racial identity as an important ingredient in decision making (Miller et al., 1985).

On the other hand, gender is also used in these procedures as a basis for team assignment. To the extent that categories crosscut one another, as when both race and gender are used as the basis for assignment to teams, the salience of either of the categories should be diffused (Brewer & Miller, 1984). Jigsaw, however, goes even further by recommending that "larger groups should ideally contain both boys and girls, assertive and nonassertive students, fast and slow readers, and members of different racial or ethnic groups" (Aronson et al., 1978, p. 36), thereby maximizing the number of dimensions on which there is heterogeneity.

Whereas public recognition of performance can make salient group level differences in performance and/or ability levels, when the method of public recognition is carefully engineered to avoid such implicit instruction, it might provide the alternative benefit of individuating group members and thereby reducing categorization effects (Wilder, 1986). The team learning procedures that advocate public recognition, however, all do so at the group rather than the individual level. Though this may enhance the salience of team boundaries and thereby counter habitual categorization along racial or ethnic boundaries, it may simultaneously increase interteam competitiveness. The heightened team cohesion produced by competition, however, may not generalize well to other out-group persons not on one's team. Much the same can be said about TGT, which, by using a form of interteam competition that requires face-to-face competition, provides more opportunity for personalized or individuated contact that is directly concerned with aspects of academic performance than does STAD, in which the competition occurs only at the group level. Although from this standpoint the social categorization model might suggest greater advantage to the former procedure, to the extent that it elicits greater competitiveness, the task focus that goes hand in hand with competition may disrupt the processing of individuating information.

Empirical Consequences of Variations
in Methods of Implementing
Cooperative Team Learning

The preceding sections, though obviously speculative, suggest differences in the specific features that theoretical positions emphasize as important in designing an ideal cooperative team learning procedure for classroom use. Additionally, they point to ingredients deemed important by one or another theoretical view, but not explicitly or ordinarily included in specific procedures.

Whereas the beneficial effects of introducing cooperative teams into classroom procedures might profit from attention to the preceding considerations, it is also possible that differences in the outcomes obtained under different conditions of implementation might be informative about variables important to a comprehensive theory of intergroup relations. The purpose of this section is not to definitively test the comparative validity of the three models.[1] Instead, it provides an example of how researchers can take advantage of the contextual variation that exists from one study to the next with respect to variables that have potential bearing on theoretical propositions of interest and use it to guide future research. The outcomes can comment on whether a given variable is indeed likely to be theoretically important and therefore a good candidate for further experimental test. Specifically, with respect to published studies that we could locate, we apply meta-analysis procedures to test six theoretically relevant dimensions on which there was variation in implementation procedures. For each case, we evaluated into which of two respective categories it fell and then compared the mean effect size of cases in each category in order to assess whether or not each moderator variable affected the mean magnitude of effect.

Literature search. To obtain a sample of published research articles that assessed the effects of cooperative contact on intergroup relations in desegregated school settings, we first examined *Psychological Abstracts* and reference sections contained within recent articles directly concerned with desegregation field interventions. We then examined their reference sections to locate additional sources, continuing this procedure until no new citations appeared.

Inclusionary criteria for studies. A study was included in the meta-analysis if it was published in either a research journal or a book, it consisted of a field experiment conducted in one or more classrooms in a desegregated school, it involved a direct comparison between students randomly assigned to an experimental group involved in a cooperative intervention and a control group in which the teacher used an individualistic or traditional classroom structure, the intervention structured cooperative contact between distinct racial or ethnic groups, dependent measures directly assessed the social relations between class members, and it contained enough statistical information to adequately estimate an effect size (including the sample N and means and standard deviations for the experimental and control groups, a t or F value directly comparing the experimental with the control group, or an χ^2 value comparing the proportions of experimental and control group subjects who displayed positive intergroup behaviors). No correlational (i.e., nonexperimental) studies or studies of cooperative interventions in settings other than desegregated schools, such as those conducted in prisons, business environments, and laboratory settings, were included.

Characteristics of the data. A total of 21 separate publications, noted with an asterisk (*) in the reference section, met these criteria. Occasionally a single publication reported more than one study, resulting in 25 independent cases. All studies were field experiments that employed one of the intervention models discussed previously, with the exception of one study by Cohen and Sharan (1980), which used a variation of Group Investigation (Sharan & Sharan, 1976). All used direct observation or sociometric questionnaires to assess the intergroup attitudes and/or behavior of all children toward those classmates who were not members of their own racial/ethnic in-group.

Effect size calculation and statistical analysis. When possible, effect size was calculated by using the pooled estimate of standard deviation (see Glass, McGaw, & Smith, 1981; Hunter, Schmidt, & Jackson, 1982). When only the F, t, or χ^2 values were reported, we used the conversion formulas found in Glass et al. Subsequent analyses used t-tests to compare the sets of individual effect size estimates of the cases that fell within each level of each moderator variable. Comparisons of effect size means are most susceptible to confounding when research designs vary greatly across studies. The constraints imposed by the study selection criteria resulted in studies equivalent in design and implementation, thereby minimizing this concern.

The mean effect size for the 25 independent comparison cases was +.415, with a standard deviation of .195. In all instances, the effect for the treatment group exceeded that of the control group, indicating a uniformly positive outcome for all cooperative interventions.

Definitions of
Moderator Variables and Results

The results are summarized in Table 2.1. In sequence, for each of six moderator variables, we discuss its definition, the results of the analysis, and their relation to the three models.

TABLE 2.1
Tests of Moderator Variables

Variable	Mean Effect Sizes [a]		N	t [b]
Task interdependence	Interdependent	Non-interdependent		
independent[c]	.658 (.244)	.375 (.186)	25	1.977****
total	.527 (.192)	.328 (.180)	60	2.485***
Reward structure	Interdependent	Individualistic		
independent	.436 (.175)	.486 (.212)	25	.171
total	.348 (.181)	.447 (.209)	60	1.371
Task role assignment	Random assignment	No assignment		
independent	.670 (.212)	.375 (.186)	24	1.906****
total	.523 (.197)	.328 (.180)	59	2.336**
Curriculum content	Language arts	Math and science		
independent	.323 (.101)	.503 (.208)	15	1.829****
total	.298 (.189)	.446 (.204)	32	2.011***
Publicized performance	Present	Absent		
independent	.322 (.104)	.390 (.165)	25	.948
total	.315 (.163)	.375 (.170)	60	.884
Numerical representation I	Equal proportion	Unequal proportion		
independent	.503 (.189)	.346 (.131)	23	2.377**
total	.434 (.175)	.297 (.163)	55	2.874*
Numberical representation II	Majority exceeds minority	Minority exceeds majority		
independent	.320 (.110)	.360 (.059)	13	.240
total	.295 (.151)	.330 (.065)	31	.223

a. Standard deviations are in parentheses.

b. All tests are two-tailed.

c. The studies in the sample reported varying numbers of hypothesis tests. In other words, one subject may have provided more than one response measure in a given study. The meta-analyst must decide whether to treat each test as an independent observation or to pool the results from those tests within a single study and provide one effect size per study. In the former procedure, the assumption of independence is obviously false. We deem this to be of serious consequence. Several researchers (e.g., Mullen, et al., 1985; Johnson, Johnson, & Maruyama, 1984) suggest, however, that potentially valuable information regarding the generality of effects in the sample population is lost when hypothesis tests are pooled within studies. For these reasons, we report effect sizes in two ways: first, we pool the multiple effect sizes from each dependent measure within a study to create a single effect size per study (independent); second, we treat the effect sizes based on each dependent measure as separate data points (total).

*Significant at p < .01; **significant at p < .05; ***significant at p < .06; ****significant at p < .075.

Task structure. Although all experiments included in the analysis used a cooperative task structure, not all tasks required interdependence among team members. We defined a task as interdependent if it explicitly required each participant to contribute to it and failure of any one team member to contribute would preclude its completion. A task was defined as noninterdependent if it encouraged cooperation but did not require interdependence for its completion.

As shown in the first rows of Table 2.1, tasks that required interdependence were associated with more benefit than those that were not.

With respect to the expectation states model, the mutual fate implicit in task interdependence might increase the salience of group-linked performance differences. This heightened salience of status-related expectations might in turn increase intergroup hostility. At the same time, however, it is important to note the consistent positive effect of these interventions on the academic performance of minority children. In settings where they occur, they do reduce academic performance gaps between black and white children. From this standpoint, interdependence might increase the salience of such academic improvements. The issue here seems to hinge, however, on relative declines versus absolute reversals in group-level performance differences. Cohen argues that absolute minority superiority, not a relative lessening of any deficit, is necessary to alter status expectations and to reduce social rejection on the part of white children toward black classmates. Perhaps, despite the consistent academic benefit produced by cooperative team learning, such relative gains are not of sufficient magnitude to be noticed by children and processes as counter-stereotypic. Further complicating this discussion, however, is the issue of the symmetry of intergroup processes. The response measures we analyze are bidirectional, including minority children's social acceptance of white classmates as well as white children's acceptance of their minority classmates. We see the expectation states model as predicting bidirectional effects. Thus, to whatever degree a decrease in group-linked performance differences affects one group, it would also affect the other.

The ignorance model suggests that heightened anxiety increases prejudice. In racially heterogeneous classes, the meaning of interdependence in conjunction with cooperative learning procedures is that students must depend on others toward whom they may have negative racial attitudes. If contact leads to intergroup anxiety, it seems likely that interdependent contact might lead to even greater anxiety, suggesting an outcome at odds with that obtained. On the other hand, interdependence may also imply greater structure, which in turn should reduce anxiety and, consequently, prejudice. The obtained outcome may reflect this latter process and thus be consistent with the ignorance model.

To the extent that task interdependence will encourage interaction with and individuation of out-group members, the social categorization model suggests it will promote positive intergroup relations. Likewise, the component of the ignorance model that sees personalized interaction as potentially disconfirming erroneous stereotypes might also suggest benefit. That is, as indicated above, task interdependence might augment the salience of the relative erroneousness of academic performance stereotypes. It is less clear, however, that it would supply added information about cultural differences. In contrast to the ignorance model, the categorization model sees any increase in personalized interaction as potentially beneficial, irrespective of whether it supplies information on the subjective culture of the groups in the setting.

Reward structure. In addition to the possibility of interdependence in performing a task, it is also possible to make participants interdependent in obtaining rewards. Reward structures were defined as interdependent when rewards were allocated to the team as a while, and as individualistic when only allocated to individual team members.

As seen in Table 2.1, comparison of interdependent and individualistic reward structures indicates little effect. Moreover, its direction is opposite when only allocated to individual team members.

To the extent that cooperative team learning improves minority performance and thereby counters expectations or stereotypes, the ignorance and expectation states models might have expected greater benefit from interdependent as opposed to individualistic rewards in that the former would seem to make such counterstereotypic gains more salient. Yet the arguments made above concerning the increased anxiety that the ignorance model might see as stemming from dependence on a disliked other complicate this expectation. To the extent that group rewards provide more individuating information, the categorization model might see them as more beneficial.

These arguments, however, ignore the previously mentioned fact that children seem to learn how their teammates performed irrespective of the objective nature of the reward structure. This may account for the general lack of effect. Alternatively, even though social psychologists have viewed mutual fate such as that explicit in reward interdependence as contributing to intrateam liking, cohesiveness, and perceived similarity, the lack of effect for reward interdependence and the positive effect for task interdependence may reflect the fact that the latter more directly affects the social interaction that underlies these intrateam processes.

Task role assignment. Individual task role assignments can be found in some interventions whereas others do not formally introduce them. Equal status contact has long been one of the most frequently espoused necessities for beneficial contact effects. There is a sense in which the random assignment of students to individual team roles implies an equivalence of status among the team members, whereas any informal differentiation or assignment by the team members themselves is more likely to reflect existing competence expectancies. As advocated by expectation states theory and found in Cohen and Roper (1972), a third possibility is reverse-status role assignment. The teacher or experimenter can explicitly assign minority team members to higher status roles. This latter procedure essentially occurs once in the published literature. Therefore, we dichotomized studies simply into those in which students are or are not formally and randomly assigned to specific task roles.

Before discussing the outcome, it is important to consider the relation of the presence or absence of task role assignments to the presence or absence of task interdependence. Conceptually, there appears to be a distinction. For instance, each member of the team of four students might be required to use a specified number of building blocks to help build a single team tower. Here there is task interdependence but no (or little) role differentiation. Alternatively, as in Jigsaw, teammates may be made individually responsible for the dissemination of distinct components of a lesson plan (e.g., Jefferson's early childhood, his adult family life, his role in framing the Constitution, his political beliefs), which they master while physically separated from their teammates. Cohen (1982) notes that with task interdependence and no (enforced) role specialization, the white children tend to assume leadership and complete the task for the team. As noted above, however, when there is role differentiation it may or may not be assigned randomly. Only in the latter case might it imply equal status.

Within the data set, there is very substantial overlap in studies characterized according to task structure and studies categorized according to task role assignment. Thus it is hard to know whether to attribute the outcomes for either variable to the equivalence of status implicit in randomly assigning team members to roles, or to the differentiation that role assignment imposes. Ideally, within those cases containing role differentiation, we might have compared those with random assignment of roles by the teacher to those in which roles are delegated by the team. Additionally, within cases containing task interdependence we might have compared those with role specialization to those without it. Unfortunately, the data set precludes such comparisons.

As seen in Table 2.1, cases with random assignment to roles are associated with greater benefit than those with no role assignment.

Although Cohen, in discussing the expectation states model, has emphasized the importance of assignments that reverse societal status patterns, it seems likely that random assignment should nevertheless be more beneficial than assignments that covary with societal patterns. Turning to the ignorance model, to the extent that lack of role assignment permits informal assignment that reflects societal status differences whereas formal random assignment by a high-status adult implies status equivalence, white students might have less anxiety in the absence of role assignments. At the same time, and counteracting this effect, minority students would have more anxiety. Thus it might be seen as making no overall prediction. Alternatively, however, it might view random assignment as a cue that disconfirms stereotypes, and thus implies benefit. From the standpoint of the categorization model, it seems more likely that it is role differentiation and its implications for the perception of differences within racial/ethnic categories that assumes more importance than does random assignment per se. In concluding this section, however, it is worth considering whether children note that role assignment is or is not random, and, if so, make the relevant attributions regarding equal status.

Task content. As discussed previously, the curriculum content of the cooperative task may moderate its effect on intergroup relations. Specifically, we thought that both social studies and language arts materials might produce different degrees of benefit than might materials from the hard sciences. Only two studies, however, used social science curricula. Therefore, we simply categorized studies into those using language arts materials and those using science or mathematics.

The results shown in Table 2.1 suggest greater benefit with the science and math curricula.

In our initial discussion we developed arguments that, from the standpoint of the ignorance model, might see either direction of effect as confirmatory, though on balance they seemed to favor the obtained result. This result also seems consistent with the social categorization model in that directing attentional focus toward difference between racial/ethnic categories should encourage category-based responding and thereby interfere with the positive effects ordinarily produced by cooperative interaction. Finally, the expectation states model seems to have little bearing on this comparison.

Publicized performance. Publicized performance was defined as present in cases in which participants' academic performance contributions were made known to the class by means of a weekly newsletter or bulletin board posting; when contributions were not made known to the class, it was defined as absent.

As seen in Table 2.1, interventions with publicized performance and those without it did not differentially affect intergroup relations in the classroom.

One might have expected publicized performance to increase the perceived relevance of status-related differences in performance and thereby heighten intergroup hostilities. Alternatively, it might appear to be a means of directing attention to individuating information about team members that might encourage positive relations. As previously indicated, however, in the instances in which performance is publicized, it is done so only at the team level. Thus, if the social categorization model has bearing, it is in terms of the increased salience of team, a category that crosscuts racial/ethnic category membership as defining a student's social identity. Note, however, that the direction of effect counters the implication of this view. Here again our earlier comments concerning the effects of competition may be relevant. Publicized performance may augment feelings of competitiveness.

Conceptually distinct from whether or not the teacher provides public recognition of performance is the issue of how the teacher scores it. In some instances, the absolute level of performance on achievement tests defined team or individual outcomes. In other cases gain scores comparing current performance to that of a previous week defined student or team outcomes. In classes in which there are group-linked academic performance differences between minority students and their white classmates, equal opportunity scoring systems such as the latter might counter negative academic stereotypes more effectively than use of absolute achievement scores. Unfortunately, however, the subsets of studies that do and do not use equal opportunity scoring overlap exactly with those that do and do not provide publicized performance.

Numerical representation on team. The nature of the numerical representation of ethnic members on teams was defined in terms of cases in which there was an equal proportion of minority and white students and those in which there was not. The latter category was further subdivided into cases in which the proportion of whites exceeded the minority proportion and conversely, those in which the minority proportion exceeded the white.

In Table 2.1, the first comparison under numerical representation, which considers the full data set, shows that equal proportions of minority and white students produced greater benefit that unequal proportions, irrespective of the direction of deviation in the latter set. Parenthetically, however, most departures from an equal proportion were in the direction of majority preponderance. The second comparison under numerical representation shows no difference, though its direction is toward greater benefit when there is minority as opposed to majority preponderance. Though not appearing in the table, we also compared each of these latter subsets to the cases with equal proportions. Inspection of the means presented in Table 2.1 suggests less benefit from either direction of deviation than from equal proportions; however, this difference was only significant in the comparison of cases of white preponderance to equal proportions, $t(19) = 2.569$, $p < 0.5$ (independent); $t(50) = 2.721$, $p < .01$ (total).

Although the bearing of the expectation states model on the effects of numerical representations may seem unclear, Cohen (1984) has argued that perceptions of minority power not only correlate positively with relative number of social categories in the setting, but also boost performance expectations. Thus equal as well as more numerous representation of students belonging to minority categories should be more beneficial than cases that mirror their societal under-representation. The second of our two comparisons in Table 2.1 seems more relevant to Cohen's theoretical analysis but is confirming only in its direction. Of the additional comparisons, only that comparing equal proportions to majority preponderance is confirming. Contrary to expectation, minority preponderance is not more beneficial than equal proportions.

With respect to the ignorance model, we might expect a numerical preponderance of minority children to lower their anxiety and thereby augment positive effects. Since the response measures are bidirectional, however, this would be countered by an opposing direction of effect among white students, whose anxiety is presumably increased by the deviation from societal representation. The response measures within studies, however, do not correct for the relative frequencies of minority and majority students. Consequently, in a case where minority students are numerically preponderant, the mean outgroup acceptance measures will be weighted more heavily by the effect of the situation upon them than by its effect on the white children because there are more of the former. Therefore, given the nature of the response measures, either direction of deviation from equal proportions should be associated with greater benefit. The outcomes, however, are opposite to this expectation.

The social categorization model finds the first comparison in Table 2.1 confirming in that the model suggests that either direction of deviation should produce less benefit than equivalent proportions. This expectation extrapolates from research on the solo effect (Taylor et al., 1975) which suggests that deviations from equal number of the respective social groups might increase category distinctiveness. The separate subgroup comparisons, however, show that this effect primarily is attributable to the subset of cases in which the majority exceeds the minority. Finally, the comparison within cases on unequal representation shows little support for the argument that an unequal representation that reflects the respective number of social groups in the larger society will increase category salience (Duval & Duval, 1983). Although equal proportions yielded more benefit than white preponderance, the anticipated similar or greater effect in the comparison of minority preponderance to white preponderance was not found.

CONCLUSION

We have argued that there is benefit to be gained from linking laboratory-based theory and research on intergroup relations with experimental field research on the use of cooperative teams in educational settings. Others have concurred in the value of these bridges between theory and practice (Johnson et al., 1984) and in the need for more detailed empirical evaluation in the aspects of cooperative team learning that moderate its effectiveness (Slavin, 1986). Elsewhere, we have begun to present data that bear on ways in which laboratory research can contribute to effective design and implementation procedures for such interventions (Brewer & Miller, 1984; Brewer & Miller, in press; Miller et al., 1985; Miller & Brewer, 1986). Here, we also have tried to illustrate the difficulty of translating general theoretical principles into more specific implications with the hope that it will encourage greater detail and specificity in theoretical formulations. Less often have mainstream social psychologists noted the potential contribution that existing field experimentation on the use of cooperative team learning in school settings might make to the development of social psychological theory on intergroup relations. We have used meta-analytic procedures to suggest this potential, and by directing our discussion to consequences of differences in the ways in which cooperative team learning is implemented, have suggested variables that may be worthy of more general theoretical concern.

NOTE

1. There are several reasons why this is an unreasonable goal. First, the derivations from the theoretical models are our own. Second, the dimensions for which information in the published studies indicates variation in their implementation procedures have been haphazardly or accidentally determined, and consequently the relevant or important dimensions of each model may not have been sampled equivalently. Nor can it be claimed that the variation with respect to the dimensions relevant to each model are "manipulated" with equivalent strength. Moreover, the tests of the moderators are not independent. Were none of the preceding points at issue, it would still not be clear what patterns of outcome (other than complete support for one model and none for the other two) could be viewed as indicating some relative superiority.

Lest these constraints be viewed as suggesting that our efforts are worthless, they should be put in the context of the inferential conclusiveness that characterizes the outcome of any typical experiment. A single study usually attempts to test only one or two propositions. Within this limitation, confirmation rests on operations that may or may not be conceptually isomorphic with the theoretical constructs. In addition, a given operationalization may not necessarily load on a single conceptual factor; operations often include other variables that covary with the manipulations. Findings may be further limited by the contextual level of other unmanipulated variables that characterize the particular experiment, and thus reflect a specific interaction that reverses the direction of effect when the contextual level of a constant factor is changed. Meta-analytic tests, of course, do not eliminate these concerns. Rather, to the degree that variation in the specific implementations of the sample studies approximates random deviations, their outcomes are less likely than those of single experiments to be affected by a particular operationalization of a key variable, a specific setting, or a single paradigm.

REFERENCES

Aronson, E., Blaney, N., Stephan, C., Sikes, J., & Snapp, M. (1978). *The jigsaw classroom.* Newbury Park, CA: Sage.

Berger, J., Cohen, B. P., & Zelditch, M., Jr. (1972). Status characteristics and social interaction. *American Sociological Review, 37,* 241-255.

*Blaney, N. T., Stephan, S., Rosenfield, D., Aronson, E., & Sikes, J. (1977). Interdependence in the classroom: A field study. *Journal of Educational Psychology, 69,* 121-128.

Brewer, M. B. (1979). Ingroup bias in the minimal intergroup situation: A cognitive-motivational analysis. *Psychological Bulletin, 86,* 307-324.

Brewer, M. B., & Miller, N. (1984). Beyond the contact hypothesis: Theoretical perspectives on desegregation. In N. Miller & M. Brewer (Eds.), *Groups in contact: The psychology of school desegregation* (pp. 281-302). New York: Academic Press.

Brewer, M. B., & Miller, N. (in press). Contact and cooperation: When do they work? In P. A. Katz & D. Taylor (Eds.), *Towards the elimination of racism: Profiles in controversy.* New York: Plenum.

Byrne, D. (1961). Interpersonal attraction and attitude similarity. *Journal of Abnormal and Social Psychology, 62,* 713-715.

Campbell, D. T. (1956). Enhancement of contrast as composite habit. *Journal of Abnormal and Social Psychology, 53,* 350-355.

Campbell, D. T. (1967). Stereotypes and the perception of group differences. *American Psychologist, 22,* 812-829.

Cohen, E. G. (1982). Expectation states and interracial interaction in school settings. *Annual Review of Sociology, 8,* 209-235.

Cohen, E. G. (1984). The desegregated school: Problems in status power and interethnic climate. In N. Miller & M. Brewer (Eds.), *Groups in contact: The psychology of desegregation* (pp. 77-96). New York: Academic Press.

Cohen, E. G., & Roper, S. (1972). Modification of interracial interaction disability: An application of status characteristic theory. *American Sociological Review, 37,* 643-657.

*Cohen, E. G., & Sharan, S. (1980). Modifying status relations in Israeli youth. *Journal of Cross-Cultural Psychology, 11,* 364-384.

Cook, S. W. (1984). Cooperative interaction in multiethnic contexts. In N. Miller & M. Brewer (Eds.), *Groups in contact: The psychology of school desegregation* (pp. 156-185). New York: Academic Press.

*Cooper, L., Johnson, D. W., Johnson, R., & Wilderson, R. (1980). The effects of cooperative, competitive, and individualistic experiences on interpersonal attraction among heterogeneous peers. *Journal of Social Psychology, 111,* 243-253.

*DeVries, D., & Edwards, K. (1973). Learning games and student teams: Their effects on classroom processes. *American Journal of Educational Research, 10,* 307-318.

*DeVries, D., & Edwards, K. (1974). Student teams and learning games: Their effects of cross-race and cross-sex interaction. *Journal of Educational Psychology, 66,* 741-749.

*DeVries, D., Edwards, K., & Slavin, R. (1978). Biracial learning teams and race relations in the classroom: Four field experiments on teams-games-tournaments. *Journal of Educational Psychology, 70,* 356-372.

Duval, S., & Duval, V. H. (1983). *Consistency and cognition: A theory of causal attribution.* Hillsdale, NJ: Lawrence Erlbaum.

Edwards, K. J., DeVries, D. L., & Snyder, J. P. (1972). Games and teams: A winning combination. *Simulation and Games, 3,* 247-269.

Fiske, S. T. (1982). Schema triggered affect: Applications to social perception. In M. S. Clark & S. T. Fiske (Eds.), *Affect and cognition: The 17th Annual Carnegie Symposium on Cognition.* Hillsdale, NJ: Lawrence Erlbaum.

Glass, G. V, McGaw, B., & Smith, M. L. (1981). *Meta-analysis in social research.* Newbury Park, CA: Sage.

Heiss, J., & Nash, D. (1967). The stranger in laboratory culture revisited. *Human Organization, 26,* 47-51.

Hendricks, M., & Bootzin, R. (1976). Race and sex as stimuli for negative affect and physical avoidance. *Journal of Personality and Social Psychology, 34,* 159-168.

Hensley, V., & Duval, S. (1976). Some perceptual determinants of perceived similarity, liking, and correctness. *Journal of Social Psychology.*

Hinkle, S., & Schopler, J. (1986). Bias in the evaluation of in-group and out-group performance. In S. Worchel & W. G. Austin (Eds.), *Psychology of intergroup relations* (pp. 196-212). Chicago, IL: Nelson-Hall.

Hochschild, J. (1984). *The new American dilemma.* New Haven: Yale University Press.

Hoffman, D., & Cohen, E. G. (1972). *An exploratory study to determine the effects of generalized performance expectations upon activity and influence of students engaged in a group simulation game.* Paper presented at the Annual Meeting of the American Educational Research Association, Chicago.

Humphreys, P., & Berger, J. (1981). Theoretical consequences of the status characteristic formulation. *American Journal of Sociology, 86,* 953-983.

Hunter, J. E., Schmidt, F. L., & Jackson, G. B. (1982). *Meta-analysis.* Newbury Park, CA: Sage.

Johnson, D. W., & Johnson, R. (1975). *Learning together and alone: Cooperation, competition and individualization.* Englewood Cliffs, NJ: Prentice-Hall.

*Johnson, D. W., & Johnson, R. (1981). Effects of cooperative and individualistic learning experiences on interethnic interaction. *Journal of Educational Psychology, 73,* 454-459.

*Johnson, D. W., & Johnson, R. (1982). Effects of cooperative, competitive, and individualistic learning experiences on cross-ethnic interaction and friendships. *Journal of Social Psychology, 118,* 47-58.

Johnson, D. W., Johnson, R., & Maruyama, G. (1984). Goal interdependence and interpersonal attraction in heterogeneous classrooms: A meta-analysis. In M. Miller & M. B. Brewer (Eds.), *Groups in contact: The psychology of desegregation* (pp. 187-203). Orlando, FL: Academic Press.

*Johnson, D. W., & Johnson, R. T. (1984). Relationships between black and white students in intergroup cooperation and competition. *Journal of Social Psychology, 125,* 421-428.

*Johnson, D. W., Johnson, R., Tiffany, M., & Zaidman, B. (1983). Are low achievers disliked in a cooperative situation? A test of rival theories in a mixed ethnic situation. *Contemporary Educational Psychology, 8,* 189-200.

*Johnson, R., Johnson, D. W., & Tauer, M. (1979). The effects of cooperative, competitive, and individualistic goals structures on students' attitudes and achievements. *Journal of Psychology, 102,* 191-198.

Johnson, S., & Johnson, D. W. (1972). The effect of others' actions, attitude similarity, and race on attraction toward others. *Human Relations, 25,* 121-130.

Kahn, A. S., & Ryen, A. H. (1972). Factors influencing the bias toward one's own group. *International Journal of Group Tensions, 2,* 33-50.

Kahneman, D., & Tversky, A. (1973). On the psychology of prediction. *Psychological Review, 80,* 237-251.

Katz, I. (1981). *Stigma: A social psychological analysis.* Hillsdale, NJ: Lawrence Erlbaum.

LeVine, R. A., & Campbell, D. T. (1972). *Ethnocentrism: Theories of conflict, ethnic attitudes, and group behavior.* New York: John Wiley.

Lippitt, R., & Gold, M. (1959). Classroom social structure as a mental health problem. *Journal of Social Issues, 15* (1), 40-49.

Merton, R. K. (1948). The self-fulfilling prophecy. *The Antioch Review, 8,* 193-210.

Miller, N. (1981). Changing views about the effects of school desegregation: Brown then and now. In M. B. Brewer & B. E. Collins (Eds.), *Scientific inquiry and the social sciences* (pp. 413-452). San Francisco: Jossey-Bass.

Miller, N., & Brewer, M. B. (1986). Categorization effects on ingroup and outgroup perception. In J. Davidio & S. Gaertner (Eds.), *Prejudice, discrimination, and racism: Theory and research* (pp. 209-230). New York: Academic Press.

Miller, N., Brewer, M. B., & Edwards, K. (1985). Cooperative interaction in desegregated settings: A laboratory analogue. *Journal of Social Issues, 41* (3), 63-79.

Miller, N., Rogers, M., & Hennigan, K. (1983). Increasing interracial acceptance: Using cooperative games in desegregated elementary schools. In L. Bickman (Ed.), *Applied Social Psychology Annual* (Vol. 4, pp. 199-216). Newbury Park, CA: Sage.

Mullen, B., Atkins, J. L., Champion, D. S., Edwards, C., Hardy, D., Story, J. E., & Vanderklok. (1985). The false consensus effect: A meta-analysis of 115 hypothesis tests. *Journal of Experimental Social Psychology, 21,* 262-283.

Nisbett, R. E., & Borgida, E. (1975). Attribution and the psychology of prediction. *Journal of Personal and Social Psychology, 32,* 932-943.

Pettigrew, T. F. (1979). The ultimate attribution error: Extending Allport's cognitive analysis of prejudice. *Personality and Social Psychology Bulletin, 5,* 461-476.

Rankin, R. E., & Campbell, D. T. (1955). Galvanic skin response to Negro and white experimenters. *Journal of Abnormal Psychology, 51,* 30-33.

Rothbart, M., & John, P. O. (1985). Social categorization and behavioral episodes: A cognitive analysis of the effects of intergroup contact. *Journal of Social Issues, 41* (3), 81-104.

Sharan, S. (1980). Cooperative learning in small groups: Recent methods and effects on achievement, attitudes, and ethnic relations. *Review of Educational Research, 50,* 241-271.

*Sharan, S., Hertz-Lazarowitz, R., & Kussel, P. (1984). Social attitudes. In S. Sharan (Ed.), *Cooperative learning in the classroom: Research in desegregated schools* (pp. 107-130). Hillsdale, NJ: Lawrence Erlbaum.

Sharan, S., & Sharan, Y. (1976). *Small-group teaching.* Englewood Cliffs, NJ: Educational Testing Publications.

Slavin, R. E. (1978a). Student teams and achievement divisions. *Journal of Research and Development in Education, 12,* 39-49.

*Slavin, R. E. (1978b). Student teams and comparison among equals: Effects on academic performance and student attitudes. *Journal of Educational Psychology, 70,* 532-538.

*Slavin, R. E. (1979). Effects of biracial learning teams on cross-racial friendships. *Journal of Educational Psychology, 71,* 381-387.

Slavin, R. E. (1980). *Using student team learning* (rev. ed.). Baltimore, MD: Johns Hopkins University, Center for Social Organization of Schools.

Slavin, R. E. (1983). *Cooperative learning.* New York: Longman.

Slavin, R. E. (1986). Cooperative learning: Engineering social psychology in the classroom. In R. S. Feldman (Ed.), *The social psychology of education* (pp. 153-171). Cambridge: Cambridge University Press.

*Slavin, R. E., & Madden, N. A. (1979). School practices that improve race relations. *American Educational Research Journal, 16,* 169-180.

*Slavin, R. E., & Oickle, E. (1981). Effects of cooperative learning teams on student achievement and race relations: Treatment by race interactions. *Sociology of Education, 54,* 174-180.

Stephan, W. G., & Stephan, C. W. (1984). The role of ignorance in intergroup relations. In N. Miller & M. Brewer (Eds.), *Groups in contact: The psychology of desegregation* (pp. 229-255). New York: Academic Press.

Stephan, W. G., & Stephan, C. W. (1985). Intergroup anxiety. *Journal of Social Issues, 41* (3), 157-175.

St. John, R. H. (1975). *School desegregation outcomes for children.* New York: John Wiley.

Stouffer, S. A., Lumsdaine, A. A., Lumsdaine, M. H., & Williams, R. M., Jr. (1949). *The American soldier* (2 vols). Princeton: Princeton University Press.

Tajfel, H. (1970). Experiments in intergroup discrimination. *Scientific American, 223,* 96-102.

Tajfel, H. (1978). Social categorization, social identity, and social comparison. In H. Tajfel (Ed.), *Differentiation between social groups* (pp. 61-76). New York: Academic Press.

Tajfel, H. (1981). *Human groups and social categories.* Cambridge: Cambridge University Press.

Tajfel, H., & Wilkes, A. (1963). Classification and quantitative judgment. *British Journal of Social Psychology, 54,* 101-114.

Taylor, S. E., Fiske, S. T., Close, M., Anderson, C., & Ruderman, A. (1975). *Solo status as a psychological variable: The power of being distinctive.* Unpublished manuscript, Harvard University.

*Warring, D., Johnson, D. W., Maruyama, G., & Johnson, R. (1985). Impact of different types of cooperative learning on cross-ethnic and cross-sex relationships. *Journal of Educational Psychology, 77,* 53-59.

*Webb, R. W. (1982). Group composition, group interaction, and achievement in cooperative small groups. *Journal of Educational Psychology, 74,* 475-484.

*Weigel, R. H., Wiser, P. L., & Cook, S. W. (1975). Impact of cooperative learning experience on cross-ethnic relations and attitudes. *Journal of Social Issues, 31* (1), 3-25.

*Wheeler, R., & Ryan, F. (1973). Effects of cooperative and competitive classroom environments on the attitudes and achievement of elementary school students engaged in social studies inquiry activities. *Journal of Educational Psychology, 65,* 402-407.

Wilder, D. A. (1986). Social categorization: Implicators for creation and reduction of intergroup bias. In L. Berkowitz (Ed.), *Advances in experimental social psychology* (pp. 291-355). New York: Academic Press.

Zander, A., Stotland, E., & Wolfe, D. (1960). Unity of group identification with group and self-esteem of members. *Journal of Personality, 28,* 463-478.

*Ziegler, S. (1981). The effectiveness of cooperative learning teams for increasing cross-ethnic friendship: Additional evidence. *Human Organization, 40,* 264-268.

3

Environmental Influences on Social Interaction and Group Development

PAUL B. PAULUS
DINESH NAGAR

Paul B. Paulus is Professor of Psychology at the University of Texas at Arlington and Senior Research Psychologist at the Walter Reed Army Institute of Research. His major research interests are in social and environmental influences on group behavior. He has edited *Psychology of Group Influence* and *Basic Group Processes* and contributed a chapter on crowding with Andrew Baum to the *Handbook of Environmental Psychology*.

Dinesh Nagar is a Postdoctoral Fellow at the University of Texas at Arlington. His research has focused on the effects of residential and laboratory crowding.

This volume exposes the reader to wide variety of issues related to group processes. Although each issue is addressed by empirical studies, typically little attention is paid to the environment in which groups exist. This approach is characteristic of most research on groups. Since most group research is done in the laboratory where the environment usually is held constant, this outcome certainly is not surprising. There are also a reasonable number of studies conducted in clinical, organizational, and other settings, but again the nature of the setting itself is rarely a focus of attention. This state of affairs does not mean that there is a lack of research on the role of environmental factors in group and interactional processes. Such research exists under the guise of a variety of labels not typically associated with the topic of group dynamics. The aim of such research generally has not been to enlighten group processes but simply to understand a particular phenomenon that happened to involve a group. For example, in a laboratory study of crowding (Paulus, Annis, Seta, Schkade, & Matthews, 1976), it was found that in a small room

AUTHORS' NOTE: The first author's preparation of this chapter was facilitated by an Intergovernmental Personnel Agreement from Walter Reed Army Institute of Research, Department of Military Psychiatry. Clyde Hendrick, Michael Kernis, and Carol Werner made helpful comments on an earlier draft of this chapter.

males perform tasks more poorly than females, while the reverse was true in a large room. If such a simple factor as size of room can completely change the direction of an observed relationship, it would seem important to know the influence of various environmental variables on a variety of group or dyadic processes.

The aim of this chapter is to highlight the research on the relationship between the environment and social interaction or group development and to explore some of the underlying processes and principles. Each of the topic areas differs in approach and specific concerns, yet all of them provide important insights into the nature of the group/environment process. It appears to us that the literature separates quite nicely into two broad categories: (1) environmental/social factors that increase positive relations in groups and group contact, and (2) those which produce negative reactions and social avoidance in groups. We will briefly summarize these two separate categories of studies and use them as a basis for suggesting a broad framework for group/environment relations. A major concern of the chapter is to promote a deeper understanding of the transactions between groups and their environments. That is, how do environments shape group interaction patterns and how and when do groups change the environments in which they live? In particular, we will highlight the role of the individual in selecting environments and the environmental factors that promote or inhibit the development of social interactions.

In our discussion we will use a variety of terms to describe group/environmental relations. Environment will refer to features of the physical or built environment that are pertinent for social interaction, in particular, the amount and arrangement of interior and exterior space. The social or group context refers to the characteristics of individuals or the nature of their interrelationship in a particular environment (e.g., similarity and cooperativeness). The term "group" will be used rather loosely to describe a variety of social entities. In most cases the research has dealt primarily with interaction among pairs of individuals. However, in most real-life settings these dyadic relationships are the basis for the development of social relations among a group of individuals in a particular environment. Our usage of the terms "group interaction" and "group development" is designed to underscore the potentially broader relevance of the present research literature.

The literature review that follows is designed to provide an overview of a set of potentially related areas of research. The review will not be extensive, detailed, or critical, since such reviews already exist in most of the topic areas. The main purpose of the review will be to provide a basis for highlighting the theoretical interrelationship of these areas of research and to lay a foundation for an integrative model of environment/social interaction relationships.

ENVIRONMENTAL FACTORS THAT
INCREASE GROUP INTERACTION AND COHESION

One recurrent theme in many studies has been that spatial and architectural features of an environment can strongly influence the development of social relations or groups. The spatial layout of a residential complex, the arrangement and positional relationship of houses, common access to facilities (e.g., mailbox, pool, lounges), and common stairways are some factors that enhance the probability of contact among residents and facilitate group development. Environmental features that increase the probability of casual contact provide the opportunity for a sequence of events necessary for group development. Initial contacts may be limited to an exchange of pleasantries, but as the residents become more familiar with each other they may get involved in extended interactions. These interactions may involve increasingly detailed and personal disclosures (Archer & Earle, 1983) and exchange of information and personal favors. As a result, relationships among residents should be characterized by increasing levels of cohesion, and definable subgroups may emerge.

Space and Human Interaction

We will briefly highlight some of the studies that have demonstrated the importance of spatial factors in promoting interaction. A classic study by Festinger, Schachter, and Back (1950) examined the influence of the physical environment and architectural design on interpersonal behavior, friendship formation, and group development of MIT married engineering students residing in two different types of housing facilities. The Westgate residential complex consisted of 100 single-family houses grouped in U-shaped courts of 7 to 13 houses. Except for those residences at the very tips of the U that faced onto the street, the houses faced a long, grassy court. In contrast, the Westgate West residential complex consisted of 17 two-story buildings that were previously Navy barracks. Each of the buildings were subdivided into 10 apartments, five on each side.

Festinger et al. (1950) found strong support for the importance of proximity factors in group development. They distinguished between physical and functional distance, physical distance being the degree of actual spatial separation and functional distance being the extent to which contact was likely because of environmental features. Thus individuals living near the stairs of an apartment complex would be likely to encounter residents using the stairs and develop relationships with them. The stairs served to put them functionally close to other residents in the building who used the stairs. Thus both physical and functional distance may influence the probability of group development and friendship formation. In Westgate, the court, and in Westgate West, the building became the social contact point because in these respective areas people were clustered both physically and functionally close to each other. The sociometric choices made by Westgate West residents indicated 65% favorable friendship choices were given to people living in the same building. Similarly, in Westgate 55.5% favorable choices were given to people in the same court.

In another classic study, Whyte (1956) examined the importance of physical factors in determining friendship patterns among residents in Park Forest. Some of the Park Foresters lived in two-story garden apartments grouped in courts. In the course of time each court developed a particular culture or activity pattern that remained relatively stable even when many residents were replaced. For Park Foresters who lived in single-family homes, activities were predominantly centered around those homes that were in close physical proximity. Whyte suggested that the location of the garden, driveways, and play areas for children were facilitative factors in the enhancement of social contact.

Many other studies have also supported the relationship between physical or functional distance and group formation or friendship choice. For example, several studies have found that locations or orientations of front doors that increased the probability of social contact were positively associated with friendships (Caplow & Forman, 1950; Kuper, 1953; Merton, 1948). More recently, Ebbesen, Kjos, & Konecni (1976) found that friendship choices were greatest among those who lived close together in an apartment complex. However, unpleasant social relationships were also most likely between those who lived in close proximity. This type of finding was also observed by Kuper (1953) and indicates that distance alone is not a sufficient factor for positive group development.

Although our discussion has focused on residential environments, a number of studies have examined social contact in public places such as airports and hospitals. Osmond (1957) observed that the arrangement of chairs in hospital halls discouraged social contact (termed sociofugal), while other arrangements seemed to facilitate such contacts (termed sociopetal). For example, in a study on a hospital ward, Sommer and Ross (1958) found that sociopetal spacing of chairs in a small circular group doubled the frequency of interaction relative to a side-by-side arrangement. Sommer (1974) has noted that many public environments are designed so as to discourage social interaction. He cited the case of airports in which chairs are arranged in long rows and cannot be easily rearranged for casual conversation among groups or individuals.

Sense of Community

The research reviewed in the preceding section suggests that environmental features can have a strong impact on group interaction and development. Features that increase the probability of social interaction seem to facilitate such a process, whereas features that hinder social contact seem to impair group interaction and development. An implicit assumption of many of these studies appears to be that people have a desire for social contact and interaction, and that outcomes of increased social contact are mostly positive. These assumptions are certainly not without merit. Research has documented a variety of interpersonal needs, including the human desire to affiliate with groups and the variety of rewards humans may provide for one another (see Schachter, 1959; Shaver & Buhrmester, 1983). The currently popular topic of social support revolves around the notion that interpersonal contact can facilitate coping with stressful life events (see Cohen & Syme, 1985). Apparently, other people may be a source of comfort or provide useful ways of coping in times of stress. There is also a substantial literature on community or neighborhood development that supports the above assumptions (Unger & Wandersman, 1985).

It appears that prolonged interaction in a neighborhood, with its associated exchange of resources (information, favors, assistance, and so forth), may lead to development of a strong sense of attachment to neighborhood, or what some have called a sense of community (Sarason, 1974). People living in a homogeneous neighborhood for a prolonged period of time are likely to become interdependent and attached emotionally to the people and places of this locality. A strong attachment to place may develop through a cost/benefit analysis by residents in which they evaluate the degree of social support in the present neighborhood in comparison to alternative neighborhoods (Proshansky, 1978; Stokols & Shumaker, 1981).

A sense of community may have a variety of positive benefits. It may enhance the inclination to interact with residents in the neighborhood and to share with them common concerns and personal problems. Neighbors may act collectively in local neighborhood organizations to solve neighborhood as well as personal problems (Kotler, 1979; Perlman, 1976; Wandersman, Florin, Chavis, Rich, & Prestby, 1985). Community development may also be a deterrent to crime. Residents may take a stronger role in monitoring activities in the neighborhood and taking responsible measures against potential intruders. Some studies indicate that supportive neighborhood ties can reduce the fear of crime (Gubrium, 1974; Sundeen & Mathieu, 1976), while Newman (1972) has provided evidence that neighborhood designs that facilitate community development and surveillance are associated with considerably lower crime rates than those that do not.

Other Variables

Mere exposure. Although we have marshalled considerable support for the rewards derived from increased social contact in various environments, some evidence exists that contact per se sometimes leads to positive reactions. Zajonc (1968) proposed that mere exposure to others may be a sufficient basis for increased liking. Much support for this hypothesis exists (e.g., Harrison, 1977), but the positive effects of repeated exposures on liking seem to be enhanced in situations in which initial attitudes are neutral or positive (Perlman & Oskamp, 1971), or the context is positive (Saegert, Swap, & Zajonc, 1973). These latter two studies have shown that in negative contexts increased exposures may in fact lead to increasingly negative reactions. Similar conclusions can be derived from research on the "contact hypothesis" (Amir, 1969). This hypothesis holds that increased contact among diverse racial and ethnic groups in neighborhoods and classrooms will reduce prejudice. Yet research indicates that for increased contact to reduce prejudice and increase favorable interpersonal attitudes the following conditions must exist: equality of status, a cooperative relationship, social norms favoring equality, a high degree of social contact, and contact with individuals who disconfirm the negative stereotypes (Cook, 1985; Stephan, 1987). If these conditions do not exist, increased contact actually may lead to more negative interpersonal attitudes and relations.

Homogeneity. Another factor that appears to play an important role in the development of relations in environments is the degree of homogeneity among the group members (i.e., degree of similarity with regard to race, professional and socioeconomic status, interests, values, and so forth). Festinger et al. (1950) and Gans (1967) pointed to the important role of homogeneity in friendship development in their studies. Other studies have noted the role of this factor in housing satisfaction (Hourihan, 1984; Michelson, 1970), with Michelson arguing that a degree of homogeneity and need for mutual assistance and contact are necessary for spatial determinism of friendship formation. Research on the contact hypothesis has shown that positive reactions to contact are facilitated if group members share similar characteristics (Stephan, 1987). Interestingly, increased contact itself may increase the presumption of similarity, and this presumption may account in part for the positive relationship between attraction and frequency of contact (Moreland & Zajonc, 1982). In fact, individuals may seek environments that allow them to be with similar others (Michelson, 1970).

Homogeneity may be a facilitative factor for several reasons. Presumption of similarity may increase interpersonal attraction and the desire to interact (Byrne, 1971). Similarity is also important in the maintenance of relationships (Murstein, 1976). It may be related to minimization of social conflict and enhances the probability of mutually rewarding interactions. Thus in environments where residents are fairly homogeneous, one should observe an enhanced impact of spatial factors both on the initiation and maintenance of social interaction and group structure.

ENVIRONMENTAL FACTORS RELATED TO
NEGATIVE GROUP INTERACTIONS AND SOCIAL AVOIDANCE

We have summarized evidence that environmental features can increase social contact and that contact can have a variety of benefits. However, there exists an equally compelling literature on the negative aspects of increased social contact. An underlying assumption of this literature is that individuals value privacy and control over their interactions with others. In situations in which the desired level of privacy or control is violated, strongly negative reactions and a desire to reduce social contact is evidenced (e.g., Altman, 1975; Baron & Rodin, 1978). We will provide a brief overview of this literature and examine its relationship to the research cited in the previous section.

Much evidence exists that individuals tend to maintain a comfortable distance from others during social interaction (Hall, 1966; Sommer, 1969). Violation of preferred distance zones by others may produce strongly negative reactions and avoidance (Evans & Howard, 1973). However, reviews and analyses of this literature (Hayduk, 1978; Patterson, 1984) suggest that negative reactions are not inevitable. In positive contexts invasion of personal space may be quite tolerable or even reciprocated in a process of developing increased interpersonal intimacy (Patterson, 1976).

In addition to sensitivity to appropriate interpersonal distances, people desire to maintain control over physical spaces or territories for which they have a sense of attachment or ownership (see Altman, 1975). Individuals may try to communicate the occupation or ownership of territory with explicit signs, environmental signals (e.g., fences or closed doors), or more subtle markers such as coats or other personal items. Violation of territorial control may lead to strongly defensive reactions. Territoriality may play a role in social interactions in public places, households (Altman, Nelson, & Lett, 1972), and in public housing projects (Newman, 1972; Yancey, 1972).

The study of personal space and territoriality provides a basis for expecting negative reactions to low degrees of control when one interacts with others in confined areas. When one encounters large numbers of people in a limited space, invasion of personal space and territorial encroachment are likely consequences. The study of crowding has been concerned with this type of situation. Crowding (too many people in too little space) can take many different forms. Residential or work places may be crowded because there are too many individuals for the resources available. Under such conditions others may be a constant source of interference or irritation (Stokols, 1976). Crowded environments may also be unpleasant because one is exposed to a lot of unpredictable and unwanted interactions with strangers (Baum & Valins, 1979). Finally, the high levels of stimulation characteristic of crowded environments may exceed optimal levels (Cohen, 1978). In a recent article, Cox, Paulus, and McCain (1984) have integrated these various components of crowding by means of a social interaction-demand model. This model suggests that involvement in social interaction in highly dense environments is often associated with three different processes: uncertainty, goal interference, and cognitive load. With high levels of density there is increased anxiety or fear because of the uncertainty about the nature and the outcome of one's interactions, frustration related to increased goal interference, and a high level of cognitive strain associated with the demands of dealing with the high degree of social stimulation. It is predicted that social interaction under high levels of density will be associated with negative psychological and physiological consequences only to the extent that these three factors are at high levels. By implication, when interactions are characterized by reasonable certainty or predictability, moderate levels of stimulation, and low degrees of goal interference, positive emotional reactions and social relationships should be evident.

The general thrust of the research on crowding is that high levels of density can be stressful, is associated with a negative impact on health, and creates strong tendencies to avoid social interaction (Baum & Paulus, 1987; Paulus, 1980). These findings apply to a wide variety of settings (e.g., college dormitories, prisons, and cities). However, the research has also pointed to the importance of degree of control over social interactions. Baron and Rodin (1978) proposed that the deleterious effects of crowding are related to the loss of control experienced (e.g., unpredictability, uncertainty, inability to escape). A number of studies have provided explicit support for the role of control in crowding related effects (Rodin, Solomon, & Metcalf, 1978; Ruback, Carr, & Hopper, 1986). Interestingly, one other factor that seems to be an important mediator of crowding effects is context. Crowding appears to be quite aversive in unpleasant or negative settings but may actually yield positive reactions in pleasant settings (Freedman, 1975; Schkade, 1977).

Thus, as with the research on social contact cited in the first section, the research on personal space, territoriality, and crowding has revealed the mediating role of a variety of factors. Invasions of personal space, violations of territory, and high levels of density are not inevitably aversive. In positive contexts and with a high degree of personal control, these situations may be quite tolerable and even lead to pleasant experiences. In their review of some of the same literature, Fleming, Baum, and Singer (1985) also concluded that with excessive or uncontrolled contacts, social interaction may be unpleasant or avoided; if contacts are controllable and not excessive, environmentally induced group development should occur.

REGULATION OF GROUP INTERACTION IN
ENVIRONMENTS: AN INTERACTIVE PERSPECTIVE

Our review of the different areas of research concerned with environmental influence on group interaction and development reveals a degree of commonality in terms of factors deemed to be important in understanding the group-environment relationship. The main factors emphasized by both areas appear to be (1) environmental features that influence the rate of social interaction, (2) the degree of positivity/negativity of the context in which the interactions take place (i.e., the extent to which group members have common characteristics, values, and goals, and relate in positive or rewarding ways), and (3) degree of perceived control over the interactions. One other factor that has been mentioned several times is the degree to which an individual desires social interaction. A variety of perspectives emphasize that humans seek an optimal level of stimulation from social interaction (Altman, 1975; Zuckerman, 1979). Having too much or too little stimulation from interaction may lead to negative reactions and attempts to achieve an optimal level. Individuals in environments that provide insufficient social contact may attempt in various ways to increase social contact (e.g., seek out friends or structure social activities). Those in environments with too much social contact may attempt to reduce social contact by actively avoiding areas where contact is likely or by being unfriendly (see Altman, 1975).

The research and ideas summarized thus far could be integrated by means of an interactive model that considers both the nature of the environmental setting and the factors that determine its impact on a group of individuals. It appears that social interaction or group formation will be facilitated to the extent that the environment encourages group contact and the following criteria are met:

1. Social contact is desired.
2. Degree of social contact can be controlled by the individual and social interactions are characterized by a low level of uncertainty.
3. The amount of experienced social contact is within the individual's range of acceptability (neither too low nor too high).
4. Group members are primarily a source of rewards (cooperation, similarity, pleasantness, support, connections, and resources, etc.).

If any of the above are not met, chances are that positive reactions to high frequencies of social contact will not ensue. Group formation should be inhibited to the extent that the environmental features discourage group contact:

1. The individual wishes to avoid social contact.
2. Degree of social contact cannot be controlled by the individual and social interactions are characterized by a high degree of uncertainty.
3. The level of social contact is outside the range of acceptability.
4. Group members are primarily a source of unpleasant outcomes (invasion of personal space, limitation of resources, interference, threats, etc.).

The interactional perspective suggests that successful prediction of the impact of the particular environment depends on one's ability to assess the degree to which the above conditions apply. One would have to determine objectively the initial social inclinations of the individuals and their range of acceptability. The degree to which exposure to social contact can be controlled or involves uncertainty in a particular environment and the degree to which fellow residents or group members are seen initially in positive or negative ways will also need to be assessed. It is important to assess these elements prior to or at the beginning of residency in a particular environment so that the influence of the time-related processes can be determined with greater clarity.

The first author's experiences in studying crowded prison conditions have strongly reinforced the above perspective. Verne Cox, Garvin McCain, and I have formally and informally examined the impact of various housing conditions on inmate health and emotional state in over 60 prisons and jails in the United States. One of our most consistent findings has been that large open dormitories with 30 or more inmates are associated with strongly negative reactions and high levels of illness complaints (Cox et al., 1984). However, in some of our visits we encountered open dormitories where there was little evidence of such negative reactions. In these cases the residents were generally a specially selected group of inmates who had achieved "honor status" by their good behavior in the prison. It seems likely that interactions among these residents would be generally positive and would be characterized by relatively high levels of predictability. In other cases, low levels of turnover of inmate residents in dormitories (and thus relatively low levels of uncertainty) were sufficient to ameliorate negative reactions to dormitory living (McCain, Cox, Paulus, & Karlovac, 1981).

Adding a Dash of Transactionalism

While the interactive model provides a useful framework for organizing much of the past research and predicting the varying impacts of environments on social interaction and group formation, it does not address another important element in the group-environment equation, the transactions of the individual with the environment. Many environmental psychologists have emphasized the need to deal with such transactions at both empirical and theoretical levels (see Altman & Rogoff, 1987; Stokols & Shumaker, 1981).[1] The individual is not seen as the passive recipient of the environmental forces but as one who can influence the environment by personal actions. Such influences may involve changing the physical environment (e.g., building fences or breaking down barriers), or choosing an environment consistent with one's needs. The full scenario is one of the individual choosing the environment, being influenced by it, influencing the environment, and choosing whether to remain or to leave based on the resulting experiences. The transactional perspective does not deny the viability of the interactive perspective but questions its completeness. Yet, so far, there has been very little empirical work explicitly assessing the processes implied by the transactional perspective. One reason may be lack of precision of the perspective and the attendant difficulty in deriving definitive predictions from the many unpredictable factors. However, we feel that with increased precision, a transactional perspective can be an important stimulus for research. In this spirit we will suggest some concrete theoretical and empirical directions.

One important issue concerns the relationship of the selection process to the impact of particular types of environments (see Michelson, 1977; Rapoport, 1985). The characteristics of people who select certain types of environments may be an important factor in determining the nature of the group/environment relationship. Individuals with certain prominent inclinations may select environments that they see as supportive of these inclinations. Sociable individuals may choose environments that facilitate the development of social contacts, while people who prefer to be left alone may choose environments that afford a degree of anonymity. These interactive effects of personality and situation in determining behavior and affect also have been of concern to personality and social psychologists, and much evidence exists that individuals do select situations that "foster and encourage behavioral expression of their own characteristic dispositions and interpersonal orientations" (Snyder & Ickes, 1985, p. 918).

The potential importance of the self-selection-to-environments issue is demonstrated by two experiences in studying housing satisfaction. About 10 years ago, the first author and his assistants interviewed residents in two different types of apartment complexes. One pair of apartments consisted of buildings that faced onto a common covered courtyard. Access to the apartments required walking through this area. Another pair of complexes faced directly onto a parking area, and residents could park in front of their apartment doors. What should one predict for these two types of apartments? Will those with the common courtyard feel crowded, complain of lack of privacy, and demonstrate social avoidance? Or will they like the social contacts and sense of community made possible by that environmental design? We were expecting a crowding effect, but to our surprise residents of the courtyard apartments felt more positive about their housing than the residents of the other apartments. They knew more of their fellow residents and felt they could rely on them more than did the residents of the other type of apartment. In fact, a number of the residents who lived in the parking lot type of apartment complained about the lack of contact with the other residents and expressed a desire to get to know more of their neighbors.

Can one conclude from this study that the apartment design differences were responsible for the observed effects and that the courtyard type of design did not contribute to crowding-related problems? Unfortunately, one cannot. One major problem is that we do not know how resident characteristics influenced apartment choice and, in turn, the observed results. Socially inclined individuals may have a preference for the courtyard design. This "problem" led us to refrain from publishing the study, but in retrospect this problem represents an important issue for future research. We need to know what personal characteristics are related to selection of different types of environments and to what extent such characteristics determine group development in such environments. Such knowledge would require a longitudinal study in which resident characteristics were assessed either prior to or early in the exposure to the environment.

Similar experiences have occurred recently during our evaluation of the quality of life in mobile home parks for the United States Army. In doing a survey of more than 40 parks near an Army base, we found several parks to be rather unpleasant-looking environments. Many of the trailers were poorly maintained, the area was littered, and the streets were in poor condition. Certainly here we would expect to find considerable resident discontent. Yet our interviews with the residents revealed positive feelings about the environment and their fellow residents in particular. There seemed to be strong social networks in these parks. Again we found results counter to our expectations. Could this finding also be attributed to a self-selection factor? Are people who choose to live in unattractive parks simply people who care little about environmental amenities but put more value in social relations?

Environmental psychologists have generally ignored the fact that many individuals willingly live in "substandard" environments. They may choose them because of convenience, proximity of friends or family, low expense, or even because of lack of sensitivity to environmental characteristics often used in determining quality (e.g., esthetics, noise, sanitation, crowding). Some may choose low-quality environments because they are consistent with their self-image (lower class or low-self-esteem). For example, a study of marital partners has provided evidence that individuals with low self-esteem may choose as partners individuals who maintain this level of esteem (Swann & Predmore, 1985). Alternatively, it is possible that residents who freely choose to live in inferior environments may experience some dissonance from their choice of housing, but they might reduce this dissonance by focusing on positive aspects of the environment (Brehm, 1956).

We have also noticed considerable differences among the mobile home parks in the reaction of residents to the survey process. Those in the generally inferior parks were more cooperative, friendlier, and less suspicious than residents of better parks. This may reflect social class differences, differences in perceived personal benefit from the survey, or basic differences in social orientation. Since our sample population consists primarily of enlisted soldiers and the range of rents in both types of parks is similar, it seems unlikely that these observed differences are entirely attributable to variations in social class. Hopefully, the results of our survey will give us some clues as to the nature of the "social" differences among the parks.

Thus both the formal literature and our personal research experience indicate that one cannot simply categorize environments as facilitative or inhibitory for group formation. Whether or not group formation is facilitated will depend on a variety of personal and social factors. Accurate prediction will require an understanding of the self-selection process and its relation to the impact of environments.

The issue of adjustment to mismatches (whether by choice or accident) also deserves serious research attention. How do people or groups adjust to mismatches? They could simply learn to tolerate the less than optimal conditions. People have shown a capacity to adapt or become less reactive to litter, crowding, and urban life (see Fisher, Bell, & Baum, 1984). Alternatively, they may attempt to change the situation. Physical or social intervention may occur. Individuals may keep their shutters drawn and minimize their time in public areas. Social norms may develop that may make the conditions more tolerable (e.g., norms of reserve and inattention in crowded environments, Milgram, 1970). Or groups may simply leave the environment to search for ones better suited to their inclinations (Toch, 1965). Although evidence exists for all of the above reactions to group/environment mismatches, there is presently little or no basis for predicting under what conditions these differing reactions may be observed. A few papers in the personality area do suggest that individuals who find themselves in situations inconsistent with their personalities or dispositions should be uncomfortable and exhibit negative emotional reactions (Emmons, Diener, & Larsen, 1986; Secord & Backman, 1965). An influential factor in this relationship appears to be the degree to which individuals have a choice of settings. Of course, if there is little choice, the relationship between situation and personality should be minimal. Moreover, it appears that individuals react most positively in chosen situations congruent with their personality and more negatively in unchosen situations inconsistent with their personality (Emmons et al., 1986). Incongruency between personality and situation may lead to psychological and behavioral attempts to restore congruency, such as reevaluation of the environment or leaving it (Secord & Backman, 1965; Snyder & Ickes, 1985). With these suggestions from the personality literature and our discussion of self-selection as a background, we will briefly suggest a basis for predicting environmental selection and adjustment behavior of groups.

The tendency to select specific environments should be strongest in individuals who have a strong self-concept and are very aware of their distinct personal characteristics and needs. Thus highly extroverted individuals would be expected to choose apartment complexes that provide many opportunities for interaction because of their sociopetal design, planned activities, and areas where contact is easily attained (e.g., pools, club houses, etc.). Such selection requires an awareness of the extent to which certain environmental features can facilitate or hinder self-expression. If such individuals are not sensitive to environmental factors, they are prone to choose inappropriate environments. They should react strongly to a mismatch once it becomes obvious since they are likely to be aware of the degree of discrepancy. These individuals should exhibit attempts at changing the environment and/or social relations to better suit their inclinations. If these attempts are frustrated, they should quickly leave to search for a more suitable environment.

Some individuals may have less strong inclinations relevant to environmental selection. For example, they may be neither strongly extroverted nor introverted. These individuals should be most prone to environmental determinism and most clearly demonstrate increased or decreased social activity in different environmental settings. Another group of individuals may be relatively insensitive to environmental features. Such features play little role in their selection of environments, and once in environments these individuals may show very little change in behavior.

Degree of adjustment to environments is also likely to be affected by the degree of choice or control the individual has over the environment. Self-adjustment would seem more likely if there are few environmental options and the individual is limited to a particular environment for a long period of time. Under such conditions individuals may learn to tolerate suboptimal conditions or develop behavioral or psychological strategies that make life in the environment more tolerable. Attempts to change or leave the environment should be most evident with individuals who have a choice of environments. They should experience some degree of reactance or frustration in the initial stage of residence (Wortman & Brehm, 1975). At this time attempts to change the environment or its impact are most likely to occur. However, if these attempts are not successful, the individual or group may leave to search for a more suitable environment. The probability of leaving and its rapidity should be related to the financial and social costs of this alternative and the perceived likelihood of finding a more suitable environment (Toch, 1965).

Most of the studies reviewed have not examined groups over long periods of time. It is possible that many of the effects discussed are limited to early phases of group interaction (e.g., Gans, 1967). Individuals may become less reactive to environments over time and less responsive to other individuals in the environment (e.g., Baum, Aiello, & Calesnick, 1978). They may reach their "quota" of contacts and social relationships may achieve a stable level.

A Specific Model and Some Questions

We have outlined the major findings of two different research traditions—one focusing on the positive impact of environmentally induced social contact and another focusing on the negative aspects of such contact. We pointed to some of the factors that seem to determine the type of impact the environment will have on groups. Figure 3.1 provides a summary of our perspective on the relationship between the environment and social interaction. We have also suggested some specific directions for research on group/environment transactions. Although there is a considerable body of knowledge in this general area, it is quite evident that some of the most interesting questions remain to be answered.

Some of the questions for future research suggested by our prior discussion are as follows:

1. What is the relationship between characteristics of the environment and characteristics of those who choose these environments? How do the characteristics of the environmental choosers influence the impact of different types of environments?
2. Are people who choose bad environments immune to the stress-related consequences of living there? Or are those who choose to live in substandard housing (e.g., slums) as prone to the impact of poor sanitation, crowding, noise, and fear of crime as residents who live there because of lack of options?
3. What is the relative importance of the various factors that appear to moderate the relationship between particular environmental arrangements and group development? Which ones are sufficient? Which are necessary?
4. What are the natural conditions under which facilitative or inhibitory effects of the environment occur? That is, what degree of certainty can we have in predicting facilitative or inhibitory effects in real work environments, using the various environmental, social, and personal criteria?
5. In what ways do individuals adjust to different types of environments outside their range of acceptability? When and under what conditions do they use cognitive or social modes of adjustment, attempt to change the environment, or leave the environment for another one?
6. What role does the degree of match between the environment and personal predispositions have in environmental influence and adjustment? For example, do unfriendly individuals who happen to find themselves in a sociopetal environment become somewhat more sociable or simply become more frustrated and search for a more suitable environment?

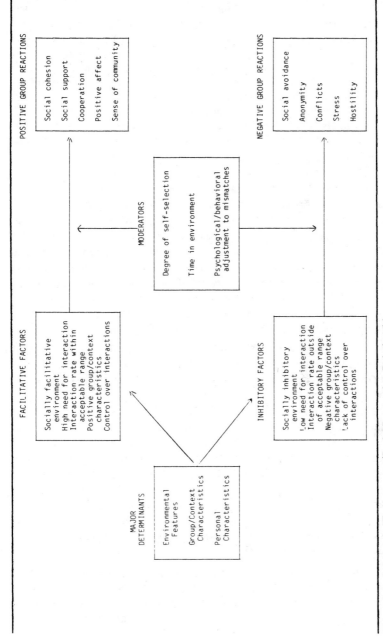

Figure 3.1 Scheme for Environment/Social Interaction Relationship

7. How does the length of time of exposure to a particular environment influence its impact and the nature of the related group processes?
8. How do the relationships observed in the United States compare with those in other countries? Are environmental factors less likely to play a role in cases where there is a high degree of residential and family stability? Will the residents of extremely crowded countries tend to be socially reserved no matter in what type of environment they live or work? Will the relative importance of the mediating and moderating factors be influenced by degree of overall crowding, societal stability, etc.?

A program of research as outlined above should do much to broaden our understanding of the group/environment relationship. Moreover, it also provides a basis for illuminating many basic questions about social-psychological processes in realistic settings. More specifically, the theoretical scheme outlined suggests a way of integrating research on personality/situation interaction with the study of people in environments. In fact, naturalistic environments may present much more appropriate settings for the study of personality and many social psychological or group processes than highly controlled laboratory situations (Emmons et al., 1986; Sears, 1986; Wachtel, 1973). Sears (1986) argues that social psychology's overdependence on the study of college students in laboratories "may have unwittingly led us to a portrait of human nature that describes rather accurately the behavior of American college students in an academic context but distorts human social behavior more generally" (p. 515).

Research on groups in natural environments is wrought with methodological and inferential difficulties. This is sufficient reason for most social psychologists to eschew such an approach. However, it should be noted that while any single naturalistic study is inevitably encumbered by ambiguities, a program of research that addresses these issues in a variety of ways over a series of environments can provide for conceptual replication and allow for accumulative elimination of alternative interpretations. In a way, this process is no different than that required for inferential certainty in experimental laboratory research.

Progress in answering some of the questions posed above will not be easy, but hopefully this chapter will help serve as a guide for those who are brave enough to attempt the task. It should also be noted that while our treatment has focused mostly on residential environments, the issues discussed are also relevant for work, recreational, and various public environments.

NOTE

1. The use of the term *transactional* varies from one scholarly treatment to another. Our usage is similar to Stokols and Shumaker's (1981) use of this term and to Altman and Rogoff's 1987) concept of an organismic approach.

REFERENCES

Altman, I. (1975). *The environment and social behavior: Privacy, personal space, territory, and crowding.* Monterey, CA: Brooks/Cole.

Altman, I., Nelson, P. A., & Lett, E. E. (1972). The ecology of home environments. *Catalog of Selected Documents in Psychology,* Washington, DC: American Psychological Association.

Altman, A. & Rogoff, B. (1987). World views in psychology: Trait, interactional, organismic, and transactional perspectives. In D. Stokols & I. Altman (Eds.), *Handbook of environmental psychology* (Vol. 1, pp. 7-40). New York: John Wiley.

Amir, Y. (1969). Contact hypothesis in ethnic relations. *Psychological Bulletin, 71,* 319-342.

Archer, R. L., & Earle, W. B. (1983). The interpersonal orientations of disclosure. In P. B. Paulus (Ed.), *Basic group processes* (pp. 289-306). New York: Springer-Verlag.

Baron, R. M., & Rodin, J. (1978). Personal control as a mediator of crowding. In A. Baum, J. E. Singer, & S. Valins (Eds.), *Advances in environmental psychology* (Vol. 1, pp. 145-190). Hillsdale, NJ: Lawrence Erlbaum.

Baum, A., Aiello, J., & Calesnick, L. (1978). Crowding and personal control: Social density and the development of learned helplessness. *Journal of Personality and Social Psychology, 36,* 1000-1011.

Baum, A., & Paulus, P. B. (1987). Density and crowding. In D. Stokols & I. Altman (Eds.), *Handbook of environmental psychology* (Vol. 1, pp. 533-570). New York: John Wiley.

Baum, A., & Valins, S. (1979). Architectural mediation of residential density and control: Crowding and the regulation of social contact. In L. Berkowitz (Ed.), *Advances in experimental social psychology* (Vol. 12, pp. 132-172). New York: Academic Press.

Brehm, J. W. (1956). Post-decision changes in desirability of alternatives. *Journal of Abnormal and Social Psychology, 52,* 384-389.

Byrne, D. (1971). *The attraction paradigm.* New York: Academic Press.

Caplow, T., & Forman, R. (1950). Neighborhood interaction in a homogeneous community. *American Sociological Review, 15,* 357-366.

Cohen, S. (1978). Environmental load and the allocation of attention. In A. Baum & S. Valins (Eds.), *Advances in environmental psychology* (Vol. 1, pp. 1-29). Hillsdale, NJ: Lawrence Erlbaum.

Cohen, S., & Syme, S. L. (Eds.). (1985). *Social support and health.* New York: Academic Press.

Cook, S. W. (1985). Experimenting on social issues: The case of school desegregation. *American Psychologist, 40,* 452-460.

Cook, V. C., Paulus, P. B., & McCain, G. (1984). Prison crowding research: The relevance for prison housing standards and a general approach regarding crowding phenomena. *American Psychologist,* 1148-1160.

Ebbesen, E. P., Kjos, G. L., & Konecni, V. J. (1976). Spatial ecology: Its effect on the choice of friends and enemies. *Journal of Experimental Social Psychology, 12,* 505-518.

Emmons, R. A., Diener, E., & Larsen, R. J. (1986). Choice and avoidance of situations and affect congruence. *Journal of Personality and Social Psychology, 51,* 815-826.

Evans, G. W., & Howard, R. B. (1973). Personal space. *Psychological Bulletin, 80,* 334-344.

Festinger, L., Schacter, S., & Back, K. (1950). *Social pressures in informal groups.* New York: Harper & Row.

Fisher, J. D., Bell, P. S., & Baum, A. (1984). *Environmental psychology.* New York: Holt, Rinehart & Winston.

Fleming, R., Baum, A., & Singer, J. E. (1985). Social support and the physical environment. In S. Cohen & S. L. Syme (Eds.), *Social support and health* (pp. 327-345). New York: Academic Press.

Freedman, J. L. (1975). *Crowding and behavior.* San Francisco: Freeman.

Gans, H. J. (1967). *The Levittowners.* New York: Pantheon Books.

Gubrium, J. F. (1974). Victimization in old age. *Crime and Delinquency, 20,* 245-250.

Hall, E. T. (1966). *The hidden dimension.* New York: Doubleday.

Harrison, A. A. (1977). Mere exposure. In L. Berkowitz (Ed.), *Advances in experimental social psychology* (Vol. 10, pp. 40-76). New York: Academic Press.

Hayduk, L. A. (1978). Personal space: An evaluative and orienting overview. *Psychological Bulletin, 85,* 117-134.

Hourihan, K. (1984). Context-dependent models of residential satisfaction. *Environment and Behavior, 16,* 369-393.

Kotler, G. (1979). Organizing for neighborhood power: New possibilities. *South Atlantic Urban Studies, 4,* 64-71.

Kuper, L. (1953). Blueprint for living together. In L. Kuper (Ed.), *Living in towns* (pp. 1-202). London: Cresset Press.

McCain, G., Cox, V. C., Paulus, P. B., & Karlovac, M. (1981). *Social disorganization as a factor in "crowding."* Paper presented to the Midwestern Psychological Association Convention.

Merton, R. K. (1948). The social psychology of housing. In W. Dennis (Ed.), *Current trends in social psychology* (pp. 163-217). Pittsburgh, PA: University of Pittsburgh Press.

Michelson, W. H. (1970). *Man and his urban environment: A sociological approach.* Reading, MA: Addison-Wesley.

Michelson, W. H. (1977). *Environmental choice, human behavior, and residential satisfaction.* New York: Oxford University Press.

Milgram, S. (1970). The experience of living in cities. *Science, 167,* 1461-1468.

Moreland, R. L., & Zajonc, R. B. (1982). Exposure effects in person perception: Familiarity, similarity, and attraction. *Journal of Experimental Social Psychology,*

18, 395-415.

Murstein, B. I. (1976). *Who will marry whom.* New York: Springer.

Newman, O. (1972). *Defensible space.* New York: Macmillan.

Osmond, H. (1957). Function as the basis of psychiatric ward design. *Mental Hospitals,* (Architectural Supplements), *8*, 23-29.

Patterson, M. L. (1976). An arousal model of interpersonal intimacy. *Psychological Review, 83*, 235-245.

Patterson, M. L. (1984). Nonverbal exchange: Past, present, and future. *Journal of Nonverbal Behavior, 8*, 350-359.

Paulus, P. B., Annis, A. B., Seta, J. J., Schkade, J. K., & Matthews, R. W. (1976). Density does affect task performance. *Journal of Personality and Social Psychology, 34*, 248-253.

Perlman, J. E. (1976). Grassrooting the system. *Social Policy, 7*, 4-20.

Perlman, D., & Oskamp, S. (1971). The effects of picture content and exposure on the evaluations of Negroes and whites. *Journal of Experimental Social Psychology, 7*, 503-514.

Proshansky, H. M. (1978). The city and self-identity. *Environment and Behavior, 10*, 147-169.

Rapoport, A. (1985). Thinking about home environments: A conceptual framework. In I. Altman and C. M. Werner (Eds.), *Home environments* (pp. 255-286). New York: Plenum Press.

Rodin, J., Solomon, S., & Metcalf, J. (1978). Role of control in mediating perceptions of density. *Journal of Personality and Social Psychology, 36*, 989-999.

Ruback, R. B., Carr, T. S., & Hopper, C. H. (1986). Perceived control in prison: Its relation to reported crowding, stress, and symptoms. *Journal of Applied Psychology, 16*, 375-386.

Sarason, S. B. (1974). *The psychological sense of community: Prospects for a community psychology.* San Francisco: Jossey-Bass.

Saegert, S. C., Swap, W., & Zajonc, R. B. (1973). Exposure, context, and interpersonal attraction. *Journal of Personality and Social Psychology, 25*, 234-242.

Schachter, S. (1959). *The psychology of affliction.* Stanford, CA: Stanford University Press.

Schkade, J. (1977). *The effects of expectancy set and crowding on task performance.* Unpublished doctoral dissertation, University of Texas at Arlington.

Sears, D. O. (1986). College sophomores in the laboratory: Influences of a narrow data base on social psychology's view of human nature. *Journal of Personality and Social Psychology, 51*, 515-530.

Secord, P. F., & Backman, C. W. (1965). An interpersonal approach to personality. In B. Maher (Ed.), *Progress in experimental personality research* (Vol. 2, pp. 91-125). New York: Academic Press.

Shaver, P., & Buhrmester, D. (1983). Loneliness, sex-role orientation and group life: A social needs perspective. In P. B. Paulus (Ed.), *Basic group processes* (pp. 259-288). New York: Springer-Verlag.

Snyder, M., & Ickes, W. (1985). Personality and social behavior. In G. Lindzey & E. Aronson (Eds.), *Handbook of Social Psychology* (Vol. 2, pp. 883-947). New York: Random House.

Sommer, R. (1969). *Personal space.* Englewood Cliffs, NJ: Prentice-Hall.

Sommer, R. (1974). *Tight spaces: Hard architecture and how to humanize it.* Englewood

Cliffs, NJ: Prentice-Hall.

Sommer, R., & Ross, H. (1958). Social interaction on a geriatrics ward. _International Journal of Social Psychiatry, 4,_ 128-133.

Stephan, W. G. (1987). The contact hypothesis in intergroup relations. In C. Hendrick (Ed.), _Review of Personality and Social Psychology._ Newbury Park, CA: Sage.

Stokols, D. (1976). The experience of crowding in primary and secondary environments. _Environment and Behavior, 8,_ 49-86.

Stokols, D., & Shumaker, S. A. (1981). People in places: A transactional view of settings. In J. H. Harvey (Ed.), _Cognition, social behavior, and the environment_ (pp. 441-488). Hillsdale, NJ: Lawrence Erlbaum.

Sundeen, R. A., & Mathieu, J. T. (1976). The fear of crime and its consequences among elderly in three urban communities. _Gerontologist, 16,_ 211-219.

Swann, W. B., & Predmore, S. C. (1985). Intimates as agents of social support: Sources of consolation or despair? _Journal of Personality and Social Psychology, 49,_ 1609-1617.

Toch, H. (1965). _The social psychology of social movements._ Indianapolis, IN: Bobbs-Merrill.

Unger, D. G., & Wandersman, A. (1985). The importance of neighbors: The social, cognitive and affective components of neighboring. _American Journal of Community Psychology, 13,_ 139-169.

Wachtel, P. L. (1973). Psychodynamics, behavior therapy, and the implacable experimenter: An inquiry into the consistency of personality. _Journal of Abnormal Psychology, 82,_ 324-334.

Wandersman, A., Florin, P., Chavis, D., Rich, R., & Prestby, J. (1985, November). Getting together and getting things done. _Psychology Today,_ pp. 64-71.

Whyte, W. H. (1956). _The organization man._ Garden City, NY: Doubleday.

Wortman, C., & Brehm, J. (1975). Responses to uncontrollable outcomes. In L. Berkowitz (Ed.), _Advances in experimental social psychology_ (Vol. 8, pp. 278-332). New York: Academic Press.

Yancey, W. C. (1972). Architecture, interaction, and social control: The case of a large scale housing project. In J. G. Wohlwill & D. H. Carson (Eds.), _Environment and the social sciences: Perspectives and applications_ (pp. 126-153). Washington, DC: American Psychological Association.

Zajonc, R. B. (1968). Attitudinal effects of mere exposure (Monograph). _Journal of Personality and Social Psychology, 8,_ 1-29.

Zuckerman, M. (1979). _Sensation seeking: Beyond the optimum level of arousal._ Hillsdale, NJ: Lawrence Erlbaum.

4

Personality and Group Performance

JAMES E. DRISKELL
ROBERT HOGAN
EDUARDO SALAS

James E. Driskell is a Research Psychologist at the Human Factors Division, Naval Training Systems Center. His research interests, in addition to this current work, include group status processes, group sentiment structure and influence, and the examination of collective orientation and group performance.

Robert Hogan is McFarlin Professor and Chair of the Department of Psychology at the University of Tulsa. His professional interests include personality theory, personality assessment, and, more recently, organizational psychology.

Eduardo Salas is a Research Psychologist with the Human Factors Division, Naval Training Systems Center. He directs and is engaged in research programs on team training and performance, performance measurement, skill acquisition, and personnel psychology. He holds a Ph.D. in industrial/organizational psychology from Old Dominion University.

Effective groups are composed of effective people. This generalization should be qualified by considerations such as intergroup relations, group structure, task demands, and group process effects. Nonetheless, a team composed of underachieving incompetents will be hard pressed to do well on most tasks, whereas a well-adjusted, skilled, and motivated work team will often succeed in the face of major obstacles.

Social psychologists have studied the behavior of people in small groups since the turn of the century (Durkheim, 1893/1933; Ross, 1908; Triplett, 1898). One useful method for studying small group performance consists of examining the impact of individual variables such as status, skills, and personality on group task behavior. If we assume that certain people will perform more effectively on some team tasks than on others, then we should be able to form groups with members who differ in terms of personality and examine the effects of these differences on group outcomes such as cohesiveness, performance decrement under stress, and task effectiveness. This research is not only theoretically interesting but practically important as well because it has implications for industrial, military, and other real world settings where effective team performance matters.

The notion that personality can influence team performance appears repeatedly in the group dynamics literature. For example, Hackman and Morris (1975) noted that personality may have both positive (enhancing and facilitative) and negative (detrimental and degrading) effects on group performance. Golembiewski (1962) suggested that personality characteristics are as important as group properties for understanding group behavior. Cattell (1951) stated that "personality factors . . . when properly combined with statements regarding the structure of a group, should enable one to predict . . . performance of the group" (p. 180). Finally, Ridgeway (1983), in a recent discussion of task groups and productivity, suggested that effectiveness "emerges from the interaction of skills and personalities of the members, the nature of the task, the groups' structure and norms, and the influence of the outside environment" (p. 281).

These claims notwithstanding, the dominant theme in the empirical literature is complexity if not actual confusion, much speculation but little factual convergence. Mann (1959) noted that the relationship between personality and team performance had been studied extensively for 50 years. However, as Sorenson (1973) observed, this work has produced an extensive but not highly cumulative body of research. Whyte (1941) remarked in his study of gang behavior that "I doubt whether an analysis in terms of personality traits will add anything to such an explanation of behavior" (p. 661). Four decades later, Kahan, Webb, Shavelson, and Stolzenberg (1985) concluded that "It does not appear promising at the present time to use personality measures in determining group composition" (p. 80). There seems to be a mismatch between what people generally believe and what is empirically supported.

We need to distinguish determinants of group behavior in general from the determinants of group effectiveness in particular. The latter topic seems to come up in 10-year cycles. For example, Hoffman (1965) made a plea for research that tested ways to promote group effectiveness. Hackman and Morris (1975) lamented the fact that, despite decades of group research, we still know little about why some groups are more effective than others. For a variety of practical and theoretical reasons, we think that understanding how to compose effective task groups is more important today than ever. Despite the ambiguous evidence, we too believe that personality affects team performance, but that these effects may only be observed under certain well-defined conditions. The purpose of this paper is to specify in more detail what these conditions may be and the conceptual reasons for their occurrence. Although it is usually preferable to light candles than to curse the darkness, we nevertheless begin with a few pointed curses. Why has there been so little progress in the research in this area?

Conceptual Status of Previous Research

At least three factors have contributed to the ambiguity of the evidence regarding the role of personality in promoting team effectiveness. The first concerns the fact that personality psychology has traditionally emphasized psychopathology. Most theories of personality come from psychiatry and clinical psychology, and a good deal of applied personality research focuses on detecting psychopathology. Therefore, many people think of personality in terms of various neurotic structures assumed to underlie behavior; this, in turn, has oriented personality-based group research in less than optimal ways. For example, Collins (1985) noted that the selection of astronaut candidates has focused on detecting psychopathology. On the one hand, this screening has been successful—there have been no cases of acute breakdown in the U.S. space program; however, there has been little emphasis on identifying people with the potential for exceptional performance. After almost a century of research, we know considerably more about undesirable people than we do about talent, competence, and effectiveness. As Hogan, Carpenter, Briggs, and Hansson (1985) noted, the absence of psychopathology does not guarantee the presence of competence. Effective task performers in normal populations have been largely ignored in traditional personality research.

A second reason for the slow accumulation of findings regarding personality and team performance may be that, until recently, there was little consensus among researchers regarding how personality should be defined and measured. In a review of research conducted prior of 1957, Mann (1959) noted that over 500 different measures of personality had been used in studies of group performance. Mann described this research, which included variables as different as oral sadism and adventurous cylothymia, as "test rich and integration poor" (p. 242). The definitional promiscuity that plagues the research on personality and group performance has produced a maze of inconsistent results, leading to the conclusion (see Shaw, 1981) that either the number of trait dimensions is very large and attempts to organize these dimensions may be futile, or that different researchers may use different names for the same trait dimensions. We believe the latter is the case.

A third reason for the inconsistent findings regarding personality and group performance lies in the fact that early research largely ignored the role of the task in determining group performance. Sanderson (1938) noted that the term *group* is as useful as the term *animal*, but it is only useful within certain limits. Precision demands that we specify types of groups, as we distinguish elephants from protozoa. Such is the case with group tasks. Hackman and Morris (1975) suggested that it is almost useless to try to predict group performance without specifying the group's task. Roby (1963) stated that any major advances in small group research depend on successfully defining task properties. However, Morris (1966) pointed out that in most prior research on group performance, the group task has been relatively unspecified. Leadership research prior to the 1950s provides a good example of this general point (see Chemers, 1983). Researchers were consumed with the search for those traits that characterized leaders regardless of the group's task. However, the search for leadership traits spanning all task domains was not productive. In a classic review, Stogdill (1948) noted that to understand the nature of leadership, we must consider the relationship between personality and the task situation. Similarly, the team task must be considered when studying the effects of personality on group performance. Hackman and Morris (1975) pointed out, however, that no fully satisfactory method for classifying group tasks has yet been developed.

In sum, three factors have impeded progress in examining personality and group effectiveness. The first is an emphasis on the psychopathological aspects of personality, an emphasis that has few implications for understanding task group effectiveness. The second is a lack of consensus regarding how personality should be operationally defined; as Cartwright and Zander (1953) succinctly put it, "personality traits are still poorly conceived and unreliably measured" (p. 537). The third is the failure to specify adequately personality effects in the context of specific task environments.

In the following sections, we review a model for conceptualizing group effectiveness. Next, we propose a method for classifying personality and selectively review research relating to the proposed categories. Finally, we suggest a method for classifying group tasks and attempt to specify the relation between personality and group performance in terms of a set of derived hypotheses.

Determinants of Group Effectiveness

As an initial strategy for thinking about group effectiveness, we will use the meta-theoretical model adopted by Gladstein (1984), Hackman and Morris (1975), McGrath (1964), Ridgeway (1983), Shiflett (1979), Steiner (1972), and others. This model, shown in Figure 4.1, illustrates the relation between input factors, group interaction processes, and group performance outcomes.

Steiner (1972) noted that a task group begins with a given set of input factors that define a group's potential for productivity. Because these factors determine a group's potential productivity, they are significant points of intervention at which to begin examining group performance. Three levels of input factors can be identified:

1. Individual-level factors: member skills, knowledge, personalities, and status characteristics.
2. Group-level factors: group size, group structure, group norms, and cohesiveness.
3. Environmental-level factors: the nature of the task, the level of environmental stress, and reward structure.

A group's potential productivity, however, does not always translate into performance. Steiner regarded the difference between potential and actual performance as a function of group process, that is, characteristics not brought to the group but which emerge out of group interaction. Process factors include coalition formation, communication structures, task performance strategies, and tendencies toward polarization. Steiner focused exclusively on process loss, that is, losses due to faulty group processes that prevent a group from reaching its potential. Social loafing, which reduced group performance, is an example of process loss (Latané, Williams, & Harkins, 1979). The degree to which individual personality is compatible with group structure also moderates productivity and is another example of process loss (Aronoff, Messé, & Wilson, 1983). Steiner defined potential productivity as the maximum possible given the initial resources; thus there is no possibility for "process gain" in his model. Sometimes, however, group interaction produces performance beyond that which might be expected on the basis of input

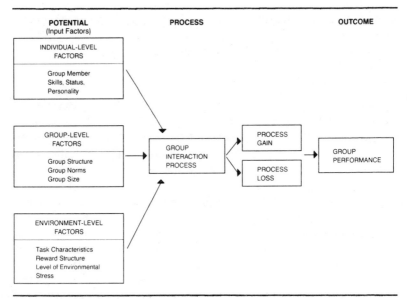

Figure 4.1 Group Performance Model

factors. For example, a group may capitalize on the opportunity to pool resources and correct errors and, as a result, outperform even its most competent member (Hill, 1982). Collins and Guetzkow (1964) refer to such phenomena as "assembly bonus effects."

Implicit in Figure 4.1 are a number of empirical questions about group performance, questions pertaining to the effect of input factors, the interaction of input factors with group process, and the interaction of group process variables. Two specific questions emerge when we consider the effect of personality on group performance. The first concerns how to use personality to compose groups so as to maximize their potential productivity. Here personality is viewed as an input variable; the question is how to compose a group in terms of personality so as to increase the resources available to it. The second question concerns the role of personality vis-à-vis process loss: How can a group minimize process losses that occur with team interaction? Here we are concerned with the effects of personality mix or complementarity that arise out of group interaction. Haythorn (1968), Schutz (1958), and others have studied this problem.

Personality affects group performance both as an input variable and in interaction with process considerations, and it is important to distinguish these two kinds of effects. One can make predictions about a team composed of ambitious (i.e., energetic and hard-working) people based on what one believes to be true about ambitious people, or one can make predictions based on what one believes to be true about the effects of trait similarity on team performance, where the trait in this case is ambition. Haythorn's (1968) review deals with the second issue; we are concerned with the first.

One may trace the effects of personality characteristics as input factors through their impact on three mediating variables. According to Hackman and Morris (1975), these variables link input factors with output measures and explain a major portion of the variance in group performance. These variables include:

1. The effort group members exert on a task.
2. The knowledge and skills group members can apply to a task.
3. The task performance strategies used to accomplish a task.

Each of these mediating variables is in fact quite complex. For example, the effort a team applies to a task is a function of individual characteristics, group norms, and task reward system, as well as process variables such as communication structure. Moreover, we expect personality to affect these summary variables differentially.

The effort each individual expends on a task and the differential coordination and application of that effort should be strongly influenced by personality, in relation to the type of task. For example, the trait of intelligence may predict performance on a problem-solving task that requires generating ideas, but it may not predict performance on a social task requiring interpersonal skills; in the latter case, a "high intelligence" member may be less able to coordinate efforts on a social task and may be unwilling to extend the needed effort.

The mediating variable of knowledge and skills is most strongly predicted by the talent of individual members. Nonetheless, intellectually motivated, well-adjusted, achievement-oriented group members will, in general, bring relatively higher levels of skill to bear on any particular task. Finally, the category of task performance strategies should also be strongly affected by personality. For example, a "high-intellectance" person may be familiar with the strategies appropriate to a problem-solving task because of experience with similar tasks, whereas a "low-intellectance" group member may never have developed appropriate schemas for problem-solving tasks.

The group performance model in Figure 4.1 allows us to examine more closely how personality as an input factor affects group performance and influences the three mediating summary variables of effort, knowledge and skills, and task performance strategies. It is also clear that this influence depends on the personality trait involved and the type of task under consideration. We now turn to these considerations.

Personality Defined

There are almost as many definitions of *personality* as there are personality psychologists. One way to clarify the meaning of personality is to examine how the word is used. MacKinnon (1944) pointed out that there are two primary uses of the word in English, and they correspond to the German terms *persönlichkeit* and *personalität*.

Personality in the first sense (P1) refers to a person's social reputation, to his or her unique stimulus value; it is a purely external view of personality. Personality in this sense in conferred or socially bestowed and is only imperfectly related to individual intrapsychic processes; "personal traits are functions of social situations" (Dewey, 1922, p. 16). Personality in the second sense (P2) refers to the structures (intrapsychic processes such as hopes, fears, aspirations, motives, complexes) within a person that explain why that person creates his or her unique social reputation (see Hogan, 1985). Both definitions are meaningful, but they serve different scientific purposes.

In this paper we will use the word in the P1 sense (i.e., personality as social reputation) because the properties of P1 are well suited to our purposes. P1 is objective; we can estimate the amount of agreement among observers regarding the nature of a person's reputation by means of Q-sorts, adjective checklists, and rating forms. Moreover, P1 is encoded in terms of trait words, which provide a vocabulary of great subtlety and richness to express a person's reputation. Finally, P1 has a well-defined and agreed-upon structure.

Factor analytic research has converged on the view that the universe of trait terms can be expressed in terms of three to six broad dimensions (the six can be recombined into the three and vice versa): intellectance, adjustment, prudence, ambition, sociability, and likability. These six dimensions are described in Figure 4.2, and cognates are presented to illustrate related trait categorizations.

TRAIT	INTELLECTANCE	ADJUSTMENT	AMBITION	PRUDENCE	SOCIABILITY	LIKEABILITY
DESCRIPTORS	Bright, creative vs. dull, un- imaginative.	Stable, self- confident vs. anxious, moody.	Achievement- oriented, energetic vs. apathetic, unassertive.	Conscientious, conforming vs. impulsive, risk-taking.	Outgoing, af- filiative vs. shy, intro- verted.	Warm, friendly vs. cold, critical.
COGNATES						
Mann, 1954	Intelligence	Adjustment	Dominance	Conservatism	Extraversion	Interpersonal sensitivity
Tupes & Christal, 1961	Culture	Adjustment	Extraversion Ascendency	Impulsivity	Extraversion Ascendency	Agreeableness
Gough, 1975	Intellectual Efficiency	Sense of well-being	Dominance	Socialization self-control	Sociability	Empathy
Costa & McCrae, 1985; Norman, 1963	Openness to experience	Neuroticism		Openness to experience	Extraversion	

Figure 4.2 Trait Dimensions

Any single individual or composite of individuals can be described in terms of these dimensions (see Goldberg, 1981; Peabody, 1984; McCrae & Costa, in press). The foregoing line of factor-analytic research provides us with a common vocabulary for describing and measuring personality. More importantly, it is possible to forecast important aspects of everyday behavior with them, including job performance (Hogan, 1986). For these reasons, we use the word personality to refer to a person's social reputation as described by peers and colleagues and encoded in the six dimensions listed in Figure 4.2.

We turn now to a review of the relevance of these dimensions to group performance.

Intellectance. There is little research relating intellectance as a personality trait to group performance. However, researchers who have examined the relation between measured intelligence of group members and group performance have found that intellectance correlates moder-ately (.30 to .60) with measured intelligence. Mann (1959) surveyed 196 studies investigating the effect of intelligence on leadership; 88% of these showed a positive relationship with correlations ranging from .10 to .25. A number of studies found intelligence to be associated with leadership in groups (Stogdill, 1948; Bass & Wurster, 1953; Simonton, 1985). Others have reported a significant relation between leader intelligence and team effectiveness (Greer, Galanter, & Nordlie, 1954; Havron & McGrath, 1961).

Several researchers have noted a positive relationship between group member aptitude and group performance. Kabanoff and O'Brien (1979) found that high-ability groups were more productive than low-ability groups on a creative task. Bouchard (1969) reported that intelligence predicted group performance on a creative task. Terborg, Castore, and DeNinno (1976) found that groups composed on the basis of high SAT scores and grade point averages outperformed low-ability groups. In a study of intact military groups, Tziner and Eden (1985) found that individual aptitude had a significant effect on performance effectiveness. On the other hand, O'Brien and Owens (1969) reported that team members' scores on the Army General Classification test were not related to performance on interactive tasks, although they were associated with performance on coactive tasks.

Adjustment. Mann (1959) and Heslin (1964) both concluded that adjustment is one of the best predictors of group performance. Mann reported that 80% of the results reviewed showed a positive relationship between adjustment and leadership status. Haythorn (1953), using the 16PF, found that emotional stability was positively related to group effectiveness, as rated by outside observers (r = .48). Greer (1955) observed that nervousness and paranoid tendencies in Army team members were negatively related to group effectiveness. In a study of group creativity, Bouchard (1969) found that the first five scales of the California Psychological Inventory (which he called *interpersonal efficiency,* but which in our terms reflect *adjustment*) were significantly related to performance on creative and problem-solving tasks.

Adjustment is also consistently correlated with leadership ratings. Cattell and Stice (1954) found that the absence of anxiety and nervous tendencies distinguish leaders from nonleaders. Richardson and Hanawalt (1952) reported that leaders were more self-confident and better adjusted than nonleaders, and Holtzman (1952) found that adjustment and leadership ratings correlated .67 to .86 in small groups.

Prudence. Hendrick (1979), examining conformity and group problem-solving, found that group members with a concrete (conforming) cognitive style took twice as long to complete a group puzzle-solving task as more abstract (and less conforming) group members. Bass (1954) and Hollander (1954) reported significant negative correlations between authoritarianism and leadership performance. Mann (1959) also noted a negative association between conservatism and leadership, based on studies showing that authoritarian persons are rated lower on leadership than nonauthoritarians. Altman and Haythorn (1968) found among

Navy teams that low dogmatism groups outperformed high dogmatism groups on abstract as well as actual Navy combat team tasks. In contrast with the foregoing, Haythorn (1953) found that conservatism (bohemianism vs. practical concernedness) was positively related to group productivity, and Stogdill (1948) reported a positive relationship between responsibility and leadership.

Ambition. French (1958) found that groups composed of high achievement-oriented members were more efficient than those composed of low achievement-oriented members under task-oriented conditions. Schneider and Delaney (1972) reported that groups with high achievement-oriented members solved complex arithmetic problems faster than did low achievement-oriented groups. Zander and Forward (1968) reported that high achievement-oriented group members were more concerned about group task success than were low achievement-oriented members.

Consistent with these results, Altman and Haythorn (1967) found that dominance—which Hogan (1986) found to be closely related to ambition—was related to task group performance. Watson (1971) reported that dominance predicted the amount of group participation as well as task orientation. Similarly, Bouchard (1969) found that dominance predicted group performance on a brainstorming task. Aries, Gold, and Weigel (1983) noted that dominance predicted 40% of the variance in dominance-oriented behavior (i.e., acts initiated, time talking) in same-sex task groups. Finally, Shaw and Harkey (1976) reported a positive association between leadership orientation and performance.

Not surprisingly, several studies reported a significant relationship between dominance and the tendency to assume a leadership role in groups (Megargee, 1969; Smith & Cook, 1973; Haythorn, 1953); however, Vertreace and Simmons (1971) found no relationship between attempted leadership and achievement motivation. Haythorn (1953) found that groups with high dominance leaders performed better; similar results are reported by Ghiselli and Lodall (1958), and Smelser (1961).

Sociability. Bouchard (1969) found that sociability was consistently related to performance on group creative and problem-solving tasks. Greer (1955) also reported a positive relation between social activeness and group effectiveness. Gurnee (1937) found that groups composed of nonsocial members made more errors on a maze task.

A number of studies have found that extraversion is related to group performance. Similarly, participation rate predicts task performance, status in the group, and emergent leadership. Morris and Hackman (1969) found a significant relationship between participation and leadership. Riecken (1958) found that the more talkative group member was more effective at generating task-oriented solutions. Sorrentino (1973) reported a significant correlation between quantity of verbal interaction and other group members' ratings of task-leadership ability.

Likability. Research has shown that positive relations in a group may be socioemotionally pleasing; for example, Stogdill (1974) found that person-oriented leadership tended to enhance group satisfaction. However, the degree to which likability enhances group performance is less obvious. Bouchard (1969) found that social insight was positively related to group performance. McGrath (1962) composed three-man rifle teams according to interpersonal orientation and found no differences in performance. Tjosvold (1984) found no direct effect of leader's warmth/coldness on team task performance, although there were significant effects on group member satisfaction, attraction, and leader's perceived effectiveness. In examining B29 aircrews in Korea, Berkowitz (1956a) observed no direct relationship between liking and crew effectiveness. Similarly, Tziner and Vardi (1982) found no effect of liking (socioeconomic choices) on the performance of military tank crews. Haythorn (1953) reported no significant relation between group member sociometric rating and group productivity. Terborg et al. (1976) used a three-person land surveying task, and found that liking (attitude similarity) had no effect on group performance.

Some studies suggest that liking may even degrade team performance. Adams (1953) used a sociometric rating of status congruency (related to group harmony) and found that in bomber crews this measure was inversely related to technical performance. Weick and Penner (1969) also found team performance to be inversely related to liking. Stimson and Bass (1964) found that relationship-oriented group members were less successful than more task-oriented group members on an intellectual team task.

The foregoing review suggests that the core personality dimensions are relevant to group performance; it also shows that attempting to specify the effect that they may have on group task performance is risky. For example, intellectance may be less associated with group performance on a mechanical or social task than on a problem-solving task (see Gibb, 1969; Cattell & Stice, 1954). Williges, Johnston, and Briggs (1966) noted that when a task requires no verbal or interpersonal interaction, sociability may have little impact on performance. In analyzing the determinants of group effectiveness, Hackman (1983) noted that "relationships obtained appear to depend substantially on the properties of the group task being performed" (p. 7). The foregoing review should be qualified in each case by the nature of the group task, because the relationship between personality and group performance depends on the type of task involved. Consequently, to evaluate this relationship further requires that we be able to classify group tasks.

Task Classification

There have been a number of attempts to classify group tasks. It is useful to distinguish between task typologies and task dimensions. Task typologies sort tasks into exclusive categories; for example, simple versus complex (Shaw, 1964); disjunctive, conjunctive, or additive (Steiner, 1972); and production, discussion, or problem-solving tasks (Hackman, 1968). These categories are rarely interchangeable because they differ in terms of the dimensions used to distinguish tasks. For example, Hackman's typology is based on the performance processes involved in a task, Steiner's is based on how members contribute to the group task, and Shaw's is based on task difficulty. Moreover, there is some disagreement about the optimum number of categories that can be used meaningfully to describe group tasks; estimates range from 5 (Shaw, 1973) to 14 (Hemphill & Westie, 1950).

The personality trait classification presented in Figure 4.2 refers to features of actors' *behaviors* that are used to describe them; a task typology compatible with this model should be developed along the same dimension. We propose sorting group tasks according to the behaviors or activities required of members to complete them: in McGrath's (1984) terms, according to the task as a set of behavior requirements. The resulting six task categories are presented in Figure 4.3. This classification system is by no means proprietary. In fact, there is a compelling similarity among attempts to classify tasks along this dimension. One of the earliest papers (Carter, Haythorn, & Howell, 1950) attempted to evaluate the relationship between leadership ability and task type. McCormick, Finn, and Scheips (1957), analyzing job requirements, found only seven factors were needed to characterize a sample of 4,000 jobs from the Directory of Occupational Titles (five of which are represented in Figure 4.3). Holland's (1966) model has been used to describe task environments as well as vocational interests. The

TASK	MECHANICAL/ TECHNICAL	INTELLECTUAL/ ANALYTIC	IMAGINATIVE/ AESTHETIC	SOCIAL	MANIPULATIVE/ PERSUASIVE	LOGICAL/ PRECISION
DESCRIPTORS	Construction, operation, maintenance of things.	Generation, exploration, or verification of knowledge.	Invention, arrangement, or production of expressive products.	Training, assisting, or serving others.	Organization, motivation, or persuasion of others.	Performance of explicit, routine tasks or tasks requiring attention to detail.
COGNATES						
Carter, Haythorn, & Howell, 1950	Motor coopera- tion/mechanical assembly	Reasoning/ intellectual construction	---	---	Discussion	Clerical
Guilford, Christensen, Bond, & Sutton, 1954	Mechanical	Scientific	Aesthetic	Social	Business	Clerical
Holland, 1959	Motoric	Intellectual	Esthetic	Supportive	Persuasive	Conforming
Holland, 1966	Realistic	Intellectual	Artistic	Social	Enterprising	Conventional
McCormick, Finn, & Scheirs, 1957	Manual	Mental	Artistic	Personal Contact	---	Precision
Hackman, 1968	---	Problem- solving	Production	---	Discussion	---
McGrath, 1984	Performances/ contests (execution)	Planning/ decision- making	Creativity	---	Cognitive conflict/mixed motive (negotiation)	Intellective

Figure 4.3 Task Classification

most developed of these typologies are presented by Holland (1966, 1985) and McGrath (1984).

The implication is that different types of tasks require specific behaviors. Furthermore, evidence suggests that tasks can be quickly and reliably classified in this manner (Gottfredson, Holland, & Owaga, 1982). More importantly, this procedure provides a means for linking group tasks with personality.

Derivations

We can specify the relationship between personality and group performance in terms of six summary hypotheses that can be confirmed or disconfirmed by empirical test (see Figure 4.4).

Hypothesis 1. The intellectance trait will be positively related to successful performance in intellectual/analytic and imaginative/aesthetic tasks. The intellectance trait reflects two general tendencies: (a) intellectual effort, the behavior most critical for intellectual/analytic tasks, and (b) originality, a prime requirement for imaginative/aesthetic

TASK TRAIT	MECHANICAL/ TECHNICAL	INTELLECTUAL/ ANALYTIC	IMAGINATIVE/ AESTHETIC	SOCIAL	MANIPULATIVE/ PERSUASIVE	LOGICAL/ PRECISION
1. INT	AV	HI	HI	AV	AV	AV
2. ADJ	HI	HI	HI	HI	HI	HI
3. PRU	HI	AV	LO	AV	AV	HI
4. AMB	HI	HI	AV	AV	HI	HI
5. SOC	LO	AV	HI	HI	AV	LO
6. LIK	AV	AV	AV	HI	HI	AV

Note. AV: Average, and not predictive
HI: Positively related to task performance
LO: Negatively related to task performance

Figure 4.4 Optimal Personality Traits for Six Task Categories

tasks. This trait will be less important for tasks requiring interpersonal skills (social and manipulative/persuasive tasks), and for tasks requiring vigilance and rule observance (mechanical/technical and logical/precision tasks). In fact, Crutchfield (1955) and others reported negative correlations between intellectual competence and conformity.

Hypothesis 2. Adjustment will predict successful performance in all task types. Poorly adjusted persons are moody and unpredictable; they tend to disrupt group interaction no matter what type of task performance may be required. All group tasks require mutually coordinated behavior: This is what defines group as contrasted with individual tasks. Poorly adjusted persons disrupt this coordination.

Hypothesis 3. Prudence will be positively related to successful performance in mechanical/technical and logical/precision tasks and negatively related to successful performance in imaginative/aesthetic tasks. Prudent people are conscientious, self-controlled, and conforming, and they perform well on tasks requiring routine, systematic, or rule-guided performance. On the other hand, lower prudence (partially in conjunction with high intellectance) is associated with creativity.

Hypothesis 4. Ambition will be positively related to performance on mechanical/technical, intellectual/analytic, manipulative/persuasive, and logical/precision tasks. Ambitious people are achievement-oriented.

Consequently, ambition will predict performance on all task types except those that depend on social coordination and support, for example, imaginative/aesthetic tasks that require coordinating the expressive output of team members to fashion products, and social tasks that require understanding or helping others.

Hypothesis 5. Sociability will be positively related to performance on imaginative/aesthetic and social tasks but negatively related to performance on mechanical/technical and logical/precision tasks. Sociability will promote effectiveness on social tasks where outgoing, affiliative behaviors are required, and on imaginative/aesthetic tasks where uninhibited, exhibitionistic behaviors are required. Conversely, tasks that require a minimum of social interaction (e.g., mechanical/technical and logical/precision tasks) tend to be disrupted by high levels of affiliative behavior.

Hypothesis 6. Likability will be positively related to performance on social and manipulative/persuasive tasks. Likability is important for tasks based on interaction and requiring social competence and interpersonal tact. Tasks that do not depend on smooth social functioning for successful performance will be less affected by this trait.

The foregoing six hypothesis are summarized in Figure 4.4. Predicted trait relevance for each task type is presented in the table rows; table columns present the optimal group member profile for each task type.

Discussion

The model presented here provides a rational basis for analyzing the effects of personality on group performance. In brief, we argued that different personality types will perform better in different task groups, because different behaviors are required in different task situations. We formalized these claims, and then derived a set of predictions in a manner than can be empirically tested.

Our derivations deal with pure or ideal types. They are the simplest, most fundamental propositions than can be derived from the preceding analysis. However, the fact that our typology is elementary does not invalidate its usefulness. Rather, the utility of our analysis is that it provides a parsimonious basis from which more complex observations can be deduced. In other words, it provides a standard against which the variations observed in actual situations may be compared (see Lundberg, 1940).

This model should be qualified in four ways. First, task situations may rarely correspond to the pure types presented in Figure 4.3. However, tasks can be classified using a profile of scores based on their resemblance to each of the ideal task types. Holland (1985) has developed a model that places the six task types in Figure 4.3 at the vertices of a hexagon. The types that are closest to each other are the most similar, whereas those across from each other are most dissimilar. For example, a social-manipulative/persuasive task, in which a group is formed to help others and to solicit donations, is relatively consistent because these two tasks share similar behavioral requirements. In contrast, an imaginative/aesthetic-logical/precision task is much less consistent. This means, on the one hand, that most real-world tasks will be classified in terms of profiles, with primary, secondary, and tertiary descriptors used, as required. On the other hand, personality will best predict performance for consistent types of tasks.

Second, the impact of personality on task performance may vary across tasks, a complexity not considered in the present model. We argued that personality affects performance by influencing three summary variables: skill, effort, and strategy. Personality will influence these variables differentially; for example, personality may determine strategy more than skill. Moreover, tasks differ in the degree to which these variables are important; that is, some tasks are primarily determined by skill, others by effort, and others by strategy. Consequently, personality may influence performance more on some tasks than others. In addition, within tasks (for example, consider a mechanical/technical task) personality may be more important for performance if the task is effort-based rather than skill-based.

Third, different phases of a task or different subtasks may have very different behavioral requirements. In these circumstances, a group task may contain separate social, technical, or persuasive roles. Teams will perform best by matching people to appropriate task roles; good managers or team leaders do this intuitively. In a sense, the present analysis is decontextualized; we assume that other group and environmental factors remain constant. This is not always the case. For example, the same trait may result in different behaviors under different group conditions. Berkowitz (1956b) placed high- and low-ascendant (ambition) persons in either central or peripheral positions in a group. During the initial trials of the experiment, low-ascendant persons were more passive than highs. But by the third trial, both lows and highs acted similarly. Furthermore, the lows in a central position were more active in task behavior than the highs in a peripheral position. Such results clearly indicate that "low-ambition" individuals can become assertive in group interaction in specific situations. Our analysis simply suggests that those not "traited" for a particular task may be less effective in its performance.

Finally, in this paper we have attempted to integrate a substantial body of work in personality, social psychology, and vocational psychology. This theoretical development yields testable hypotheses and points to an obvious research agenda. The theory makes general predictions about both individual and team performance in specific situations. The inability to make such predictions has plagued research for some time.

REFERENCES

Adams, S. (1953). Status congruency as a variable in small group performance. *Social Forces, 32,* 16-22.

Altman, I., & Haythorn, W. W. (1967). The effects of social isolation and group composition on performance. *Human Relations, 20,* 313-340.

Aries, E. J., Gold, C., & Weigel, R. H. (1983). Dispositional and situational influences on dominance behavior in small groups. *Journal of Personality and Social Psychology, 44,* 779-786.

Aronoff, J., Messé, L. A., & Wilson, J. P. (1983). Personality factors in small group functioning. In H. H. Blumberg, P. Hare, V. Kent, & M. Davies (Eds.), *Small groups and social interaction* (Vol. 1, pp. 79-88). New York: John Wiley.

Bass, B. M. (1954). The leaderless group discussion. *Psychological Bulletin, 51,* 465-492.

Bass, B. M., & Wurster, C. R. (1953). Effects of company rank on LGD performance of oil refinery supervisors. *Journal of Applied Psychology, 37,* 100-104.

Berkowitz, L. (1956a). Group norms among bomber crews: Patterns of perceived crew attitudes, 'actual' crew attitudes, and crew liking related to aircrew effectiveness in Far Eastern combat. *Sociometry, 19,* 141-153.

Berkowitz, L. (1956b). Personality and group position. *Sociometry, 19,* 210-222.

Bouchard, T. J. (1969). Personality, problem-solving procedure, and performance in small groups. *Journal of Applied Psychology Monograph, 53,* 1-29.

Carter, L., Haythorn, W., & Howell, M. (1950). A further investigation of the criteria of leadership. *Journal of Abnormal and Social Psychology, 45,* 350-358.

Cartwright, D., & Zander, A. (Eds.). (1953). *Group dynamics: Research and theory.* Evanston, IL: Row, Peterson.

Cattell, R. B. (1951). New concepts for measuring leadership, in terms of group syntality. *Human Relations, 4,* 161-184.

Cattell, R. B., & Stice, G. F. (1954). Four formulae for selecting leaders on the basis of personality. *Human Relations, 7,* 493-507.

Chemers, M. M. (1983). Leadership theory and research: A systems-process integration. In P. Paulus (Ed.), *Basic group processes* (pp. 9-39). New York: Springer-Verlag.

Collins, B. E., & Guetzkow, H. (1964). *A social psychology of group processes for decision-making.* New York: John Wiley.

Collins, D. L. (1985). *Psychological issues relevant to astronaut selection for long-duration spaceflight: A review of the literature* (Technical Paper No. 84-41). Brooks Air Force Base, TX: Air Force Human Resource Laboratory.

Costa, P. T., & McCrae, R. R. (1985). *The NEO Personality Inventory Manual.* Odessa, FL: Psychological Assessment Resources.

Crutchfield, R. S. (1955). Conformity and character. *American Psychologist, 10,* 191-198.

Dewey, J. (1922). *Human nature and conduct.* New York: Holt.

Durkheim, E. (1933). *The division of labor in society.* New York: Macmillan. (Original work published in 1893).

French, E. (1958). Effects of the interaction of motivation and feedback on task performance. In J.W. Atkinson (Ed.), *Motives in fantasy, action, and society* (pp. 400-408). Toronto: Van Nostrand.

Ghiselli, E., & Lodall, T. M. (1958). Patterns of managerial traits and group effectiveness. *Journal of Abnormal and Social Psychology, 57,* 61-66.

Gibb, C. A. (1969). Leadership. In G. Lindzey & E. Aronson (Eds.), *Handbook of social psychology* (Vol. 4, pp. 205-282). Reading, MA: Addison-Wesley.

Gladstein, D. L. (1984). Groups in context: A model of task group effectiveness. *Administrative Science Quarterly, 29,* 499-517.

Goldberg, L. R. (1981). Language and individual differences: The search for universals in personality lexicons. In L. Wheeler (Ed.), *Review of Personality and Social Psychology* (Vol. 2, pp. 141-165). Newbury Park, CA: Sage.

Golembiewski, R. T. (1962). *The small group: An analysis of research concepts and operations.* Chicago: University of Chicago Press.

Gottfredson, G. D., Holland, J. L., & Ogawa, D. K. (1982). *Dictionary of Holland occupational codes.* Palo Alto: Consulting Psychologists Press.

Gough, H. G. (1975). *Manual for the California Personality Inventory.* Palo Alto: Consulting Psychologists Press.

Greer, F. L. (1955). *Small group effectiveness.* (Institute Report No. 6). Philadelphia: Institute for Research on Human Relations.

Greer, F. L., Galanter, E. H., & Nordlie, P. G. (1954). Interpersonal knowledge and individual and group effectiveness. *Journal of Abnormal and Social Psychology, 49,* 411-414.

Guilford, J. P., Christensen, P. R., Bond, N. A., & Sutton, M. A. (1954). A factor analysis study of human interests. *Psychological Monographs, 68,* (Whole No. 375).

Gurnee, H. (1937). Maze learning in the collective situation. *Journal of Psychology, 3,* 437-443.

Hackman, J. R. (1968). Effects of task characteristics on group products. *Journal of Experimental Social Psychology, 4,* 162-187.

Hackman, J. R. (1983). *A normative model of work team effectiveness* (Technical Report No. 2). New Haven, CT: Yale School of Organization and Management.

Hackman, J. R., & Morris, C. G. (1975). Group tasks, group interaction process, and group performance effectiveness: A review and proposed integration. In L. Berkowitz (Ed.), *Advances in experimental social psychology* (Vol. 8, pp. 45-99). New York: Academic Press.

Havron, M. D., & McGrath, J. E. (1961). The contribution of the leader to the effectiveness of small military groups. In L. Petrullo & B. M. Bass (Eds.), *Leadership and interpersonal behavior* (pp. 167-178). New York: Holt.

Haythorn, W. (1953). The influence of individual members on the characteristics of small groups. *Journal of Abnormal and Social Psychology, 48,* 276-284.

Haythorn, W. W. (1968). The composition of groups: A review of the literature. *Acta Psychologica, 28,* 97-128.

Hemphill, J. K., & Westie, C. M. (1950). The measurement of group dimensions. *Journal of Psychology, 29,* 325-342.

Hendrick, H. W. (1979). Differences in group problem solving behavior and effectiveness as a function of abstractness. *Journal of Applied Psychology, 64,* 518-525.

Heslin, R. (1964). Predicting group task effectiveness from member characteristics. *Psychological Bulletin, 62,* 248-256.

Hill, G. W. (1982). Group versus individual performance: Are N+1 heads better than one? *Psychological Bulletin, 91,* 517-539.

Hoffman, L. R. (1965). Group problem solving. In L. Berkowitz (Ed.), *Advances in experimental social psychology* (Vol. 2, pp. 99-132). New York: Academic Press.

Hogan, R. (1985). *Personality psychology: Back to basics.* Third Biennial Henry A. Murray Symposium in Personality Psychology. East Lansing, MI: Michigan State University.

Hogan, R. (1986). *Manual for the Hogan Personality Inventory.* Minneapolis: National Computer Systems.

Hogan, R., Carpenter, B. N., Briggs, S. R., & Hansson, R. O. (1985). Personality assessment in industry: A historical and conceptual overview. In H. J. Bernardin & D. A. Bownas (Eds.), *Personality assessment in industry* (pp. 21-52). New York: Praeger.

Holland, J. L. (1959). A theory of vocational choice. *Journal of Counseling Psychology, 6,* 35-44.

Holland, J. L. (1966). A psychological classification scheme for vocations and major fields. *Journal of Counseling Psychology, 13,* 278-288.

Holland, J. L. (1985). *Making vocational choices: A theory of vocational personalities and work environments* (2nd ed.). Englewood Cliffs, NJ: Prentice-Hall.

Hollander, E. P. (1954). Authoritarianism and leadership choice in a military setting. *Journal of Abnormal and Social Psychology, 49,* 365-370.

Holtzman, W. H. (1952). Adjustment and leadership. *Journal of Social Psychology, 36,* 179-189.

Kabanoff, B., & O'Brien, G. E. (1979). Cooperation structure and the relationship of leader and member ability to group performance. *Journal of Applied Psychology, 64,* 526-532.

Kahan, J. P., Webb, N., Shavelson, R. J., & Stolzenberg, R. M. (1985). *Individual characteristics and unit performance.* Santa Monica, CA: Rand.

Latané, B., Williams, K., & Harkins, S. (1979). Many hands make light the work: Causes and consequences of social loafing. *Journal of Personality and Social Psychology, 37,* 822-832.

Lundberg, G. A. (1940). Some problems of group classification and measurement. *American Sociological Review, 5,* 351-360.

MacKinnon, D. W. (1944). The structure of personality. In J. McV. Hunt (Ed.), *Personality and the behavior disorders* (Vol. 1, pp. 3-48). New York: Ronald Press.

Mann, R. D. (1959). A review of the relationships between personality and performance in small groups. *Psychological Bulletin, 56,* 241-270.

McCormick, E. J., Finn, R. H., & Scheips, C. D. (1957). Patterns of job requirements. *Journal of Applied Psychology, 41,* 358-364.

McCrae, R. R., & Costa, P. T., Jr. (in press). Validation of the five factor model of personality across instruments and observers. *Journal of Personality and Social Psychology.*

McGrath, J. E. (1962). The influence of positive interpersonal relations on adjustment and effectiveness in rifle teams. *Journal of Abnormal and Social Psychology, 65*, 365-375.

McGrath, J. E. (1962). *Social psychology: A brief introduction.* New York: Holt.

McGrath, J. E. (1984). *Groups: Interaction and performance.* Englewood Cliffs, NJ: Prentice-Hall.

Megargee, E. I. (1969). Influence of sex roles on the manifestation of leadership. *Journal of Applied Psychology, 53*, 377-382.

Morris, C. G. (1966). Task effects on group interaction. *Journal of Personality and Social Psychology, 5*, 545-554.

Morris, C. G, & Hackman, J. R. (1969). Behavioral correlates of perceived leadership. *Journal of Personality and Social Psychology, 13*, 350-361.

Norman, W. T. (1963). Toward an adequate taxonomy of personality attributes. *Journal of Abnormal and Social Psychology, 66*, 574-583.

O'Brien, G. E., & Owens, A. G. (1969). Effects of organizational structure on correlations between member ability and group productivity. *Journal of Applied Psychology, 53*, 525-530.

Peabody, D. (1984). Personality dimensions through trait inferences. *Journal of Personality and Social Psychology, 46*, 384-403.

Richardson, H. M., & Hanawalt, N. G. (1952). Leadership as related to the Bernreuter personality measures. *Journal of Social Psychology, 36*, 141-154.

Ridgeway, C. L. (1983). *The dynamics of small groups.* New York: St. Martin's.

Riecken, H. W. (1958). The effect of talkativeness on ability to influence group solutions of problems. *Sociometry, 21*, 309-321.

Roby, T. B. (1963). *Process criteria of group performance.* Paper presented as part of the task and criterion work group of the small groups in isolation project of the Neuropsychiatric Division, NMRI, Bethesda, MD.

Ross, E. A. (1908). *Social psychology.* New York: Macmillan.

Sanderson, D. (1938). Group description. *Social Forces, 16*, 309-319.

Schneider, F. W., & Delaney, J. G. (1972). Effect of individual achievement motivation on group problem solving efficiency. *Journal of Social Psychology, 86*, 291-298.

Schutz, W. C. (1958). *FIRO: A three dimensional theory of interpersonal behavior.* New York: Rinehart.

Shaw, M. E. (1964). Communication networks. In L. Berkowitz (Ed.), *Advances in experimental social psychology* (Vol. 1, pp. 111-147). New York: Academic Press.

Shaw, M. E. (1973). Scaling group tasks: A method for dimensional analysis. *JSAS Catalog of Selected Documents in Psychology, 3* (8) (Ms. No. 294).

Shaw, M. E. (1981). *Group dynamics: The psychology of small group behavior* (3rd ed.). New York: McGraw-Hill.

Shaw, M. E., & Harkey, B. (1976). Some effects of congruency of member characteristics and group structure upon group behavior. *Journal of Personality and Social Psychology, 34*, 412-418.

Shiflett, S. (1979). Toward a general model of small group productivity. *Psychological Bulletin, 86*, 67-79.

Simonton, D. K. (1985). Intelligence and personal influence in groups: Four nonlinear models. *Psychological Review, 92*, 532-547.

Smelser, W. T. (1961). Dominance as a factor in achievement and perception in cooperative problem-solving interactions. *Journal of Abnormal and Social Psychology, 62,* 535-542.

Smith, R. J., & Cook, P. E. (1973). Leadership in dyadic groups as a function of dominance and incentives. *Sociometry, 36,* 561-568.

Sorrentino, R. M. (1973). An extension of theory of achievement motivation to the study of emergent leadership. *Journal of Personality and Social Psychology, 26,* 356-368.

Sorenson, J. R. (1973). Group member traits, group process, and group performance. *Human Relations, 26,* 639-655.

Steiner, I. D. (1972). *Group process and productivity.* New York: Academic Press.

Stimson, D. V., & Bass, B. M. (1964). Dyadic behavior of self-interaction-and task-oriented subjects in a task situation. *Journal of Abnormal and Social Psychology, 68,* 558-562.

Stogdill, R. M. (1948). Personal factors associated with leadership: A survey of the literature. *Journal of Personality, 25,* 37-71.

Stogdill, R. M. (1974). *Handbook of leadership: A survey of theory and research.* New York: Free Press.

Terborg, J. R., Castore, C., & DeNinno, J. A. (1976). A longitudinal field investigation of the impact of group composition on group performance and cohesion. *Journal of Personality and Social Psychology, 34,* 782-790.

Tjosvold, D. (1984). Effects of leader warmth and directiveness on subordinate performance on a subsequent task. *Journal of Applied Psychology, 69,* 422-427.

Triplett, N. (1898). The dynamogenic factors in pace-making and competition. *American Journal of Psychology, 9,* 507-533.

Tupes, E. C., & Christal, R. E. (1961). *Recurrent personality factors based on trait ratings* (Technical Report ASD-TR-61-97). Lackland Air Force Base, TX: USAF Personnel Laboratory.

Tziner, A., & Eden, D. (1985). Effects of crew composition on crew performance: Does the whole equal the sum of its parts? *Journal of Applied Psychology, 70,* 85-93.

Tziner, A., & Vardi, Y. (1982). Effects of command style and group cohesiveness on the performance of self-selected tank crews. *Journal of Applied Psychology, 67,* 769-775.

Vertreace, W. E., & Simmons, C. H. (1971). Attempted leadership in the leaderless group discussion as a function of motivation and ego involvement. *Journal of Personality and Social Psychology, 19,* 285-289.

Watson, D. (1971). Reinforcement theory of personality and social systems: Dominance and position in a group power structure. *Journal of Personality and Social Psychology, 20,* 180-185.

Weick, K. E., & Penner, D. D. (1969). Discrepant membership as an occasion for effectivce cooperation. *Sociometry, 32,* 413-424.

Williges, R. C., Johnston, W. A., & Briggs, G. E. (1966). Role of verbal communication in teamwork. *Journal of Applied Psychology, 50,* 473-478.

Whyte, W. F. (1941). Corner boys: A study of clique behavior. *American Journal of Sociology, 46,* 647-664.

Zander, A., & Forward, J. (1968). Position in group, achievement orientation, and group aspirations. *Journal of Personality and Social Psychology, 8,* 282-288.

5

Group Rapport and Nonverbal Behavior

LINDA TICKLE-DEGNEN
ROBERT ROSENTHAL

Linda Tickle-Degnen is a doctoral candidate in social psychology at Harvard University. Her current research interests are focused on gaining an understanding of the development and outcome of rapport, particularly as it relates to health care and rehabilitation, and of differences between actors and observers in their impressions of interacting individuals.

Robert Rosenthal is Professor of Social Psychology at Harvard University. He is the author of *Experimenter Effects in Behavioral Research* and *Pygmalion in the Classroom* (with Lenore Jacobson), and of several books on nonverbal communication, research methods, and quantitative procedures in the social sciences. His current work is in the areas of interpersonal self-fulfilling prophecies, data analysis in the social sciences, and nonverbal communication in teacher-student, doctor-patient, manager-employee, and psychotherapist-client interaction.

No sensation . . . can endure the test of a moment's inspection when compared with a social enjoyment. It is then only that a man is truly pleased, when pulse replies to pulse, when the eyes discourse eloquently to each other, when in responsive tones and words the soul is communicated. (Godwin, 1802, p. 72)

Godwin's protagonist may not have exaggerated too much when he proclaimed that only with social enjoyment, man, and, we add, woman, is truly pleased. The social enjoyment that he described as a process during which "the soul is communicated" is infrequent in our daily encounters with others, and, therefore, of particular value to us. This infrequency is due partly to the fact that many of our social interactions are ones in which we do not wish to, or do not have the time to, communicate our souls, but also it is due to the seeming lack of control we have over its occurrence. These encounters that are characterized by a high degree of rapport among the interactants are attributed to "chemistry," meaning that it was the *combination* of the elements, in this case, the participants, not the elements alone that constituted the character of the interaction.

Among other reasons, because a high degree of rapport feels good and is valued, it is a powerful determinant of the outcome of interactions. We would probably wish to be around individuals for longer periods of time and more often when we experienced a high rather than a low level of rapport with them. We would most likely listen to, be responsive to, and be influenced by individuals with whom we feel we are communicating our souls. In fact, this responsiveness to another's influence appears to have been the key element in the use of the term *rapport* earlier in this century. Rapport was used to indicate a quality of a relationship in which at least one of the members of an interaction became highly suggestible and dependent in relation to another, such as during hypnosis, the development of a collective mind in a crowd (Park & Burgess, 1924), and the process of transference in psychoanalytic treatment (Freud, 1914/1924).

More recently, the concept of rapport seems to have been used in a broader sense to describe a generally good interaction among individuals, with the implication remaining that it is a crucial factor contributing to the outcome of the interaction. For example, investigators have been interested in rapport as good interaction in relation to psychotherapeutic (Rogers, 1957; Truax & Carkhuff, 1967) and medical (Friedman & DiMatteo, 1982; Szasz & Hollender, 1956) outcomes. Not only does a high degree of rapport increase the likelihood that clients or patients continue therapeutic interactions and prescribed regimens, but it also appears to promote good health itself (White, Tursky, & Schwartz, 1985).

The concept of rapport is not limited in its current usage to health professional interactions, though most of the relevant research has been done in this area. We tend to associate its usefulness to any situation in which individuals come together to work to achieve an explicit and formal goal, such as in buyer-seller interactions, survey interviews, organizational committee work, and work teams. The degree of rapport present may determine the efficiency and quality of the progress toward goal achievement, and whether, in fact, the goal is ever achieved.

Despite its recognized importance to the outcome of interactions, the concept of rapport has not been very clearly delineated. It is so familiar to psychologists, psychiatrists, counselors, social workers, ministers, managers, and the general public that almost everyone has a rough and ready working definition of the concept. These working definitions, usually descriptive of a generally positive interaction, are perfectly adequate for workaday applications. They are also acceptable in research when the investigator is interested in an intuitively appealing and clinically appropriate summarizing label for positive interactional attributes; however, such a practice neglects the richness of the implications of the term *rapport*.

One of the major purposes of this chapter is to suggest a more explicit and detailed conceptualization of rapport than that used in most previous research. A second major purpose of the chapter is to explore the role that nonverbal behavior plays in the "chemistry" of the interaction. Evidence is provided to show that nonverbal behavior is (a) an important determinant of rapport, (b) a consequent of rapport, and (c) an indicator of the level of rapport present in an interaction. A third major purpose of the chapter is to offer some methodological suggestions for the investigation of group rapport and nonverbal behavior. There are many "gaps" in research in this area, factors and issues that have been underinvestigated or have remained in a conundrum of ambiguous results. We focus our attention on two issues that have important implications for future research: (1) the distinction between the experience and observation of rapport as mediated through nonverbal behavior, and (2) the temporal aspects of rapport as it relates to nonverbal behavior.

THE CONCEPTUALIZATION OF GROUP RAPPORT

Our approach to a conceptualization of rapport is by way of an informed lay psychology. We draw upon our own experiences and the language used in everyday conversation to gain some sense of what is meant by the term, and then add insight derived from a review of the research to suggest structural and dynamic components that seem to be required for a useful conceptualization of rapport. The discussion begins by eliminating some things rapport is not so that we can encircle a "conceptual territory" in which to locate the construct.

What Rapport Is Not

First, rapport cannot exist where there is no interaction between individuals. Rapport is not a personality trait, although an individual may be particularly skilled at developing rapport in certain situations, or, as with psychotherapists, be trained to exhibit qualities that will facilitate rapport (Rogers, 1957; Truax & Carkhuff, 1967). Rapport is intrinsically interactional, and describes a quality of relationship.

Although interaction is necessary, it is not sufficient for the emergence of rapport. We would not expect rapport to develop in what Goffman (1963) calls an unfocused gathering. Such a gathering is one in which individuals are merely aware of the copresence of another, such as when several pedestrians are waiting for a traffic light to change so that they may cross the street. Communication occurs, in that minimal impressions may be formed and individuals coordinate their movements and positions so as not to bump into one another, but that communication does not imply the involvement with one another required for rapport to develop. Greater opportunities for rapport to develop occur in focused interactions, when individuals cooperate to sustain a single focus of attention through communication with one another.

Furthermore, the concept of rapport is not typically thought to apply in very brief focused interactions, such as the exchange of greetings between two acquaintances passing one another on the street, or the buying of a hot dog from a clerk at a sandwich shop. In both cases, the individuals are involved in an exchange during which they sustain a single focus of attention, but that exchange is too brief for us to label it as having or lacking a quality of rapport. We usually tend to think of rapport as developing over time and as existing in focused interactions of more than a brief instant. In fact, we would expect that the frequency with which the word *rapport* would co-occur in everyday speech with the words *build, develop, maintain,* or other verbs of a temporal nature, would be very high. For example, health professionals and sales personnel often speak of building rapport with their clients.

Typically, the word *rapport* does not imply negative interaction, but, rather a positive involvement of interactants. When researchers design self-report measures of rapport, it is usually assumed that rapport will be manifested as positive ratings on adjective scales such as *friendly, good, pleasant* (e.g., Harrigan & Rosenthal, 1986), and other terms of positive valence.

Although positive involvement is a general characteristic of rapport, rapport does not require a cheerful atmosphere. LaFrance (1982), drawing upon an example from Scheflen (1964), points out that a situation in which old friends are arguing is not necessarily one in which there is a lack of rapport, and yet the content of the interaction could be seen as negative. In the example, the friends are arguing, thus expressing negative verbal content in their interaction, but they are also sharing each other's posture, possibly a nonverbal expression of the underlying

TABLE 5.1
Examples of the Crossing of State and Trait Rapport

		Trait Rapport	
		Low	High
State Rapport	Low	argument in a bad relationship	argument in a good relationship
	High	agreement in a bad relationship	agreement in a good relationship

ties in their friendship. The Scheflen example suggests that we could think of rapport as having enduring aspects and short-term aspects analogous to trait and state aspects of an individual. Thus, relationships may be characterized by high and low rapport that is long-term (trait), for example, good and bad marriages, or therapy relationships, or high and low rapport of a more transient short-term nature (state), such as that occurring during single interactions in which the interactants are agreeing or disagreeing with one another. Table 5.1 shows examples of the crossing of these dimensions of rapport.

So far from our discussion of what rapport is not, we have learned that rapport occurs in nontrivial, focused interaction, is of a positive nature, and has a developmental quality. But there is more.

What Rapport Is

The terms *balance, harmony,* and *"in sync"* come to mind when thinking of the experience of rapport, and even though these terms have positive connotations, there is something more to them than just positive valence. In an interpersonal context they convey an image of equilibrium, of regularity and predictability, of coordination between the interactants. Although all interactions to some extent involve coordination and predictability of action in order for communication to take place among the participants (Duncan & Fiske, 1977), one would expect groups that are characterized by high rapport to have a higher level of these qualities than those that show low rapport. This coordination of behavior in informal social interaction has been described using analogies such as the smooth actions of a well-functioning athletic team (Altman & Taylor, 1973), or the rhythm and synchronization of the members of an orchestra (Scheflen, 1963). Park and Burgess (1924) aptly describe this coordination aspect of rapport:

> *Rapport* implies the existence of a mutual responsiveness, such that every member of the group reacts immediately, spontaneously, and sympathetically to the sentiments and attitudes of every other member. (p. 893)

In summary, the conceptualization of rapport can be outlined in terms of structural and dynamic components. The two structural components are the prerequisites of rapport. They are those features of an interaction that identify it as one in which rapport can be assessed, either by the participants or observers. First, the context of rapport is an interaction that is of a focused nature. And, second, it is an interaction that is sustained for more than a brief period of time; it is not of a trivial or transient nature. The three dynamic components of rapport are those features of an interaction that have a developmental and changing quality and that can be assessed in a 'state' or 'trait' manner: the degree of (1) mutual attention and involvement, (2) positivity, and (3) coordination among the participants of an interaction. An interaction involving high state and trait rapport would, by definition, have a high degree of mutual attention, positivity, and coordination among the participants.

NONVERBAL BEHAVIOR AND GROUP RAPPORT

We turn now to an examination of the role of nonverbal behavior as a correlate, determinant, and consequence of rapport in groups. Following from the conceptualization of group rapport, we examine those nonverbal behaviors or behavioral patterns, such as facial expressions, body movements, and vocal characteristics, that seem to be most related to participant attentiveness, positivity, and coordination. Our intention is to review some representative samples of the research, not to provide an extensive description of the literature.[1]

Nonverbal Behavior and Mutual Attention

Through direct observational studies it has been established that focused interaction is typified by a pattern of group spatial behavior. When people spontaneously gather and carry on a conversation, the configuration that their bodies form is usually circular or semicircular (Ciolek, 1978). Kendon (1976) has explained the configuration as functioning to place each individual within each other's transactional segment, a space extending in front of the person that is used for conducting current activities in which the person is engaged. The configurational system, called an F-formation, has a bounding function that serves to define the individuals as a group separate from its surroundings. The maintenance of the F-formation is achieved by the active cooperation of the participants when they are standing and by the furniture arrangement when they are seated. Sheflen (1964) has observed, however, that seated individuals are able to include or exclude individuals from an interaction by trunk and extremity posture. For example, in three-person groups, turning the upper body toward one individual and the lower body toward another, serves to maintain the relationship among all three individuals.

In experimental studies, nonverbal spatial behavior has been treated as an independent variable in an attempt to determine whether it can increase or decrease the level of involvement of participants with one another. For example, Patterson, Kelly, Kondracki, and Wulf (1979) manipulated the spatial configuration of four-member groups by positioning the interactants' chairs in either a circular or L-shaped seating arrangement. They found that the circular configuration was characterized by greater involvement as indicated by fewer pauses in conversation and fewer signs of discomfort, but the type of seating configuration did not significantly affect the participants' self-reported ratings of feeling part of a group. It is interesting to note that the L-shaped arrangement was characterized by more postural adjustments on the part of the participants, possibly due, as the investigators pointed out, to active and somewhat successful maneuvering (in light of the nonsignificant results of the effect of postural alignment on the rating scales) to overcome the interactional limitations of the configuration.

When participants are unable to increase the involvement of another person through their own verbal and nonverbal responses, it appears that they feel less involved themselves. Hale and Burgoon (1984) examined the effect of a confederate's manipulated nonverbal behavior on the interaction ratings by the other participant of a dyadic interaction. When the confederate sat at a greater distance, with an indirect body orientation, backward lean, crossed arms, and low eye contact, the subject felt a greater degree of detachment from the interaction than did those subjects who interacted with a confederate demonstrating a pattern consisting of more close and intimate behaviors. These findings and the results of the Patterson et al. (1979) investigation suggest that the degree of involvement of an individual in an interaction is affected both by that individual's own nonverbal behavior as well as the behavior of the other person.

Outside observers of an interaction also appear to be influenced in their ratings of the involvement in an interaction by the nonverbal behavior of the participants. Scherer and Schiff (1973) found that the perceived opportunity for gazing at one another in an interaction affected ratings of intimacy. Judges rated photographs in which the interactants were physically oriented toward one another as demonstrating greater intimacy than those in which the interactants were less oriented toward each other. It appeared to be sufficient for the participants' heads to be directly oriented, regardless of the rest of the body's orientation, for a rating of high intimacy.

In the studies discussed so far, the interaction itself was rated. In other studies, the relationship between a particular participant's nonverbal behavior and subsequent ratings of his or her attentiveness has been examined. Fretz, Corn, Tuemmler, and Bellet (1979) found observers of a counselor to rate the counselor as more attentive when he or she demonstrated greater eye contact, forward trunk lean, and direct body orientation relative to low degrees of these behaviors. They also found, however, that clients who were actually participating in the interaction with counselors appeared to be unaffected in their ratings of the counselors' attentiveness. Kleinke, Staneski, and Berger (1975) controlled eye contact in interviews between a female confederate and male subjects. In this study, greater eye contact was given higher ratings of attentiveness by the male participants.

The studies we have described demonstrate that nonverbal behavior is a correlate or antecedent of focused attention. In order to understand how focus of attention would affect nonverbal behavior, we would have to examine research in which focus of attention was manipulated and subsequent nonverbal interaction observed. There appears to be little research on this topic. It would be difficult to manipulate a subject's focus of attention without also manipulating nonverbal behavior. Ellis and Holmes (1982) employed a potentially useful methodology to investigate focus of attention. They had their subjects either focus inward on the self or focus outward on another participant. The degree of warmth of the nonverbal behavior of the subjects appeared to be unaffected by their focus of attention. Specific behaviors were not examined.

Overall, we may conclude that nonverbal behavior is a correlate of focused interaction, and a factor contributing to participants' and observers' perceptions of interactional involvement and attentiveness. Whether it is also a consequence of increased attentiveness is unsubstantiated. In summary, through postural alignment and orientation, the participants convey to each other as well as to outsiders that they constitute a group. Their bodies, in creating a boundary to the interaction, serve to focus the attention of the group inward into the "location" (Kendon, 1976) of the interaction, thus allowing the maintenance of a focused interaction. The opportunity for mutual observation seems to be a crucial factor in the involvement of the participants. The ability to observe easily another person's face and body may serve many functions (Argyle & Cook, 1976; Kleinke, 1986), one of which appears to be the gathering of information about that person, including how he or she is responding to one's own behaviors. This information would be used to determine the level and type of involvement of the other individual and to determine what types of responses to make (Patterson, 1983). Through nonverbal behavior a participant develops a feeling of involvement and through the observation of another participant assesses the attentiveness of others and their wish for continued involvement. To our knowledge, no one has investigated the temporal effect of these behaviors on an interaction, for example, how long focus and attentiveness would be maintained during various conditions of nonverbal behavior, or how attentiveness would grow or decline over time nonverbally.

Closely related to the degree of attentiveness and focus is the level of positivity in an interaction. A high level of one component, however, does not necessarily imply a high level of the other component. There may be a high involvement and attention of a negative nature, for example, as in teenage boys confronting one another in verbal combat, and low involvement and mutual attention of a positive nature, as individuals in a stadium cheering their team's scoring. In high state rapport, however, both high attention to one another and positivity would be present.

Nonverbal Behavior and Positivity

The relationship between nonverbal behavior and positivity in an interaction is a complex one. The same types of nonverbal behavior may occur in negative or positive interactions, and their interpretation is dependent on the roles that participants are playing in an interaction, the history of the relationship of the individuals, and the perceived function of the interaction for the participants (Ekman, 1965; Patterson,

1983). Most of the research on this issue of the context-dependent meaning of nonverbal behavior has been done employing eye contact (Kleinke, 1986). Under conditions of cooperative tasks among peers, for example, eye contact is indicative of positive feelings, yet under conditions in which the interactants feel personal threat or competitiveness toward one another, it may be indicative of aggressiveness. Likewise, the behavior of smiling may be a positive expression of warmth or a negative expression of anxiety (Ekman, Friesen, & Ancoli, 1980), such as in situations of anticipated unpleasant interactions (Ickes, Patterson, Rajecki, & Tanford, 1982). Given that it is understood that the context of an interaction is generally one in which the individuals have basically friendly, cooperative goals, we can determine what types of nonverbal behavior appear to be correlates of rapport.

The study of nonverbal behavior and the positivity of an interaction has taken place primarily with counselor-client dyads and informal get-acquainted sessions between peers. In these investigations there are several methodological practices that limit the generalizability of their results to our present discussion of rapport. First, the interaction is usually dyadic. Second, the analysis typically centers on how impressions are formed about one member of the dyad, not about the interaction of the members. Third, the interactions are generally short so that the relationship between nonverbal behavior and positivity is not explored as it develops over time within an interaction and across many interactions. Fourth, the interactants often are strangers participating in a staged interaction in a psychology laboratory. Despite these limitations, the findings of the studies provide us with some insight into the possible role of nonverbal behavior in the positivity of group interaction.

Positive feelings in an interaction appear to be related to a variety of nonverbal behaviors, behaviors that Mehrabian (1972) calls "immediacy" behaviors, for example, forward leaning, direct body orientation, and eye contact. Correlational research in which naturally occurring nonverbal behavior is examined shows that the relationship is not straightforward and consistent. For example, in a study reported by Harrigan and Rosenthal (1986), physicians who displayed direct body orientation, less asymmetrical posturing of arms, greater posturing of the legs in open positions, and less mutual gaze with a patient, were rated more positively by judges than were physicians who did not follow this pattern. Smiling, trunk lean, openness of arms, head nodding, and smiling were unrelated to the ratings. In a correlational investigation by Ickes, Robertson, Tooke, and Teng (1986), participants' positive thoughts and feelings during an interaction were positively related to their duration and frequency of gazing toward the other interactant, to smiling, and to gesturing. Fretz (1966) found that client forward lean was positively related to the client's rating of the relationship with a counselor, though counselor forward lean was slightly negatively related to the counselor's evaluation of the relationship. The counselors' amount of smiling and hand movements, however, were positively related to their perception of the quality of the interaction. Taken together, these studies indicate that nonverbal behavior is related to positivity, but specific behaviors are not consistently indicative of positivity.

Studies in which nonverbal behavior is specifically manipulated, in order to determine its effect on perceived positivity of an interaction, yield findings more consistent than the findings of correlational research. For example, there appears to be a general postural pattern of a seated individual that is usually rated as positive by observers and participants. This pattern is one in which the individual being judged is leaning forward, directly facing the other member of the dyad, with uncrossed arms (e.g., Harrigan & Rosenthal, 1986; Kelly, 1972; Mehrabian, 1968, 1970).

In a meta-analysis (Tickle-Degnen, Rosenthal, & Harrigan, 1986) of 37 studies using correlational or experimental designs, preliminary results show that the mean correlation between trunk lean and positivity of impression was approximately .53, with forward lean being associated with more positive ratings. Meta-analytic results for the relationship between the other nonverbal behaviors and positive ratings yielded r's of .39 for direct body orientation (22 studies), and .36 for open arms (six studies). Uncrossed legs showed a small positive effect on ratings (mean $r = .12$) in the meta-analysis of seven studies.

There was significant variability in the findings of the separate studies included in the meta-analysis, some of which was probably due to using both experimental and correlational studies in the analysis, but some of which appear to be related to differences in the findings of observer and participant decoding studies. There were enough studies in the trunk lean and body orientation categories to perform separate analyses for those using observers and those using participants as decoders. The general result of these separate analyses was that the relationship between observers' ratings and the dyad members' nonverbal behavior was significantly greater than the same relationship for the participants' ratings. For trunk lean and body orientation respectively, the relationship for observers was .72 and .52; for participants it was .27 and .21. Therefore, it appears that nonverbal behavior has differential influence in the perception of positivity by outside observers and by participants. We will discuss the possible reasons for this difference in a later section on the experience and observation of rapport.

In addition to correlational investigations, and studies in which nonverbal behavior has been manipulated, a few studies (see Mehrabian, 1972, for a review) have been performed in which the felt positivity of one interactant for another has been manipulated and its effect on the other interactant's behavior observed. Again, individuals tend to demonstrate the same behaviors identified above, such as forward leaning, direct body orientation, and eye contact, when they have a positive attitude toward the other member of a dyad. Individuals who do not have a positive attitude toward another interactant but who may be attempting to increase the positivity of an interaction also tend to exhibit greater amounts of 'positive' types of nonverbal behavior. Ickes et al. (1982) found that a greater amount of smiling, directed gazes, and verbalizations occurred in situations in which subjects expected either an unfriendly or a friendly interaction, relative to having no expectations about the interaction. They suggested that the subjects were acting in a reciprocal manner under the friendly condition, but in a compensatory manner under the unfriendly condition possibly as a strategy to change the anticipated unpleasant course of the interaction. In both cases, subjects were conveying positivity through their behavior, in the former case, possible as a genuine expression of their feelings, and in the latter, as a contrived means of manipulating the outcome of the interaction.

In summary, feelings of positivity tend to be conveyed and interpreted as such through participants' demonstrating greater amounts of forward lean, direct body orientation, mutual gaze, smiling, and gestures. No specific nonverbal behavior appears to be a consistent cue and expression of positivity. Rather, a global pattern of behaviors, indicative not only of attentiveness and involvement on the part of the participants, but also of a desire to approach and to get closer both emotionally and physically, is related to positivity in the interactions.

We continue our analysis of rapport and nonverbal behavior by turning to the coordination component of the conceptualization of rapport. The positivity and coordination components of rapport are closely linked. But, again, as with positivity and attentiveness, coordination, though related to positivity, is not equivalent to it. There may be a high degree of positivity and a low degree of coordination in an interaction, in which individuals, with unrestrained eagerness, vie with one another to tell a funny story to a newcomer to the group. Alternatively, an interaction may display low positivity and high coordination, as in the Scheflen (1964) example described earlier, in which old friends were arguing. The attentional component of rapport, likewise, is associated with coordination, but not equivalent to it. Individuals coordinating their movements in a busy crosswalk do not usually pay much attention to one another.

Nonverbal Behavior and Coordination

Regulation of interaction that coordinates the behavior of participants and provides predictable patterns of behavior has been studied in terms of three types of nonverbal behavior. One type involves the coordination of speakers and listeners as they exchange speaking and listening roles during a conversation. Another type is interactional synchrony, a rhythm to interaction that implies smooth coordination. Finally, postural mirroring is a behavior pattern that may signal to the participants that they are "with" one another, acting as a unit.

Observational and correlational research has shown that paralinguistic features, gestures, and head movements are important in the smooth exchange of speaker and listener roles during a conversation. Duncan and Fiske (1977), for example, carried out detailed structural analyses of get-acquainted conversations and found that when individuals were taking over the speaker role, they would typically signal this transition with a head shift and/or a gesticulation. Nonverbal behaviors also appear to be correlated with maintaining the speaker role and with eliciting reactions of understanding, agreement, or attention from the listener. Rosenfeld and Hancks (1980) found that the listener typically acknowledged the speaker's utterances with a number of head nods during a brief verbal response ("mhm," or "Yeah, okay," for example), and showed interest in the utterance prior to a verbal response by leaning forward and maintaining visual regard of the speaker. Although these studies were performed with dyads, Duncan and Fiske (1977) pointed out that they are relevant to larger groups as well.

Some investigators have noted that all interaction appears to have a rhythm to it, in which both speakers and listeners engage. Condon and Ogston (1967), based upon the observation and detailed linguistic and nonverbal transcription of a 5½-second interaction among a mother, father, and son at a dinner table, defined interactional synchrony as the synchronization of movement of all individuals in a group. Kendon (1970) also observed interactional synchrony in the transcript and film of a gathering of men and women at a private lounge in a London hotel. He suggested that speaker and listener turn-taking may be coordinated through synchrony. He described a situation in which one individual appeared to "beat time" to another's speech, possibly to facilitate the timing of his own entry as a speaker. Kendon suggested that while visual input was used by the interactants to maintain synchrony, it appeared sufficient for the listener merely to hear the speech of the speaker.

The existence of interactional synchrony is far from established in that investigators using different methodologies do not obtain similar results (e.g., McDowell, 1978; see Cappella, 1981, for a review). Recently, Bernieri, Resnick, and Rosenthal (1986) have used a new methodology to explore interactional synchrony. Rather than analyzing the specific movement changes in the interactants, these researchers attempted to determine whether judges would make differential judgments about the synchrony present in three forms of split-screen interactions recorded on videotape: (1) those between a mother and her own child, (2) a mother and an unfamiliar child, and (3) an artificial interaction created by the experimenter splicing together mothers and children who were not actually interacting with each other at the time. In this way, the researchers were able to determine a baseline level of synchrony from the perceived degree of synchrony in "interactions" that never really took place. Against this baseline, then, the researchers could examine the levels of synchrony perceived in real interactions. As it turned out, the judges did indeed perceive synchrony above baseline in real interactions, and the perceived level of synchrony was greater between the familiar than between the unfamiliar interactants.

The research discussed so far has addressed the correlation of nonverbal behavior with interactional coordination, as well as the effect of interactional synchrony on the perceptions of outside observers. No research, to our knowledge, has investigated the subjective experience of the interactants who are demonstrating different levels of coordination in turn-taking behavior and synchrony.

Both participants' and observers' ratings have been employed to explore another nonverbal phenomenon, postural mirroring, that appears to indicate coordination or "togetherness" among interactants (Charny, 1966; Kendon, 1970; LaFrance, 1979, 1985; Scheflen, 1964). Mirroring occurs when individuals produce mirror image reflections of one another with their extremities. Preliminary findings of a meta-analysis of 10 experimental and correlational investigations (Tickle-Degnen et al., 1986) indicate that mirroring is positively correlated with ratings of the degree of togetherness in an interaction with a moderate and significant mean effect size r of .25. There was no difference in these studies between ratings by participants or outside observers. The experimental evidence indicates that mirroring (a) positively affects perceptions of rapport (Storms, 1983; Trout & Rosenfeld, 1980), and (b) is a consequence of cooperativeness among participants (LaFrance, 1985).

In all but one study (LaFrance & Ickes, 1981), the correlation between mirroring and rapport ratings was positive. In this study, previously unacquainted individuals were unobtrusively observed as they spontaneously interacted while waiting to participate in an experiment. Postural mirroring was associated with subsequent ratings of feeling that the interaction was awkward. LaFrance and Ickes interpreted the finding as the mirroring being an indication of an active concern to achieve rapport when it was too early to have been attained. In the other studies in which mirroring was found to be positively related to aspects of rapport, the situations were highly structured by the experimenter (LaFrance, 1985; Trout & Rosenfeld, 1980) or involved interactions among acquainted individuals in naturalistic settings (LaFrance, 1979; LaFrance & Broadbent, 1976).

The work of LaFrance and her colleagues sheds light on the development of rapport and its relation to nonverbal behavior. Coordinated behavior in the early stage of a relationship may be an attempt to establish rapport, whereas at a later stage it may be an indication of achieved rapport. Furthermore, the degree of coordination in the early part of an interaction may not be predictive of how coordinated the interaction will be later. Charny (1966), for example, found postural mirroring to increase over the course of a session between a client and her therapist. Bernieri et al. (1986) found that at the beginning of five-minute mother-child interactions, mothers with their own children did not demonstrate greater synchrony than mothers with unfamiliar children, although over the course of the interaction, synchrony was perceived to increase for the former interactions and decrease for the latter.

We would expect that behavioral patterns indicating a well-regulated interaction, besides serving different functions at different stages, would be more consistent and readily identified in the latter part of interactions, or repeated interactions, than in early interactions. As individuals developed a mutual history, they would learn what to expect from one another behaviorally, and would know how best to coordinate their behavior with others so as to attain mutual satisfaction in the interaction (Duncan & Fiske, 1977; Kendon, 1981; Patterson, 1983). In addition, a group of frequently interacting individuals may develop idiosyncratic conventions that identify to the members how to behave during different events in their interaction with one another (Duncan & Fiske, 1977). For example, group interactants may employ a specific behavioral pattern as a cue for "what I'm saying is not to be taken too seriously," or "pay attention to me," or "leave me alone for a minute."

Summary of the Relationship Between
Nonverbal Behavior and Group Rapport

The evidence suggests that nonverbal behavior is a correlate, antecedent, and consequence of rapport. First, nonverbal behavior appears to be a correlate of the attentiveness, positivity, and coordination in an interaction. High levels of focused attention by group participants would be signaled through the spatial configurations produced by their body placement, and the amount of directed gazing. High levels of positivity would be related to behaviors of approach and warmth, such as forward leaning, open posturing of the arms and legs, and smiling. High levels of coordination would be indicated through smooth and efficient turn-taking among speakers and listeners, high interactional synchrony, and postural mirroring. As has been pointed out, the degree to which these various nonverbal behaviors indicate high levels of rapport is dependent on the context of the interaction.

Second, nonverbal behavior appears to function as an antecedent to feelings and ratings of rapport. Manipulated nonverbal behavior affects individuals' impressions of one another's level of involvement and positivity, and the degree of coordination occurring in an interaction. There is evidence, particularly for the positivity component of rapport, that participants in an interaction may be influenced less by nonverbal behavior in their feelings of rapport than are observers in their assessment of rapport.

Third, nonverbal behavior appears to be influenced by participants' feelings associated with rapport. A few studies on positivity in an interaction and on postural mirroring indicate that participants' expectations of positivity and cooperativeness influence their nonverbal behavior. More studies are required in this area, however, before firm conclusions can be drawn.

The three dynamic components of rapport are closely related but not equivalent. The degrees of attentiveness, positivity, and coordination probably develop mutually and influence one another over the course of a single interaction or a series of interactions. Individuals probably feel more positively about an interaction in which their own attention as well as that of the other participants was highly focused toward the interaction. The more focused their attention, the more able the participants to adjust their behavior to one another, resulting in a smoothly coordinated interaction. A well-regulated interaction would provide predictability to the interaction and create a feeling of similarity among the participants, at least in terms of the conventions to which they complied, thus leading to feelings of positivity (Duncan & Fiske, 1977; Heider, 1958). Generally, the three components of rapport would be likely to transform and be transformed by each other during interaction, with the outcome being that the separate participants of an interaction would be pulled toegther into a behavioral unit.

THE EXPERIENCE AND OBSERVATION OF GROUP RAPPORT

Throughout our discussion of the different components involved in rapport, we have referred to research in which rapport-relevant ratings of an interaction were made either by participants within the interaction or by observers outside of it. Based upon that review, it becomes evident that nonverbal behavior may differentially affect ratings by participants and observers. It appears, particularly from research related to the positivity component of rapport, that participants' ratings are less related to nonverbal behavior than are observers' ratings. Two possible reasons for this difference are (1) the experience and observation of rapport are not related to nonverbal behavior in the same way, and (2) the methodological procedures used in the investigation of observer versus participant ratings are different. Such differences have important implications for the conceptualization of rapport and its measurement.

Nonverbal Behavior in the Experience and Observation of Rapport

Attempts to achieve higher degrees of mutual involvement and positive and coordinated interaction cannot necessarily be distinguished behaviorally from achievement of these qualities in an interaction.[2] The conclusions from the results of the Ickes et al. (1982) study, that subjects' smiling seemed to be a compensatory response to an expected unfriendly interaction, and of the investigation by LaFrance and Ickes (1981), that postural mirroring among previously unacquainted individuals was an attempt to achieve rapport, support this contention. The participants in an interaction know to what degree they themselves actually feel rapport and to what degree they are trying to achieve it. Participants may generalize from their own feelings and behaviors to other participants as well, thus not perceiving another's behavior as a genuine expression of feelings, but as an active attempt to develop or manipulate those feelings. We would expect that nonverbal behavior would be most related to participants' ratings when the situation was one in which impression management was not the overriding concern of the participants.

Unlike the participants, observers would not have direct access to the participants' feelings, nor would they be caught up in the immediacy of the interaction that would cause a search for participant motives. The observers would have access to participant feelings only through behavior, thus being influenced by nonverbal behavior to a greater degree in their assessments of rapport.

Not all types of nonverbal behavior appear to follow this pattern of showing different relationships to participant versus observer ratings. Possibly, those behaviors that are less obvious means for managing impression equally influence ratings because they provide similar information to the participant and observer. For example, posture sharing, a group behavior that seemed equally to affect participant and observer ratings, may be used less in impression management than other behaviors, such as trunk lean and body orientation. Posture sharing and other group behaviors implying coordination among participants, such as interactional synchrony and smooth turn-taking behavior in speech, would be less under the control of each participant because of the mutual interaction required to achieve them.

Methodological Explanations
for Participant-Observer Differences

The participant-observer differences were more pronounced within the positivity component than the coordination component of rapport possibly because of the way that research falling within the two components differed in the operationalization of nonverbal behavior.[3] As noted earlier, most of the investigations reported in the section of the paper dealing with the positivity component of rapport were designed to investigate how the nonverbal behavior of one participant affects another participant's or an observer's impression of that participant. The focus was on only one interactant's behavior. In observer studies, raters often rated the behavior of that interactant from videotapes without having visual or audio access to the second member of the dyad. On the other hand, in participant studies, the participant raters would have visual and audio access to the other, as well as proprioceptive and physiological feedback from their own behavior. The participant raters, therefore, could potentially include information from both participants' behaviors when making the rating.

Other methodological differences that may have been influential were the variation in primary tasks of the two types of raters and the subsequent differences in the point of time at which they made their ratings. The participants' primary task was to interact, whereas the observers' was to evaluate. Participants could not make their ratings of an individual while interacting, so they made the ratings after the interaction, based on the recall of the interaction. Observers, on the other hand, made the ratings during the interaction, either unobtrusively behind one-way mirrors or while watching a videotape of the interaction.

For future research on rapport and nonverbal behavior, it would be important to control these and other methodological differences, and to include both participants and observers in the same study, in order to determine whether nonverbal behavior plays a different role in the experience versus the observation of group rapport. Furthermore, since rapport is an interactional variable, group nonverbal behaviors, such as those found in the coordination studies, might prove to be of greater interest than the discrete behaviors of each individual. Finally, as Kendon (1981) argues, it may prove important first to understand what distinctions participants make when classifying behaviors in others during naturalistic interactions, and then to investigate nonverbal behavior in terms of these distinctions. We need to learn the degree to which participants are aware of group nonverbal behavior during interaction, including their own, and the types of behavior they generally associate with feelings of high rapport.

CONCLUSION

The operationalization of group rapport should follow directly from its conceptual definition. Therefore, the elements of the degree of (a) group-directed focus of attention by the participants, (b) positivity of the interaction, and (c) coordination of the interaction, should all be addressed when studying rapport. If one or more of these components were lowered, then state rapport would be lowered based upon our conceptual definition. If one or more of these components were consistently lowered over time, then trait rapport would be lower. Furthermore, if would be expected that trait rapport would emerge as the components of rapport interacted with one another through the development of mutual experiences and shared conventions, so the degree of attentiveness, positivity, or coordination may be found to show a temporal and possibly quite complex progression across interactions.

Besides an examination of trait rapport across many interactions, it may be possible to see configurations of nonverbal behavior in single interactions that are indicative of the level of trait rapport in a continuing relationship. Table 5.2 depicts a categorization system for the formulation of research questions to be examined in the investigation of the relationship between group rapport and nonverbal behavior based on single interactions. For example, the lowest levels of nonverbal attentiveness, positivity, and coordination would be predicted to be found in interactions in which there is a low state/low trait rapport, whereas the highest levels of these three components would be expected for high state/high trait rapport interactions. These predictions would be equivalent for both observers and participants.

It is unclear what types of predictions could be made for the types of nonverbal behavior occurring in interactions falling within the categories of low state/high trait rapport and high state/low trait rapport. Recall the Sheflen example that was presented earlier and that fell within the low state/high trait category. Coordination and attention between the arguing old friends was high, but positivity was low. It may be that such a configuration of behavior is typical for this category or, on the other hand, is restricted to particular situations or types of relationships, such as those between friends. In high state/low trait rapport, higher degrees of all three components would be expected to be present than in the low state conditions, because of the very nature of state rapport, but relative to high state/high trait rapport interactions, we would expect the degrees of these components to be lower.

The empirical value of our conceptualization of group rapport lies in its stimulation of research ideas and its provision of structure for the initiation and organization of research. From a practical standpoint, it would also be of value in determining configurations of behavior that

TABLE 5.2
Categorization of Research Questions and Preliminary Predictions
for the Study of Group Rapport

		Trait Rapport			
		Participant Rating		Observer Rating	
		Low	High	Low	High
State Rapport	Low	ATTN: Low POS: Low COORD: Low	ATTN: Med POS: Med COORD: Med	ATTN: Low POS: Low COORD: Low	ATTN: Med POS: Med COORD: Med
	High	ATTN: Med POS: Med COORD: Med	ATTN: High POS: High COORD: High	ATTN: Med POS: Med COORD: Med	ATTN: High POS: High COORD: High

NOTE: ATTN = Degree of focused attention. POS = Degree of positivity. COORD = Degree of coordination. Low, Med (Medium), and High correspond to contrast weights of -1, 0, and $+1$, respectively, as a first pass to assess the model. (See Rosenthal & Rosnow, 1985, for a discussion of the use of contrast weights in the testing of hypotheses.)

are predictive of desirable outcomes to group interaction. For example, nonverbal behavior of a high state/high trait rapport quality would possibly be predictive in a group psychotherapy setting of the emergence of group cohesiveness and the length of individuals' participation in the course of therapy. In a labor-management negotiation meeting, where the development of trait rapport is not to be expected, nonverbal behavior indicative of high state/high trait or high state/low trait interactions may be equally predictive of successful negotiations. Convergence of participant and observer ratings in these situations would be expected to increase the power of the prediction. With the explicit conceptualization that has been provided, rapport may be a more useful construct to employ in these types of research as well as those concerned with the basic issue of what makes some human interactions feel, and look, so right, and others, so wrong.

NOTES

1. Patterson (1983) provides a thorough review of the nonverbal behavior literature which includes issues relevant to rapport. Harrigan and Rosenthal (1986) review research

related to clinical rapport and nonverbal behavior.

2. Patterson (1983) would recognize the nonverbal behaviors in the former situation as fulfilling a social control function, and in the latter, an informational function.

3. Not enough information on participant-observer differences in the influence of nonverbal behavior on ratings of attentiveness was available at the time of the current writing to assess the attentional dimension.

REFERENCES

Altman, I., & Taylor, D. A. (1973). *Social penetration: The development of interpersonal relationships.* New York: Holt, Rinehart & Winston.

Argyle, M., & Cook, M. (1976). *Gaze and mutual gaze.* Cambridge: Cambridge University Press.

Bernieri, F., Resnick, J. S., & Rosenthal, R. (1986). *Synchrony, pseudosynchrony, and disynchrony between mothers and children.* Manuscript submitted for publication.

Capella, J. N. (1981). Mutual influence in expressive behavior: Adult-adult and infant-adult dyadic interaction. *Psychological Bulletin, 89,* 101-132.

Charny, E. J. (1966). Psychosomatic manifestations of rapport in psychotherapy. *Psyhcosomatic Medicine, 28,* 305-315.

Ciolek, M. T. (1978). Spatial arrangements in social encounters: An attempt at taxonomy. *Man-Environment Systems, 8,* 52-59.

Condon, W. S., & Ogston, W. D. (1967). A segmentation of behaviour. *Journal of Psychiatric Research, 5,* 221-235.

Duncan, S. D., Jr., & Fiske, D. W. (1977). *Face-to-face interaction: Research, methods, and theory.* Hillsdale, NJ: Lawrence Erlbaum.

Ekman, P. (1965). Communication through nonverbal behavior: A source of information about an interpersonal relationship. In S. S. Tomkins & C. E. Izard (Eds.), *Affect, cognition, and personality* (pp. 390-442). New York: Springer.

Ekman, P., Friesen, W. V., & Ancoli, S. (1980). Facial signs of emotional experience. *Journal of Personality and Social Psychology, 39,* 1125-1134.

Ellis, R. J., & Holmes, J. G. (1982). Focus of attention and self-evaluation in social interaction. *Journal of Personality and Social Psychology, 43,* 67-77.

Fretz, B. R. (1966). Postural movements in a counseling dyad. *Journal of Counseling Psychology, 13,* 335-343.

Fretz, B., Corn, R., Tuemmler, J., & Bellet, W. (1979). Counselor nonverbal behaviors and client evaluations. *Journal of Counseling Psychology, 26,* 304-311.

Freud, S. (1924). On the history of the psycho-analytic movement. In *Collected papers* (Vol. I, pp. 287-359) (J. Riviere, Trans.). London: Hogarth Press. (Original work published in 1914.)

Friedman, H. S., & DiMatteo, M. R. (Eds.). (1982). *Interpersonal issues in health care.* New York: Academic Press.

Godwin, W. (1802). *St. Leon: A tale of the sixteenth century* (Vol. I). Alexandria, VA: R. & J. Gray.

Goffman, E. (1963). *Behavior in public places.* New York: Free Press.

Hale, J. L., & Burgoon, J. K. (1984). Models of reactions to changes in nonverbal intimacy. *Journal of Nonverbal Behavior, 8,* 287-314.

Harrigan, J. A., & Rosenthal, R. (1986). Nonverbal aspects of empathy and rapport in physician-patient interaction. In P. D. Blanck, R. Buck, & R. Rosenthal (Eds.), *Nonverbal communication in the clinical context* (pp. 36-73). University Park, PA: Pennsylvania State University Press.

Heider, F. (1958). *The psychology of interpersonal relations.* Hillsdale, NJ: Lawrence Erlbaum.

Ickes, W., Patterson, M. L., Rajecki, D. W., & Tanford, S. (1982). Behavioral and cognitive consequences of reciprocal versus compensatory responses to preinteraction expectancies. *Social Cognition, 1,* 160-190.

Ickes, W., Robertson, E., Tooke, W., & Teng, G. (1986). Naturalistic social cognition: Methodology, assessment, and validation. *Journal of Personality and Social Psychology, 51,* 66-82.

Kelly, F. E. (1972). Communicational significance of therapist proxemic cues. *Journal of Consulting and Clinical Psychology, 39,* 345.

Kendon, A. (1970). Movement coordination in social interaction. *Acta Psychologica, 32,* 100-125.

Kendon, A. (1976). The F-formation system: The spatial organization of social encounters. *Man-Environment Systems, 6,* 291-296.

Kendon, A. (1981). Introduction: Current issues in the study of "nonverbal communication." In A. Kendon (Ed.), *Nonverbal communication, interaction, and gesture: Selections from Semiotica* (pp. 1-53). The Hague: Mouton.

Kleinke, C. L. (1986). Gaze and eye contact: A research review. *Psychological Bulletin, 100,* 78-100.

Kleinke, C. L., Staneski, R. A., & Berger, D. E. (1975). Evaluation of an interviewer as a function of interviewer gaze, reinforcement of subject gaze, and interviewer attractiveness. *Journal of Personality and Social Psychology, 31,* 115-122.

LaFrance, M. (1979). Nonverbal synchrony and rapport: Analysis by the cross-lag panel technique. *Social Psychology Quarterly, 42,* 66-70.

LaFrance, M. (1982). Posture mirroring and rapport. In M. Davis (Ed.), *Interaction rhythms: Periodicity in communicative behavior* (pp. 279-297). New York: Human Sciences Press.

LaFrance, M. (1985). Postural mirroring and intergroup relations. *Personality and Social Psychology Bulletin, 11,* 207.

LaFrance, M., & Broadbent, M. (1976). Group rapport: Posture sharing as a nonverbal indicator. *Group and Organization Studies, 1,* 328-333.

LaFrance, M., & Ickes, W. (1981). Posture mirroring and interactional involvement: Sex and sex typing effects. *Journal of Nonverbal Behavior, 5,* 139-154.

McDowell, J. J. (1978). Interactional synchrony: A reappraisal. *Journal of Personality and Social Psychology, 36,*963-975.

Mehrabian, A. (1968). Relationship of attitude to seated posture, orientation, and distance. *Journal of Personality and Social Psychology, 10,* 26-30.

Mehrabian, A. (1970). A semantic space for nonverbal behavior. *Journal of Consulting and Clinical Psychology, 35,* 248-257.

Mehrabian, A. (1972). *Nonverbal communication.* New York: Aldine.

Park, R. E., & Burgess, E. W. (1924). *Introduction to the science of sociology.* Chicago: University of Chicago Press.

Patterson, M. L. (1983). *Nonverbal communication: A functional perspective.* New York: Springer-Verlag.

Patterson, M. L., Kelly, C. E., Kondracki, B. A., & Wulf, L. A. (1979). Effects of seating arrangement on small-group behavior. *Social Psychology Quarterly, 42,* 180-185.

Rogers, C. (1957). The necessary and sufficient conditions of therapeutic change. *Journal of Consulting Psychology, 21,* 95-105.

Rosenfeld, H. M., & Hancks, M. (1980). The nonverbal context of verbal listener responses. In M. R. Key (Ed.), *The relationship of verbal and nonverbal communication* (pp. 193-206). The Hague: Mouton.

Rosenthal, R., & Rosnow, R. L. (1985). *Contrast analysis.* New York: Cambridge University Press.

Scheflen, A. E. (1963). Communication and regulation in psychotherapy. *Psychiatry, 26,* 126-136.

Scheflen, A. E. (1964). The significance of posture in communication systems. *Psychiatry, 27,* 316-331.

Scherer, S. E., & Schiff, M. R. (1973). Perceived intimacy, physical distance and eye contact. *Perceptual and Motor Skills, 36,* 835-841.

Storms, R. J. (1983). A study of verbal and non-verbal pacing procedures as methodologies for the establishment of counselor-client rapport. *Dissertation Abstracts International, 43,* 2360B-2361B.

Szasz, T. S., & Hollender, M. H. (1956). The basic models of the doctor-patient relationship. *Archives of Internal Medicine, 97,* 585-592.

Tickle-Degnen, L., Rosenthal, R., & Harrigan, J. (1986). Nonverbal behavior and evaluative ratings: A meta-analysis. Unpublished data.

Trout, D. L., & Rosenfeld, H. M. (1980). The effects of postural lean and body congruence on the judgment of psychotherapeutic rapport. *Journal of Nonverbal Behavior, 4,* 176-190.

Truax, C. B., & Carkhuff, R. R. (1967). *Toward effective counseling and psychotherapy.* Chicago: Aldine.

White, L., Tursky, B., & Schwartz, G. E. (Eds.). (1985). *Placebo: Theory, research, and mechanisms.* New York: Guilford.

6

Affective and Cognitive Factors in Intragroup and Intergroup Communication

GALEN V. BODENHAUSEN
LISA GAELICK
ROBERT S. WYER, Jr.

Galen V. Bodenhausen is Assistant Professor of Psychology at Michigan State University. He has published several articles and chapters in the general area of social information processing. His primary research interests include prejudice and stereotyping, interpersonal and intergroup conflict, and person and event memory.

Lisa Gaelick is currently completing her dissertation in clinical psychology at the University of Illinois. She has published several journal articles and book chapters, and her interests include the descriptive modeling of interpersonal behavior, the development of friendship, and self-management methods and self-control.

Robert S. Wyer, Jr., is Professor of Psychology at the University of Illinois in Urbana-Champaign. He is a past recipient of the Alexander von Humboldt Special Research Prize and is coeditor of the *Handbook of Social Cognition.* He is the author of numerous books and journal articles on social information processing.

The study of communication processes requires a shift from the analysis of individual actions to an analysis of the relations between actors (Rogers, Millar, & Bavelas, 1985). In this analysis, the focus is on the patterned regularities of communicative acts that occur over a period of time. Such an analysis may be applied both to statements and behaviors of individuals within a group and to those occurring between two groups. A model of communication, and of interaction behavior more generally, must also be able to describe and account for changes in communication patterns over time. Ideally, it should also permit both interpersonal and intergroup communication to be conceptualized in

AUTHORS' NOTE: Preparation of this chapter was supported by grant MH 3-8585 BSR from the National Institute of Mental Health. We are grateful to Clyde Hendrick and Dina Zinnes for their helpful criticisms and suggestions.

terms of a common set of parameters. In this chapter, we present a general approach to the study of communication processes that was developed with these criteria in mind.

The widespread scientific analysis of communication and interaction processes has generated a number of general approaches to the topic (e.g., Bales, 1950; Duncan & Fiske, 1977; Gottman, 1979; Ickes, 1983; Kelley et al., 1983; Kenny & LaVoie, 1984; Shannon & Weaver, 1949), and our approach has benefitted from the insights of the many theorists who have previously explored the interaction domain. One obvious conclusion that can be drawn from these various approaches is that human interaction is a frustratingly complex phenomenon. Consequently, difficult choices must be made by researchers interested in studying interaction as to which variables will be examined and incorporated into theoretical systems.

In this chapter we propose a conceptual framework that is generic enough to be applied to any type of dynamic interaction, allowing a variety of theoretical and empirical issues to be examined in various types of dyadic, as well as intergroup, relations. Despite its generality, the proposed framework reflects a number of specific choices as to the aspects of the communication process that are examined and the perspective from which they are viewed, and these will be elaborated. In discussing the approach, we will focus on one particular type of communication, namely the communication of affect during conflict. As we will point out, however, the parameters of the formulation we propose are applicable to nonconflict situations as well, and they apply to the communication of descriptive material as well as emotion.

A MODEL OF COMMUNICATION PROCESSES

Preliminary Considerations

The framework we propose was previously applied in an empirical analysis of emotional communication occurring in the conflicts of heterosexual couples (Gaelick, Bodenhausen, & Wyer, 1985). It focuses on the patterns of affective interchange that characterize interactions between two parties (i.e., two individuals or two social groups). Before presenting the model, several definitions and assumptions should be made explicit.

In our framework, the term *message* refers to actions performed by one party that are observed by another party. This definition underscores the potential communicative function of any overt behavior, which may be either verbal, nonverbal, or both. However, in order for a message to serve a communicative function, it must actually influence the behavior of the receiver in some way. The term *communication* as we use it refers to the pattern of relations among messages that have an impact on one another in the course of an interaction by virtue of the meanings they are given by the interactants.

Messages often contain several different types of information. On one hand, they may describe a person, object, or event, or may convey one's beliefs and opinions about these entities. In addition, messages may convey information about the communicator's perception of the relationship between the parties to the communication (Watzlawick, Beavin, & Jackson, 1967; Ericson & Rogers, 1973). This *relationship component* of a message may concern the relative status or power of the sender and receiver, or it may convey the affect, or degree of acceptance or rejection, that is felt by one party toward the other.

The relationship component of a message is often more difficult to interpret than the descriptive component. For example, an individual's statement, "I think you should see a psychiatrist" conveys information at the descriptive level about the speaker's belief concerning what the recipient should do. At the relationship level, it could convey that the communicator either feels superior to the recipient, feels hostile and rejecting, or wishes to be helpful. Analogously, a country's decision to violate a nuclear test ban treaty may communicate a change of policy at the descriptive level, but may convey either fear, distrust, or hostility toward another country at the relationship level.

The conceptualization we propose could in principle be applied to both descriptive and relationship components of messages. In this chapter, however, we will apply it primarily to the relationship component and, in particular, to the communication of affect. In doing so, we will divide relationship messages into two broad categories of affective meaning, to be denoted *love* and *hostility*. Loving messages convey themes of trust, admiration, understanding, and sympathy. Hostile messages convey themes of anger, resentment, and criticism. A more differentiated classification system may ultimately be desirable (see Gottman & Levenson, 1986). However, the research we have performed to date reveals that these two dimensions, which are independent of one another (Gaelick et al., 1985; see also Bradburn,

1969; Diener & Emmons, 1984), are sufficient to provide substantial insight into emotional communication.

Communicative behavior may be analyzed either from the vantage point of an observer who views the interaction from outside of the interaction system, or from the perspective of the participants themselves. Each has advantages and disadvantages. An outside observer is able to evaluate the entire system as a whole, providing a complete description of the ongoing interaction. However, an observer's interpretation of the messages that are transmitted in an interaction may often differ markedly from that of the interaction participants. This is especially true of affective relationship messages, which can be subtle and ambiguous from the perspective of an outside observer. As Folger, Hewes, and Poole (1984) have noted, the great majority of available objective coding schemes are used without any evidence as to their validity. As will become evident from the following discussion, our theoretical analysis hinges on the intentions and perceptions of interacting parties, and these variables simply cannot be directly inferred by observing the overt behavior of the parties. We have chosen to conceptualize communicative behavior in terms of variables defined from the perspectives of the participants because we believe that interactants' intentions and perceptions play a critical role in the communication process, but this role has remained largely unexamined in research involving the perspective of outside observers. In choosing this "insider" perspective, we recognize that the participants themselves are unable to evaluate the communication process at the systems level. However, by combining each interactant's perceptions, it is possible to mathematically derive a systems perspective.

Statement of the Model

The basic unit of affective communication in the conceptualization we propose is a two-message sequence involving a message sent by one participant (A) and the response to this message by a second participant (B). Of course, B's response may itself be considered a message to A, to which A presumably responds. Thus communication units are inherently overlapping, with each message simultaneously serving both roles defined above. In characterizing this sequence and the factors that influence it, several measurable variables come into play:

1. the affect that the sender (A) intends to convey to the receiver (*Intent*)
2. the receiver's (B) perception of the sender's intention (*PercInt*)

3. the receiver's affective reaction to the message (*React*)
4. the sender's expectancy for how the receiver will react (*Exp React*)
5. the sender's perception of how the receiver actually reacted (*Perc React*).

These variables can be defined separately for each type of affect under consideration (i.e., love or hostility). The postulated relations among these variables are shown in Figure 6.1 as they pertain to the communication of a particular type of affect (X). As the figure shows, A's intentions to convey a given emotion in a message to B ($Intent_{X,A}$) may influence B's perception of these intentions ($PercInt_{X,B}$). These perceptions may influence the feelings that B attempts to convey to A in return ($React_{X,B}$). A's perception of B's reaction ($PercReact_{X,A}$) may be determined in part by B's actual reactions, as manifested in B's message, and in part by A's expectancies for how B would react ($ExpReact_{X,A}$). In practice, these various relations may not always exist. In fact, the theoretical and empirical issues raised by the conceptualization we propose involve specification of the relative strength of these relations across different types of relationships and interaction sequences.

The parameters of the model in Figure 6.1 can be used to conceptualize three communication characteristics that are of particular interest. One, *accuracy,* refers to the correspondence between a sender's perception of a message and the receiver's perception of the message (i.e., in Figure 6.1, the correspondence between $Intent_{X,A}$ and $PercInt_{X,B},$ or between $React_{X,B}$ and $PercReact_{X,A}$).[1] Two other variables concern the tendency for a given type of message to be reciprocated. *Intended reciprocation*, or the intention to reciprocate the affective content of another's message in one's own communication, is inferred from the correspondence between the recipient's perception of the affect conveyed in the sender's message ($PercInt_{X,B}$) and the recipient's reactions to the message ($React_{X,B}$). The *actual reciprocation* of the sender's message is inferred from the correspondence between the sender's actual intentions ($Intent_{X,A}$) and the recipient's actual reactions ($React_{X,B}$).

These three variables are interrelated. That is, a recipient's actual reciprocation of the emotion a communicator intends to convey is a joint function of the accuracy with which the receiver perceives these intentions and whether or not he or she attempts to reciprocate. More specifically, the functional relation between B's reactions to an emotion that A intends to express, the accuracy with which B perceives A's intentions, and B's intentions to reciprocate is conveyed conceptually by the equation:

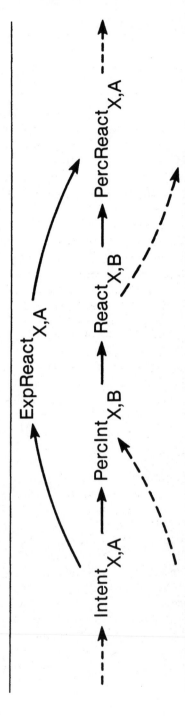

Figure 6.1 Theoretical relations among components of a communication of an emotion (X) between a sender (A) and a recipient (B). Dashed paths denote relations involving components of communicative acts that either precede or follow the one shown. (Thus, for example, the dashed line leading to $PercInt_{X,B}$ could reflect a contribution of B's expectations for the emotion that A intended to convey or the effect of A's intentions to convey some other emotion that B misperceived as X.) [From "Emotional Communication in Close Relationships" by L. Gaelick, G. V. Bodenhausen, and R. S. Wyer, 1985, *Journal of Personality and Social Psychology*, 49, p. 1248. Copyright 1985 by the American Psychological Association, Inc. Reprinted by permission.]

Actual reciprocation = Accuracy × Intended reciprocation

$$= f(r_{\text{Intent, PercInt}}) \times g(r_{\text{PercInt, React}}) \quad [1]$$

where f and g are functions of the correlations (r) between the parameters that define accuracy and intended reciprocation as indicated earlier (see Note 1).

Although this equation is simple, it is a powerful tool in conceptualizing the dynamics of communication and the probable effects of a sequence of communicative acts. Several aspects merit attention. First, note that as we have defined them, accuracy and reciprocation may each be either positive, negative, or zero, depending on whether the correspondence between the two parameters defining it is either greater than, less than, or equal to chance. To the extent that participants' intentions to convey a particular emotion are generally reciprocated (i.e., actual reciprocation is high), the intensity and frequency of expressing the emotion is likely to increase over the course of the interaction. Thus, for example, an interaction in which hostility is more often reciprocated than love is likely to deteriorate, whereas an interaction in which love is more often reciprocated than hostility may be maintained and strengthened. According to Equation 1, however, the extent to which the reciprocation of one emotion predominates over that of another depends not only on the participants' attempts to reciprocate but also on the accuracy with which they perceive one another's intentions. If one type of emotion is perceived more accurately than the other, for example, the former emotion is likely to predominate even though participants try to reciprocate both emotions to an equal degree. By analyzing the conditions that independently influence both accuracy and intended reciprocation, one can begin to obtain an understanding of the dynamics of the communication sequence being investigated and its likely long-term effects on the relationship.

A further value of Equation 1 lies in its specification of the factors that theoretically underlie accuracy and intended reciprocation. This permits the effects of situational and individual difference variables to be pinpointed in terms of their influence on specific model parameters (*Intent, PercInt*, etc.). In this regard, Kenny and LaVoie (1984) point out that communication accuracy is a function not only of characteristics of the dyadic situation itself, but also of more general differences in (a) the sender's overall ability to produce behavior that adequately conveys the intended message (*transmission accuracy*), and (b) the recipient's overall ability to interpret specific types of messages (*reception accuracy*). Both of these factors may combine to affect overall accuracy, as defined in terms of the correspondence between *Intent* and *PercInt*. Situational and individual differences in intended reciprocation can be similarly localized.

One aspect of the model is made salient by this discussion. Although general cross-situational differences in transmission and reception accuracy may contribute to the accuracy with which one member of a dyad perceives the other's intentions, they are not taken into account directly. That is, the model does not distinguish between the emotions that a participant intends to convey and the emotion that the individual "objectively" expresses. This is both a strength and a weakness of the conceptualization. That is, "objective" expressions of emotion are typically defined in terms of observers' ratings or other criteria that are external to the relationship itself. If the interacting parties have been in a relationship with one another for some time, however, they may have developed a "private meaning system" (Gottman & Porterfield, 1981) to which outside observers are not privy. Consequently, the extent to which observers' ratings of the emotion conveyed are more "objective" than the ratings made by the involved parties themselves is questionable. By defining our interaction parameters in terms of the judgments of the interacting parties rather than external criteria, the proposed conceptualization circumvents this ambiguity.

This aspect of our model distinguishes it from many other formulations of emotional communication phenomena. Many analyses of the dynamics of close relationships recognize the important role that the reciprocation of emotion can play (see Gottman, 1979; Pike & Sillars, 1985). However, this literature generally focuses on the *actual* reciprocation of emotions, as inferred either from ratings of observers (e.g., Gottman, 1979) or, in some cases, from direct assessment of partners' physiological reactions to one another's communications (Levenson & Gottman, 1983, 1985). There is, of course, a relation between intended expressions of emotions and what is actually expressed (as interpreted, for example, by an observer), and therefore research on reciprocation of actual emotional behavior (for a review, see Bradbury & Fincham, in press) can often be conceptualized in terms of the framework we propose here. However, by focusing on the relations among interaction participants' perceptions and intentions, the conceptualization is likely to capture a number of important phenomena that may otherwise be obscured, thus providing a more general picture of communication processes.

To the extent that the parameters summarized in Figure 6.1 can be assessed, alternative hypotheses suggested by such an analysis can be evaluated empirically. A study we have conducted demonstrates the utility of the formulation in conceptualizing communication phenomena in a particular type of dyadic interaction situation, namely interpersonal conflict in heterosexual couples. After describing this specific application of the proposed formulation, we will apply it to conceptualize the communication patterns of other types of interactions between individuals, and also between groups.

AN EMPIRICAL APPLICATION

In our previous research (Gaelick et al., 1985), we studied conflict in romantic relationships by videotaping couples discussing a specific conflict they were having in their relationship. Later, both partners independently viewed selected segments of the tape depicting specific exchanges that occurred during the discussion and made judgments relevant to the assessment of the various model parameters outlined in Figure 6.1. That is, message senders made ratings of (a) the feelings (love or hostility) they intended to convey[2], (b) their expectations of how their partner would react to their communication, and (c) their perception of their partner's actual reactions. Their partners, in turn, indicated (d) the feelings they believed the sender intended to convey, (e) their reactions to the communication, and (f) their perception of how the sender would interpret their reactions. These ratings were analyzed separately for male senders and female senders to produce a single score for each partner for each communication parameter. Correlational and path analyses were then conducted to examine the nature of the causal relations hypothesized in Figure 6.1.

Although a detailed presentation of the findings is beyond the scope of this chapter, two sets of findings are particularly noteworthy:

(1) Both males and females attempted to reciprocate the emotion (love or hostility) that they perceived their partner intended to convey to them. However, they perceived their partner's intentions accurately only in the case of hostility. As a consequence, the hostility that partners intended to convey to one another was actually reciprocated, whereas the love they intended to convey was not.

(2) Two types of misperception occurred. First, males' (but not females') perceptions of the hostility that their partners intended to

communicate were negatively related to the love their partners had actually tried to convey. On the other hand, females' (but not males') perceptions of the love their partners conveyed were negatively related to the hostility that their partners intended to communicate. These misperceptions are particularly interesting in light of the fact that hostility and love were independent affective dimensions (see Note 2). Gaelick et al. interpreted these results in terms of the gender-based role expectations prevalent in our society. That is, females may be expected to be nurturant and loving. When their behavior deviates from these expectations, males interpret it as indicative of hostility. In contrast, males are expected by females to be aggressive, and their failure to conform to these expectancies is interpreted by them as an indication of love.

The nature of these findings is more fully summarized in Figure 6.2. This figure shows the positive and negative relations among variables pertaining to the communication of both love and hostility between both female and male partners. Solid lines denote significant causal relations between variables pertaining to different emotions. The top section of the figure shows that the sequence of communications, perceptions, and reactions by each partner along the love dimension proceeds independently of the other partner's behavior and perceptions along this dimension. In contrast, partners' perceptions of one another's hostility, and the hostility of their communications in response to these perceptions, are highly interdependent. That is, one partner's expression of hostility elicits hostility on the part of the other, which stimulates further hostility by the first, and so on.

Considered in isolation, these data would imply that expressions of negative affect are likely to persist or increase over the course of an interaction, whereas expressions of positive affect will not (see Equation 1). A communicator who fails to convey one type of affect does not automatically convey the other type (Note 2). Nevertheless, our data indicate that when the female partner intends to behave in a way that does not particularly convey love, her partner does tend to misperceive this behavior as hostile, and this may increase the hostility he expresses to her in return. When this occurs, the woman may see his reactions as not only hostile but also unloving. This may reduce further the love she expresses in her next communication, leading the man to perceive her as even more hostile and to increase the hostility of the next message. Significantly, analogous effects do not occur when men fail to convey love or when women express hostility. Specifically, men who do not

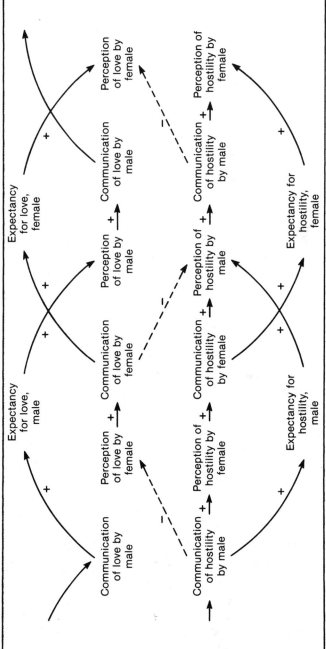

Figure 6.2 Composite path diagram showing positive (+) and negative (−) influences of communications and perceptions on one another. Solid lines refer to influences involving a single emotion (love or hostility); dashed lines indicate influences of a communication of one emotion on perceptions of the other emotion. [From "Emotional Communication in Close Relationships" by L. Gaelick, G. V. Bodenhausen, and R. S. Wyer, 1985, *Journal of Personality and Social Psychology, 49*, p. 1258. Copyright 1985 by the American Psychological Association, Inc. Reprinted by permission.]

intend to convey love are perceived by their partner to be neither unloving nor hostile, and therefore their behavior does not affect the feelings their partner expresses in return. Moreover, women's expressions of hostility are not necessarily perceived by their partner as unloving, and therefore these expressions do not affect the love he communicates. This asymmetry has potential implications for the conditions in which expressions of positive feelings can be maintained, and communications of hostility can be averted. That is, positive feelings can be most easily maintained, if not increased, if men (but not necessarily women) avoid responding to their partners in a way that they believe conveys hostility. Moreover, to prevent an escalation of hostility, women (rather than men) must avoid responding in a way that they believe conveys a lack of love.

We do not claim that the relations identified by Gaelick et al. (1985) will generalize to all situations and types of communications. Rather, we argue that the parameters involved in these relations may be relevant to an understanding of communication processes in general, and that differences in these processes and their consequences can be conceptualized in terms of differences in the model's parameters. In the remaining sections of this chapter, we attempt to support this contention.

DETERMINANTS AND CONSEQUENCES
OF EMOTIONAL COMMUNICATION

The parameters of our conceptualization of interpersonal and intergroup communication must ultimately be tied empirically to the variables that presumably affect them and are affected by them. Although we cannot do justice to a discussion of these matters in this chapter, two bodies of literature may be worth noting briefly in this context. Again, we will focus our discussion on emotional communication between persons involved in heterosexual relationships.

Relationship Satisfaction

As we have noted, the reciprocation of hostility during the course of an interaction without a corresponding reciprocation of love is likely to result in its deterioration, whereas the reciprocation of love but not hostility should result in its maintenance. To the extent that the interaction in which communication characteristics are assessed is representative of those that typically occur between the parties involved, variables that influence reciprocation in the observed interaction

(*Intent, PercInt, React*, etc.) should be related to participants' general satisfaction with the relationship in which they are involved.

In Gaelick et al.'s study, women who expressed dissatisfaction with their relationship were more likely than satisfied women to perceive that their partners conveyed hostile feelings toward them. They were also more inclined to believe that their partners viewed them as hostile, and these beliefs were, in fact, correct. In contrast, males' satisfaction was not strongly related to any communication patterns associated with hostility. Moreover, neither partner's satisfaction was related to parameters pertaining to the communication of love. These results suggest that women's satisfaction is more adversely affected by communication of hostility than is men's, and that neither partner's satisfaction is influenced by the communication of love. Bear in mind, however, that the communication parameters were assessed during a conflict situation. In situations in which the focus of attention is less likely to be on problems that partners are having with one another, the communication of love (or at least the perception that it is being conveyed) may be more important.

Accuracy. Accuracy in communicating hostility seems to be lower in dissatisfied couples than in satisfied couples, and this may be reflected in differences in both *Intent* (transmission accuracy) and *PercInt* (reception accuracy). For example, Noller (1984) found that dissatisfied marriage partners communicated more hostility to one another (based on observers' ratings) than they intended. Their actual feelings of hostility, which were stronger than they intended to transmit, were apparently conveyed through nonverbal behaviors that they were unable to control effectively. On the other hand, Rausch, Barry, Hertel, and Swain (1974) suggested that unhappy couples typically interpret one another's messages from a "defensive" or critical standpoint, as if they expect hostility and conflict. In terms of our formulation, these results suggest that expectations for the hostility conveyed by one another is a more important contributor to dissatisfied partners' perceptions of hostility than to satisfied partners' perceptions of it.

Reciprocation. Most of the literature bearing on reciprocation has focused on the extent to which actual expressions of emotion, as described by an outside observer, are reciprocated. Our research complements this literature by providing an analysis of reciprocation from the participant's perspective. The use of this perspective allows us to distinguish two types of reciprocation (intended and actual).

Gottman (1979) found that dissatisfied and nondissatisfied married partners both tended to reciprocate expressions of emotion. However, dissatisfied couples tended to be locked into a pattern of immediate reciprocation, whereas happy couples were more flexible in their patterns of reciprocation, sometimes deferring their reactions until later in the conversation. The communications involved in these interactions are predominately negative (Pike & Sillars, 1985). This means that although satisfied partners delay their reciprocation of love and hostility, this delay has its greatest effect on hostility. In the present framework (which takes into account only immediate reciprocations of emotion), this difference in communication strategy may be reflected in a lower tendency to reciprocate hostility (and also love) by satisfied couples than dissatisfied ones. In other words, the negative spiral of hostility we postulated to result from the communication pattern implied by Figure 6.2 may be less likely to occur in the case of satisfied couples.

There is an obvious ambiguity in evaluating the implications of these conclusions. That is, relationship satisfaction may be either a determinant or an effect of communication processes. Levenson and Gottman (1985) found that physiological indices of couples' emotional reactions to one another's communications predicted their level of marital satisfaction several years later. However, the causal relatedness of reciprocation and satisfaction could nonetheless be bidirectional.

Gender Differences
in Affective Communication

The results reported by Gaelick et al. suggest that males and females may differ in important ways in their perceptions of one another's emotions, and also in the effect these perceptions have on relationship satisfaction. Results of other studies provide more general insight into gender differences that are relevant to the proposed conceptualization.

Accuracy. As noted earlier, differences in accuracy may be the result of factors that are unique to the relationships in which the communications take place and types of emotions being communicated. However, they may also reflect more general differences in either transmission accuracy or reception accuracy. Noller (1984) found that whereas males and females are both able to communicate hostility in a way that reflects their underlying feelings, females are superior to males in conveying positive emotions. Some research suggest that males may demonstrate better reception accuracy than females (Zuckerman, Lipets, Koivumaki, & Rosenthal, 1975). However, the evidence reported by Gaelick et al. (1985) suggests that both sexes may be prone to reception distortion, but the nature of those distortions differs as a function of sex. That is, women tend to bias their interpretations of men's behavior in a positive direction, whereas males saw neutral behavior as indicative of hostility.

Reciprocation. General gender differences in intended reciprocation may result in part from differences in social power (see Brehm, 1985). Specifically, subordinates may be more inhibited than superiors in reciprocating expressions of negative affect, whereas superiors may be relatively less motivated than subordinates to reciprocate expressions of positive affect. To the extent that women have less social power than men, this implies that in heterosexual relationships women will be more inclined than men to try to reciprocate positive affect, but men will be more likely than women to try to reciprocate negative affect.

In close relationships, however, these power differences may diminish or even reverse. That is, although men in such relationships may often maintain control over tangible resources, women may have more power over the exchange of love and sex (see Howard, Blumstein, & Schwartz, 1986; Sprecher, 1985). This shift may be reflected by a change in males' and females' intentions to reciprocate positive and negative affect as their relationship becomes more intimate.

This analysis implies that a critical variable in conceptualizing communication processes is the type of relationship that exists between the parties involved. This contingency is elaborated in the next section.

AFFECTIVE COMMUNICATION
AND RELATIONSHIP INTERDEPENDENCE

Interdependence broadly refers to the degree to which the behavior of each party in a relationship influences the behavior of the other party (Kelley et al., 1983). The couples studied by Gaelick et al. were highly interdependent, as they were living together. In contrast, relationships that are defined by more superficial social or vocational roles (e.g., relationships among coworkers, student-faculty relationships, etc.) in which behavior is defined by normative standards are much less interdependent. The dynamics of affective communication among persons involved in relatively noninterdependent relationships may differ in several ways from those identified by Gaelick et al. These differences may be conceptualized within the framework we propose.

Type and Intensity of Affective Messages

Noninterdependent relationships are usually characterized by less intense expressions of emotion than highly interdependent ones (see Levinger, 1980), and the affect that is expressed is more likely to be positive than negative. In role-defined (student-teacher, employer-employee) interactions, expressions of negative affect are contrary to social norms and guidelines for appropriate behaviors (Sillars & Weisberg, in press). The nature of conflict resolution is also likely to differ as a function of interdependence. In formal situations where interaction behavior is often defined by social roles, one participant in the interaction often has power to simply dictate how a conflict will be resolved. In more informal, equal-status relationships of low interdependence (e.g., casual acquaintances), the conflicts that occur may be resolved by termination of the relationship, since neither partner may be willing to expend the time and effort required to achieve a mutually agreeable resolution.

Interactions among participants in noninterdependent relationships are particularly likely to be constrained by social or cultural norms. In these relationships, expressions of respect, politeness, and friendliness are considered socially desirable, whereas displays of intense negative affect are not acceptable. These norms are applied more frequently in noninterdependent than interdependent relationships (Fitzpatrick & Winke, 1979; Vincent, Weiss, & Birchler, 1975). In formal relationships, for example, role occupants are often expected to "act in a professional manner," and therefore not to express openly any strong negative feelings they may be experiencing.

Because of role expectations and social norms, the emotions that individuals intend to convey in noninterdependent relationships may differ substantially from the affect they are actually experiencing. This is particularly likely to be true when the emotion involved is negative. Such emotions may be directly expressed only outside the relationships, to persons who are not directly involved. This discrepancy between the emotions that one experiences and those that one intends to communicate (which is less likely to occur in highly interdependent relationships) is an important consideration in predicting the accuracy and reciprocity of emotions that are expressed.

Accuracy in Perceiving Emotional Communications

As we have noted, the emotional content of messages transmitted in noninterdependent relationships is often dictated by externally defined social norms. To the extent that the participants in such relationships conform to these norms, one might expect higher levels of accuracy in highly interdependent relationships. However, several additional considerations arise:

(1) To the extent that intense expressions of affect in noninterdependent relationships are counternormative, the range of emotions that the participants in these relationships intend to convey in their messages is likely to be low. Therefore, differences in these emotions may be more difficult to detect.

(2) The ways that persons communicate affect are often idiosyncratic. Consequently, it may sometimes require substantial contact with a person before the person's affective messages are understood. As noted earlier, persons involved in highly interdependent relationships (e.g., married couples) may form "private meaning systems" (Gottman & Porterfield, 1981) that guide their interpretation of one another's messages, thereby increasing accuracy (see Sillars & Scott, 1983). These meaning systems are less apt to exist in noninterdependent relationships, since the partners have not shared a lengthy and diverse interaction history.

(3) Perceptions of the affect conveyed in a message are partly determined by expectancies for the affect that the communicator is likely to express (see Figure 6.1). To the extent that the affect expressed in noninterdependent relationships is governed by social norms, such expectancies may be well established and may have a larger influence on perceptions than they do in interdependent relationships. Although these expectancies may increase the accuracy of perceiving intentions to convey normatively appropriate affect, they may decrease the accuracy of perceiving intentions to convey affect that is counternormative.

(4) Although a communicator in a noninterdependent relationship may intend to convey emotions that conform to social norms or role expectations, he or she may not always be successful in doing so. This may be particularly true when the emotion actually experienced deviates from these norms. These spontaneous, unintended communications may involve nonverbal cues that are difficult to control (for a summary of research bearing on this, see Buck, 1984). To the extent that recipients are sensitive to these cues, their accuracy in perceiving the communicator's actual emotions may increase, but their accuracy in perceiving the emotions the communicator intends to convey may decrease.

Thus the effects of relationship interdependence on the accuracy of perceiving affective messages is not at all clear. An understanding of this component of communication in noninterdependent relationships is complicated by the fact that in these relationships, to a greater extent than in highly interdependent ones, there may be a greater difference between the affect that communicators intend to convey and the affect that they are actually experiencing (and may unwittingly communicate).

Intended Reciprocation

In our study of communication processes in heterosexual couples, we found that partners generally attempted to reciprocate the type and intensity of affect that they believed their partners intended to convey to them. This was true for both positive and negative affect. It may be unlikely that this reciprocity principle will be applied as often in noninterdependent relationships. We have argued that relationship messages in these interactions are governed by social norms and expectancies that exist independently of the particular individuals involved. Thus attempts to conform to these norms may take precedence over attempts to reciprocate emotions.

To the extent that participants' perceptions of the affect the other communicates has an influence on the affect they try to convey in return, the nature of this influence may differ as a function of level of interdependence. For example, an interactant who perceives that the affect conveyed in another's message deviates from social norms or expectancies may not attempt to reciprocate this affect. Instead, he or she may attempt to conform to normative standards even more. Thus a person who perceives that a casual acquaintance has communicated hostility during an informal conversation may respond in a positive manner in an attempt to reestablish the normative rules governing the interaction rather than by responding in kind. Analogous reactions may occur if a participant is perceived to convey more intense positive feelings than the other considers normatively appropriate.

Actual Reciprocation

For a communicator's intentions to express affect to be actually reciprocated, the recipient must not only try to reciprocate but also must perceive the communicator's intentions correctly (see Equation 1). Since the expectancies and behavior of participants in noninterdependent relationships are likely to be guided by social norms to be polite and friendly, expressions of positive affect should more often be perceived accurately than expressions of negative affect. Therefore, if a reciprocity rule guided communications in noninterdependent relationships, positive affect should increasingly dominate the interaction as time goes by. This tendency would of course be contrary to the conclusions we drew from our analysis of conflictual exchanges in highly interdependent relationships.

As speculated earlier, however, a reciprocity principle actually may be less likely to be applied to noninterdependent relationships than in interdependent ones. To this extent, the actual reciprocation of affect may be relatively unlikely regardless of the accuracy with which it is perceived. Further theoretical and empirical work is necessary to come to grips with these alternative possibilities.

Transitions from Noninterdependent
to Interdependent Relationships

The above considerations suggest that the dynamics of communication are quite different in noninterdependent relationships than in highly interdependent ones. However, the distinction between noninterdependent and interdependent relationships involves a continuum rather than a dichotomy. For one thing, noninterdependent relationships often evolve into highly interdependent ones; acquaintances become close friends or even lovers. As the nature of a relationship changes, one type of communication pattern may be transformed into another. The specific dynamics of such a shift are of considerable interest. For example, we have argued that reciprocity norms operate more frequently in interdependent relationships than in noninterdependent ones. Moreover, accuracy in perceiving one another's intentions to convey affect is a more important determinant of the actual reciprocation of emotions (and therefore of the consequences of affective communication) in interdependent relationships. It is unclear, however, whether accuracy and intended reciprocation are determinants or effects of the development of high interdependence. On one hand, accuracy in perceiving one another's affective messages could be a precondition for the development of a close relationship, and the adoption of a reciprocation rule could be a consequence of developing this sort of relationship. On the other hand, one could as easily hypothesize that the motivation to reciprocate the affect conveyed by another person is a precondition for the development of an intimate personal relationship, and that accuracy in perceiving one another's affect comes later, as a result of the knowledge acquired through participation in such a relationship.

An equally important question arises from the fact that individuals are often involved in different role relationships with one another, and the role requirements of these relationships may differ. For example, an employer may have an affair with an employee, or a professor with a colleague. In such conditions, it is unclear whether the patterns of communication between the parties involved vary with the demands of the particular relationship to which the communication is relevant, or whether the communication rules defined in the context of one type of relationship generalize to the other. In the latter case, role conflict may interfere with effective communication in both types of relationship.

Our discussion in this section obviously does not do justice to the many theoretical and empirical issues that might be raised concerning the differences between interdependent and noninterdependent relationships. Moreover, we have raised more questions than we have answered concerning the differences in communication processes that may exist at different levels of interdependence. In doing so, however, we have attempted to demonstrate that a consideration of these differences within the conceptual framework we have proposed calls attention to several empirical issues that might not otherwise be identified, and permits these issues to be conceptualized using a common set of theoretical constructs.

CONFLICT BETWEEN SOCIAL GROUPS

Thus far, our discussion has focused on intragroup interaction and communication. However, the conceptualization we propose can be applied to the interaction and communication processes occurring between groups as well. In many circumstances, groups of individuals act as a unit in communicating with one another, either directly (verbally) or indirectly (through behaviors or actions that potentially affect one another). These groups may be as small as divisions within a department, or as large as nations. In an age of inconceivably destructive nuclear weaponry, an understanding of the nature of conflict occurring between groups assumes particular importance. One testimony to the importance of this problem is its ubiquitous presence in the research agendas of all of the major branches of social science. Each discipline undoubtedly has important contributions to make in the endeavor to understand social conflict. In this section, we examine some of the psychological processes that are involved in intergroup conflict.

Before launching into an application of a framework developed for the study of conflict and communication in close interpersonal relationships to the intergroup domain, it is wise to consider some of the limitations of this sort of extrapolation. Some theorists (e.g., Brown & Turner, 1981; Tajfel, 1978a) have argued quite emphatically than an understanding of interindividual processes may shed relatively little light onto intergroup phenomena. This is because factors come into play at the intergroup level that are ignored in models of interindividual behavior. Although others are more optimistic about the contributions of research on the behavior of individuals toward an understanding of intergroup processes (e.g., de Mesquita, 1980; Frank, 1973), the case against such generalization deserves consideration.

In addition to the psychological sense of social identity that is likely to emerge in intergroup situations (see Erikson, 1985; Tajfel, 1978b), numerous economic, political, historical, and cultural forces may emerge to complicate intergroup behavior. Nevertheless, intergroup conflict, like interindividual conflict, ultimately rests upon a phenomenological foundation. To determine the reasons why a given intergroup conflict has constructive or destructive consequences, it is necessary to understand the social perceptions of the conflicting parties and the reciprocal relations between these perceptions and the communicative exchanges to which they give rise (see Eldridge, 1979). Even though multiple factors may contribute to these exchanges, these factors necessarily exert their influence through their impact on the beliefs that the parties hold about one another and their perceptions of the implications of one another's communications for their ultimate well-being. So, independently of whether specific findings concerning the dynamics of communication in interpersonal conflict situations, the framework we have proposed may be sufficiently generic to be useful in conceptualizing intergroup situations in terms of similar constructs.

Our adoption of this approach does not imply that universal agreement exists among members of a group in their perceptions of and emotional reactions to communications from other groups, and in the statements and actions that they communicate in the name of the group they represent. When different representatives of a group make statements or engage in behaviors that appear contradictory, the recipient of these communicative acts has a particularly difficult task in construing the intentions of the group as a whole. In many instances, perceptions of intentions may be based more on the actions taken by the group than their verbal statements. Nevertheless, these behaviors constitute the equivalent of "relationship messages" as we have defined them. The affective content of these messages (whether conveying friendliness or hostility) is subject to interpretation by other groups and may elicit responses that also convey positive or negative affect. To this extent, the series of messages transmitted by the two groups over a period of time can be conceptualized in terms of factors very similar to those we have defined in the context of our analysis of interpersonal communication, and characteristics defined in terms of these parameters (e.g., accuracy, intended reciprocity, actual reciprocity, etc.) may be useful in diagnosing the nature of communications between the countries and the likely outcome of these communications.

The framework we propose is not likely to be useful in characterizing communications among ill-defined groups that do not engage in structured communicative exchanges. For example, a general under-standing of racial conflict may be well beyond the scope of our approach, especially given the institutionalized forms of discrimination that pervade our society and create conflict without direct confrontation. On the other hand, a specific conflict (e.g., between two citizen's groups that disagree about a school desegregation plan) could very likely be scrutinized in terms of the parameters of our framework. In fact, a large number of intergroup conflict situations appear to be amenable to the approach we are advocating. Business organizations, for instance, are often involved in conflict with one another, or departments within an organization may be at loggerheads. Labor disputes between corporate management and unions are also clear candidates. In this section, we will elaborate on only one variety of intergroup conflict, which we consider to be of by far the greatest importance, namely, conflict between nations. However, our examination of international conflict will reveal several ways in which our framework could contribute to an understanding of intergroup communication processes more generally.

One particularly noteworthy aspect of selecting international conflicts as an example is that the circumstances surrounding such conflicts often have the character of highly interdependent relationships. That is, the countries involved are economically dependent on one another, and conflicts that develop cannot easily be resolved simply by "terminating the relationship" or avoiding contact. To this extent, the pattern of communications in international conflict situations may bear some resemblance to the pattern that exists in interpersonal conflict situations when persons are highly interdependent. This possibility will become clear in the course of considering the various components of communi-cation that may be relevant to an understanding of communication processes in general.

Accuracy

To reiterate, accuracy is defined in terms of the correspondence between the meaning of a message a communicator intended to convey and the recipient's perception of these intentions. In the present context, it is the extent to which the type of affect (positive regard, belligerence, distrust, and so forth)[3] that one country intends to convey through its actions is correctly perceived by the "recipient" country. The idea that misperception is a key ingredient in international conflict has received extensive consideration (e.g., Bar-Tal & Geva, 1986; Deutsch, 1983; Mandel, 1986; Tetlock & McGuire, 1986; Vertzberger, 1982), especially since the influential work of Jervis (1976). As Mandel, Vertzberger, and others have emphasized, however, this body of work needs to be placed within a integrative conceptual framework. The approach that Vertzberger has taken toward this end focuses primarily on the causes and effects of substantive international misperceptions. In contrast, our concern here is with the emotional misperceptions that may underlie conflict.

As we have noted, an important contingency in the accuracy of interpersonal perceptions of intentions appears to be whether the affect intended is positive or negative. That is, intentions to convey hostility are perceived more accurately than intentions to convey positive feelings. Whether a similar contingency exists at the international level is hard to assess. However, some inferences may be drawn from postmortem analyses of international conflict based on historical documentation of the intentions, perceptions, expectancies, and reactions of the political elites of the nations involved. One such analysis, of the Falkland/Malvinas Islands conflict between Argentina and Great Britain (Furlong & Albiston, 1985), suggests that in contrast to research on interpersonal conflict, the participants in this particular intergroup conflict failed to perceive accurately the hostility communicated to one another. Consequently, each side expected a much milder reaction to their own aggressive actions than ultimately occurred.

Although the issue of misperception has received a good deal of theoretical attention, there appears to be relatively little evidence directly bearing on the extent of accuracy in international perception of affect. One explanation for this lack is the substantial logistical problems involved in finding historical documents establishing one nation's intentions in performing some action and other documents corresponding to another nation's perceptions of the intentions of the first nation. Another factor that may contribute to the lack of attention to this issue is the concern that perceptions of specific episodes may play a very negligible role in directing behavior at the international level (see Hopmann & King, 1976). In fact, Zinnes (1980) reviews research suggesting that international conflict may be rather autistic in nature. Several studies support the idea that, for example, country B's reactions to the behavior of country A are better predicted by country B's previous behavior toward country A than by knowing something about the nature of country A's recent behavior or the interpretations given to it by country B. To the extent that this is true, the nature of perceptual accuracy assumes a tangential or epiphenomenal status. However, there are other studies (also reviewed by Zinnes) that suggest that nations may in fact actually engage in true communicative interaction in the sense that one country's behavior has some apparent influence on that of the other. It appears therefore premature to conclude that perceptual accuracy is an irrelevant or unimportant issue at the international level, and the difficult work of empirically assessing accuracy may in fact be a matter worth pursuing.

Intended Reciprocation

Communication in highly interdependent interpersonal relationships is generally governed by a reciprocity principle. That is, individuals reciprocate the affect they believe that others have conveyed to them. It is interesting to speculate that in highly interdependent intergroup relationships, a similar rule may apply. A casual observation of the actions and communicative exchanges between Russia and the United States over the past several decades suggests the existence of such a principle. Consider, for example, the unending spiral of nuclear testing and defense spending. More direct evidence of an affective reciprocity rule was obtained by Zinnes (1968) in an archival study of the events preceding World War I. (The completeness and authenticity of documents revelant to this conflict have made it the subject of similar analyses by other researchers as well; see Holsti & North, 1966; Holsti, North, & Brody, 1968). Using elaborate procedures for coding both written communications and behavior, Zinnes was able to identify both perceptions and expressions of hostility that occurred during the crisis and to examine the relations between them. Among other things, she found clear evidence that perceptions of hostility resulted in hostile reactions. In other words, the interactions of the countries in this conflict were indeed governed in part by a reciprocity rule. Comparable analyses of perceived and actual expressions of positive affect (cooperation) were not undertaken by Zinnes, and appear to be generally lacking in the international research arena (see Mandel, 1986).

Actual Reciprocation

An evaluation of actual reciprocation and its determinants requires knowledge of the accuracy of communicators' perceptions of one another's intentions to convey affect as well as their intentions to reciprocate. Unfortunately, Zinnes did not directly consider the accuracy of communicators' perceptions. In light of the data available, the deterioration of relations that ultimately led to World War I might be attributable to two factors. First, the parties involved may have attempted to reciprocate one another's expressions of both positive and negative affect, but they were less accurate in perceiving expressions of positive affect than expressions of hostility. This interpretation would parallel the conclusions drawn by Gaelick et al. in their study of interpersonal communication. As noted before, however, the conclusions drawn by Furlong and Albiston (1985) from their analysis of the Falklands/Malvinas crisis suggest that countries are not necessarily accurate in interpreting hostile communications. A second possible account of the events leading up to World War I is that the parties were equally accurate (or inaccurate) in perceiving one another's intentions to convey both positive and negative affect, but that they only attempted to reciprocate this affect if it was negative. Further analyses of the data collected by Zinnes might allow these alternative possibilities to be evaluated.

Whatever the case may be, Zinnes' study represents an important demonstration of systematic patterns of affective communication in intergroup conflict, and suggests that the application of a conceptual framework of the sort we propose may be useful in conceptualizing the dynamics of this type of conflict.

Other Considerations

Level of interdependence. In our analysis of international conflict, we have assumed that the countries involved were in highly interdependent relationships. However, there are obviously differences in the degree of interdependence. In many cases, the interdependence of countries may be determined by economic considerations (e.g., the extent to which each country relies on the other for natural resources and material goods). When countries are economically independent, they may be less motivated to apply a reciprocity rule in their communications. The role of interdependence in international communications, and in intergroup communication phenomena more generally, is clearly a subject for further theoretical and empirical consideration.

The role of power differences in intergroup relations. In our analysis of both intergroup and interpersonal communication, we have focused on situations in which the communicating parties have relatively equal power status. When power differences exist, the communication patterns that emerge may be quite different. For one thing, parties who have the power to control the outcomes of the other party have little need to engage in a real dialogue with the other party, since they can simply dictate the terms of any dispute that arises. To this extent, the nature of emotional expressions may have relatively little influence in comparison to its impact in equal power relationships.

The parameters of our conceptual framework can be applied to the dynamics of communication processes in unequal power relationships as well as equal power ones. For example, subordinates are less likely to express and reciprocate hostility toward superiors, but are more sensitive to signs of hostility expressed toward them. Furthermore, superiors may be less inclined to reciprocate expressions of positive affect toward subordinates. These possibilities require further empirical exploration at both the interpersonal and the intergroup level.

CONCLUDING REMARKS

As the diversity of the chapters contained in this volume testifies, the issues surrounding intergroup and intragroup relationships are numerous, and the factors that must ultimately be considered in developing a comprehensive understanding of them are manifold. No single theoretical formulation is likely to be able to address all of these issues or to incorporate the effects of all of the factors that must be taken into account. However, communication processes are a central ingredient in most if not all interpersonal and intergroup interaction, and a formulation that permits these processes to be conceptualized in terms of a common set of theoretical constructs is clearly desirable. The framework we have proposed is admittedly incomplete, and will ultimately require modification and elaboration. However, it appears to be a fruitful first step in the development of such a formulation.

As we have hoped to convey, one particularly promising direction for future research is the investigation of the systematic ways in which different types of relationships are characterized by different patterns of perceptual accuracy and reciprocity. In this chapter, we have focused on the dimension of interdependence as one means of categorizing relationships into subtypes that may exhibit different patterns of affective communication. Eventually, a more elaborate taxonomy of relationships, including dimensions other than interdependence, will undoubtedly prove to be desirable. The typology developed by Fitz-patrick (1984) in the domain of marital interaction may prove to be very useful in this regard.

At the present time, a consideration of interpersonal and intergroup processes from the perspective we have taken raises more questions than it answers. Further empirical work will hopefully fill in some of the gaps in our knowledge that the proposed conceptualization identifies. Our own research in this area is directed toward this goal.

NOTES

1. As Cronbach (1955) has noted, many factors may affect this correspondence, not all of which may be reflected in any given index. For our present purposes, we will use correlations as indices of correspondence. However, these indices do not take into account more general "level" differences that may influence the actual discrepancy between one person's intentions or expressions of emotions and the other's perceptions of them. A more precise statement of the formulation would require that these differences be accounted for as well.

2. In fact, several different ratings were made, and these ratings were factor analyzed, producing two orthogonal factors, one of which was interpreted as pertaining to love and the other to hostility. Scores on these factors were used to define the parameters noted above.

3. As was the case in our interpersonal analysis (Gaelick et al., 1985), the positive and negative affect dimensions have been found to be independent in intergroup interaction settings as well (Burrowes & Garriga-Pico, 1974).

REFERENCES

Bales, R. F. (1950). *Interaction process analysis: A method for the study of small groups.* Cambridge, MA: Addison-Wesley.

Bar-Tal, D., & Geva, N. (1986). A cognitive basis of international conflicts. In S. Worchel & W. G. Austin (Eds.), *Psychology of intergroup relations* (pp. 118-133). Chicago: Nelson-Hall.

Bradburn, N. M. (1969). *The structure of psychological well-being.* Chicago: Aldine.

Bradbury, T. N., & Fincham, F. D. (in press). Affect and cognition in close relationships: Review and integration. *Cognition and Emotion.*

Brehm, S. S. (1985). *Intimate relationships.* New York: Random House.

Brown, R. J., & Turner, J. C. (1981). Interpersonal and intergroup behavior. In J. C. Turner & H. Giles (Eds.), *Intergroup behavior* (pp. 33-65). Chicago: University of Chicago Press.

Buck, R. (1984). *The communication of emotion.* New York: Guilford Press.

Burrowes, R. & Garriga-Pico, J. (1974). The road to the Six Day War: Relational analysis of conflict and cooperation. *Papers of the Peace Science Society (International), 22,* 47-74.

Cronbach, L. J. (1955). Processes affecting scores on "understanding of others" and "assumed similarity." *Psychological Bulletin, 12,* 177-193.

de Mesquita, B. B. (1980). Theories of international conflict: An analysis and an appraisal. In T. R. Gurr (Ed.), *Handbook of political conflict.* New York: Free Press.

Deutsch, M. (1983). The prevention of World War III: A psychological perspective. *Political Psychology, 4,* 3-32.

Diener, E., & Emmons, R. A. (1984). The independence of positive and negative affect. *Journal of Personality and Social Psychology, 47,* 1105-1117.

Duncan, S., Jr., & Fiske, D. W. (1977). *Face-to-face interaction: Research, methods, and theory.* Hillsdale, NJ: Lawrence Erlbaum.

Eldridge, A. F. (1979). *Images of conflict.* New York: St. Martin's Press.

Ericson, P. M., & Rogers, L. E. (1973). New procedures for analyzing relational communication. *Family Process, 12,* 245-267.

Erikson, E. H. (1985). Pseudospeciation in the nuclear age. *Political Psychology, 6,* 213-217.

Fitzpatrick, M. A. (1984). A typological approach to marital interaction: Recent theory and research. In L. Berkowitz (Ed.), *Advances in experimental social psychology* (Vol. 18, pp. 1-47). New York: Academic Press.

Fitzpatrick, M. A., & Winke, J. (1979). You always hurt the one you love: Strategies and tactics in interpersonal conflict. *Communication Quarterly, 47,* 3-11.

Folger, J. P., Hewes, D. E., & Poole, M. S. (1984). Coding social interaction. In B. Dervin & M. J. Voight (Eds.), *Progress in communication sciences* (Vol. 4, pp. 115-161). Norwood, NJ: Ablex.

Frank, J. D. (1973). Statement on psychological aspects of international conflict. In D. E. Linder (Ed.), *Psychological dimensions of social interaction* (pp. 266-276). Reading, MA: Addison-Wesley.

Furlong, W. L., & Albiston, C. L. (1985). Sovereignty, culture, and misperceptions: The Falkland/Malvinas war. *Conflict, 6,* 139-168.

Gaelick, L., Bodenhausen, G. V., & Wyer, R. S. (1985). Emotional communication in close relationships. *Journal of Personality and Social Psychology, 49,* 1246-1265.

Gottman, J. M. (1979). *Marital interaction: Experimental investigations.* New York: Academic Press.

Gottman, J. M., & Levenson, R. W. (1986). Assessing the role of emotion in marriage. *Behavioral Assessment, 8,* 31-48.

Gottman, J. M., & Porterfield, A. (1981). Communicative competence in the nonverbal behavior of married couples. *Journal of Marriage and the Family, 43,* 817-824.

Holsti, O. R., & North, R. C. (1966). Comparative data from content analysis: Perceptions of hostility and economic variables in the 1914 crisis. In R. L. Merritt & S. Rokkan (Eds.), *Comparing nations: The use of quantitative data in cross-national research* (pp. 169-190). New Haven, CT: Yale University Press.

Holsti, O. R., North, R. C., & Brody, R. A. (1968). Perception and action in the 1914 crisis. In J. D. Singer (Ed.), *Quantitative international politics (pp. 123-158).* New York: Free Press.

Hopmann, P. T., & King, T. (1976). Interactions and perceptions in the Test Ban negotiations. *International Studies Quarterly, 20,* 105-142.

Howard, J. A., Blumstein, P., & Schwartz, P. (1986). Sex, power, and influence tactics in intimate relationships. *Journal of Personality and Social Psychology, 51,* 102-109.

Ickes, W. (1983). A basic paradigm for the study of unstructured dyadic interaction. In H. T. Reis (Ed.), *Naturalistic approaches to studying social interaction: New directions in methodology for social and behavioral science* (Vol. 15, pp. 5-21). San Francisco: Jossey-Bass.

Jervis, R. (1976). *Perception and misperception in international politics.* Princeton, NJ: Princeton University Press.

Kelley, H., Berscheid, E., Christensen, A., Harvey, J., Huston, T., Levinger, G., McClintock, E., Peplau, A., & Peterson, D. (1983). *Close relationships.* New York: Freeman.

Kenny, D. A., & LaVoie, L. (1984). The social relations model. In L. Berkowitz (Ed.), *Advances in experimental social psychology* (Vol. 18, pp. 141-182). New York: Academic Press.

Levenson, R. W., & Gottman, J. M. (1983). Marital interaction: Psychological linkage and affective exchange. *Journal of Personality and Social Psychology, 45,* 587-597.

Levenson, R. W., & Gottman, J. M. (1985). Physiological and affective predictors of change in relationship satisfaction. *Journal of Personality and Social Psychology, 49,* 85-94.

Levinger, G. (1980). Toward the analysis of close relationships. *Journal of Experimental Social Psychology, 16,* 510-544.

Mandel, R. (1986). Psychological approaches to international relations. In M.G. Hermann (Ed.), *Political psychology: Contemporary problems and issues* (pp. 251-278). San Francisco: Jossey-Bass.

Noller, P. (1984). *Nonverbal communication and marital interaction.* New York: Pergamon.

Pike, G. R., & Sillars, A. L. (1985). Reciprocity of marital communication. *Journal of Social and Personal Relationships, 2,* 303-324.

Rausch, H. L., Barry, W. A., Hertel, R. K., & Swain, M. E. (1974). *Communication, conflict, and marriage.* San Francisco: Jossey-Bass.

Rogers, L. E., Millar, E. E., & Bavelas, J. B. (1985). Methods for analyzing marital conflict discourse: Implications of a systems approach. *Family Process, 24,* 175-187.

Shannon, C. E., & Weaver, W. (1949). *The mathematical theory of communication.* Urbana, IL: University of Illinois Press.

Sillars, A. L., & Scott, M. D. (1983). Interpersonal perception between intimates: An integrative review. *Human Communication Research, 10,* 153-176.

Sillars, A. L., & Weisberg, J. (in press). Conflict as social skill. In M. E. Roloff & G. R. Miller (Ed.), *Further explorations in interpersonal communication.* Newbury Park, CA: Sage.

Sprecher, S. (1985). Sex differences in bases of power in dating relationships. *Sex Roles, 12,* 449-462.

Tajfel, H. (1978a). Interindividual and intergroup behaviour. In H. Tajfel (Ed.), *Differentiation between social groups* (pp. 27-60). New York: Academic Press.

Tajfel, H. (1978b). Social categorization, social identity, and social comparison. In H. Tajfel (Ed.), *Differentiation between social groups* (pp. 61-76). New York: Academic Press.

Tetlock, P. E., & McGuire, C. B. (1986). Cognitive perspectives on foreign policy. In R. K. White (Ed.), *Psychology and the prevention of nuclear war* (pp. 255-273). New York: New York University Press.

Verzberger, Y. (1982). Misperception in international politics: A typological framework for analysis. *International Interactions, 9,* 207-234.

Vincent, J. P., Weiss, R. L., & Birchler, G. R. (1975). Dyadic problem solving as a function of marital distress and spousal vs. stranger interactions. *Behavior Therapy, 6,* 475-487.

Watzlawick, P., Beavin, J. H., & Jackson, D. D. (1967). *The pragmatics of human communication.* New York: Norton.

Zinnes, D. A. (1968). The expression and perception of hostility in prewar crisis: 1914. In J. D. Singer (Ed.), *Quantitative international politics* (pp. 85-119). New York: Free Press.

Zinnes, D. A. (1980). Three puzzles in search of a researcher. *International Studies Quarterly, 24,* 315-342.

Zuckerman, M., Lipets, M., Koivumaki, J., & Rosenthal, R. (1975). Encoding and decoding nonverbal cues of emotion. *Journal of Personality and Social Psychology, 32,* 1068-1076.

7

Social Loafing and Social Facilitation

NEW WINE IN OLD BOTTLES

STEPHEN G. HARKINS
KATE SZYMANSKI

Stephen G. Harkins is an Associate Professor of Psychology at Northeastern University. He received his Ph.D. at the University of Missouri-Columbia in 1975. His research interests include group processes and the effects of social context on attitude change.

Kate Szymanski is a graduate student at Northeastern University. She received a master's in social psychology at the University of Warsaw in 1979 and a master's in experimental psychology at Northeastern University in 1985. Her research interests include group processes, private aspects of the self, and the ecological approach to person perception.

In the first published experiment in social psychology, Triplett (1898) found that children reeled more fishing line when working alongside another child similarly occupied than when reeling alone. Some fifteen years later, Ringelmann (1913, summarized by Kravitz & Martin, 1986) reported that students working together pulled on a rope with less force than was expected on the basis of their individual outputs. Reeling line and pulling rope are both very simple tasks. Yet on one, working together led to better performance than working alone, while on the other, the opposite effect was obtained. These two experiments represent the initial efforts in what have come to be considered two separate lines of research, social facilitation and social loafing. The fact that these two phenomena fall into separate research domains may account for the fact that nothing has been made of the apparently contradictory nature of the findings. However, we will argue that these findings are intimately related, and are not contradictory. In fact, the two research paradigms are complementary.

SOCIAL FACILITATION AND
SOCIAL LOAFING AS UNRELATED PHENOMENA

Actually, these experiments were seen at one time as falling in the same domain. In an early review, Dashiell (1935) included Ringelmann's study in a section entitled "The effects of coworkers upon the individual's work" along with other experiments on social facilitation (e.g., Allport, 1920). Given the inconsistencies that already characterized the research in this area, the discrepancy between the findings of Triplett and Ringelmann must not have appeared noteworthy. As Dashiell (1935) wrote: "Looking backward over this section it appears that results with tests on the effect of the presence of other workers alongside are not in agreement on all points. Very generally there seems to emerge a recognition of contrasted kinds of influence from coworkers, facilitating and inhibiting"(p. 1115). Matters had not progressed by the 1950s when Solomon Asch (1952) wrote:

> When performance increases under group conditions it is because social facilitation is at work; if under the same conditions the opposite effect is obtained, an opposed factor is responsible, social inhibition. Why one factor is effective at one time and not at another, with one person and not another, remains obscure. The suspicion then arises that the proferred concepts are simply restatements of the quantitative results. (p. 67)

After several decades of research, there was no convincing refutation of Asch's suspicion, and interest in this area waned.

In 1965, Zajonc suggested a resolution to the muddle. He hypothesized that the "mere presence" of others leads to increased drive, which enhances the tendency to emit dominant responses. If the dominant response is correct, facilitation is obtained; if incorrect, performance is debilitated. Of course, on simple or well-learned tasks, the dominant response is likely to be the correct one, leading to facilitated performance, as in Triplett's case. However, on complex or not well-learned tasks, the dominant response is likely to be incorrect, leading to debilitated performance. Zajonc's (1965) review suggested that this analysis made sense of a large body of research.

But what of Ringelmann's finding? The task was quite simple and people worked together, yet there was no facilitation effect. Ringelmann's research was not included in Zajonc's review, apparently because, by now, it was considered to be part of the group process literature. In Zajonc's (1966) text, social facilitation effects were presented in a chapter entitled *Coaction,* while Ringelmann's findings appeared in the *Group Performance* chapter, and why not? In Triplett's study, *working together* meant working individually, side by side, on the same task. Ringelmann's students actually *worked together,* pulling on the same rope. In the latter case, as Zajonc (1966) noted, the participants had to coordinate their efforts to achieve their full potential. If the participants reached their peak pulls at slightly different times, or if they pulled along slightly different axes, coordination loss would occur, leading to suboptimal performance. As Steiner (1972) has shown, the performance decrements exhibited by Ringlemann's students were directly proportional to the number of coordination links among the participants. The potential for coordination loss is clearly a consequence of working with others. Therefore, it makes sense to consider the Ringelmann effect as a *group process,* while Triplett's study and the subsequent research are placed in the domain of *coaction* (i.e., the effects of the presence of others working independently on the same task). Following this classification scheme, Forsyth (1983) presented coaction research in a section of his book entitled *Performance when others are present,* while social loafing was presented in *Performance in interacting groups.* In most social psychology textbooks, these two phenomena appear in separate sections and no consideration is given to their relationship.

SOCIAL FACILITATION AND SOCIAL LOAFING
AS COMPLEMENTARY PHENOMENA

Subsequent research, however, has shown that coordination loss alone is insufficient to account for Ringelmann's findings, and that working together can lead to less output even when there is no opportunity for coordination loss. Ingham, Levinger, Graves, and Peckham (1974), after replicating Ringelmann's rope-pulling experiment, arranged things in a second experiment so that, on certain trials, participants were given the impression that they were pulling with others, when they actually pulled alone. This arrangement provided no opportunity for coordination loss. On these pseudogroup trials, participants put out less effort than when they thought they were pulling alone. This reduction in effort has been termed *social loafing* (Latané, Williams, & Harkins, 1979), and this effect has been demonstrated for both sexes on tasks requiring both physical effort (clapping, Harkins, Latané, & Williams, 1980; pumping air, Kerr & Bruun, 1981; shouting, Latané et al., 1979) and cognitive effort (reacting to proposals, Brickner, Harkins, & Ostrom, 1986; brainstorming and vigilance, Harkins & Petty, 1982; solving mazes, Jackson & Williams, 1985; evaluating essays, Petty, Harkins, Williams, & Latane, 1977). Applying Steiner's

(1972) typology, some of these tasks were "maximizing" (requiring the participant to put out as much effort as possible, such as rope-pulling, shouting, pumping air, and brainstorming), while others were "optimizing" (requiring the participant to achieve some criterion performance, such as evaluating essays, vigilance, and solving mazes). On all of these tasks, "groups" failed to achieve even the potential suggested by their individual performances, though the possibility of coordination loss was eliminated, either by using pseudogroups (e.g., Ingham et al., 1974; Latané et al., 1979), or by using tasks on which individual performances added, with no possibility of coordination loss (e.g., vigilance and brainstorming, Harkins & Petty, 1982; solving mazes, Jackson & Williams, 1985).

Paradigms Examined

While the potential for coordination loss may have consigned Ringelmann's findings to the group domain, this difference between the paradigms is not sufficient to account for the contradictory findings. In fact, a close examination of the two experimental paradigms reveals many more similarities than differences.

Social facilitation. In the prototypic coaction experiment, the outputs of the coacting participants are individually identifiable, and these outputs are compared to the output of a single participant performing the same task. The usual finding in social facilitation research is that working together leads to enhanced performance on simple tasks and debilitated performance on complex ones. As noted previously, Zajonc (1965) offered a drive interpretation of this phenomenon, which proposed that the presence of others increased arousal, which enhanced the tendency to emit dominant responses. If the dominant response was correct, facilitation occurred; if not, performance was debilitated. Over the next decade, this drive account was seen as the most parsimonious theoretical explanation for facilitation effects (e.g., Geen & Gange, 1977), although there was controversy over whether it was the mere presence of the others that increased drive (Zajonc, 1965, 1980), or the fact that these others were associated with evaluation and/or competition (Cottrell, 1972).

However, in a review of the facilitation literature since 1977, Geen (in press) concluded that "today such a confident assertion of the primacy of the drive theoretical approach is not warranted. . . . Instead several sophisticated alternatives have found considerable support in experimental studies." Geen organized these theoretical approaches into three broad classes. One class of theories incorporates those approaches that continue to rely on the notion that the presence of others increases drive (e.g., distraction/conflict, Baron, 1986; evaluation apprehension, Cottrell, 1972; social monitoring, Guerin & Innes, 1982; compresence, Zajonc, 1980). The second class of theories includes those approaches that suggest that "the presence of others creates either explicit or implicit demands on the person to behave in some way" (Geen, in press) (e.g., self-presentation, Bond, 1982; self-awareness, Carver & Scheier, 1981), while the third class consists of Baron's information processing view of distraction/conflict, which proposes that the presence of others affects focus of attention and information processing.

Although there are a number of theories that attempt to account for facilitation effects, and "none appears to command the high ground as drive theory did in the 1960s and 1970s" (Geen, in press), each of these theories focuses on the effects of one or both of the same two features of the facilitation paradigm: the mere presence of others, and/or the potential for evaluation that these others represent. The "number" theories argue that the mere presence of others leads to the feeling of uncertainty that leads to increased drive (Zajonc, 1980); the presence of others leads to uncertainty and increased drive, when the behavior of these others cannot be monitored (Guerin & Innes, 1982); or the simple presence of others may be distracting enough to trigger attentional conflict or increased drive (Brown, 1986); or the simple presence of others may be distracting enough to create an attentional overload affecting focus of attention (Baron, 1986). The "evaluation" theories argue that the presence of others can come to be associated with evaluation and/or competition, and the resulting evaluation apprehension leads to increased drive (Cottrell, 1972); the possibility of evaluation leads to distraction that increases drive (Baron, 1986); the potential for evaluation makes one self-aware which leads to greater attention to how performance matches some standard (Carver & Scheier, 1981); the prospect of evaluation leads to concerns about self-presentation (Bond, 1982); or the potential for evaluation affects focus of attention (Baron, 1986). Thus each of these explanations represents an attempt to account for the effects of number and/or evaluation.

Social loafing. In the prototypic social loafing experiment, the outputs of the participants are pooled. That is, the outputs of the participants are summed, the "group's" performance is represented by this sum, and individual outputs are "lost in the crowd." Social loafing has been described as the finding that participants working together put out less effort that participants working alone (e.g., Latané et al., 1979). This description suggests that the performances of participants in the "loafing" condition are compared to the performances of participants working by themselves. However, in virtually all of these studies the number of participants has been held constant. In the within-subjects loafing designs (e.g., Harkins et al., 1980; Ingham et al., 1974; Latané et al., 1979; Williams et al., 1981), a fixed number of participants performed individually and in various sized groups. In this research, care has been taken to ensure that when participants performed alone or with others, their outputs could not be monitored by the other participants. For example, in Latané et al., participants wore blindfolds and headsets over which a loud masking noise was played, making it virtually impossible for participants to hear anyone on any trial. Thus the trials on which participants were asked to shout individually were like facilitation trials on which participants performed sequentially rather than simultaneously.

In the between-subjects designs (e.g., Brickner et al., 1986; Harkins & Jackson, 1985 ; Harkins & Petty, 1982), groups of participants, whose outputs were individually identifiable, performed the task simultaneously (e.g., vigilance, brainstorming), exactly as in facilitation research. Thus in loafing research the performances of a set of participants whose outputs are pooled are compared to the performances of a set of participants whose outputs are individually identifiable.

Latané et al.'s description of the loafing effect suggests that loafing is a "group versus individual" effect. However, our analysis suggests that loafing would be more appropriately viewed as an evaluation effect. In fact, Latané et al. suggested that the "information reducing" nature of the "group" trials (Davis, 1969) may have been responsible for the loafing effect. When participants' performances were pooled, individual outputs were lost in the crowd, submerged in the total, and were not individually recoverable by the experimenter. Because participants could receive neither praise nor blame for their performances, they loafed. Consistent with this explanation, Williams et al. (1981) found that when participants were led to believe that their individual outputs could be monitored even when they performed "together" (i.e., pooled outputs), there was no loafing. Also, when participants were led to believe that interest centered on "group" performance and their individual outputs were to be summed, they loafed as much when they performed individually as when they performed "together." Williams et al. (1981) concluded on the basis of these findings that identifiability of individual outputs is an important mediator of social loafing.

However, Williams et al. (1981) did not manipulate identifiability alone. The participants all worked on the same task; thus, when their performances were individually identifiable, they could be directly compared to the performances of the other participants. This opportunity for comparison may have led participants to believe that their outputs could be evaluated, and it was this potential for evaluation, not identifiability alone, that motivated performance. To test this possibility, Harkins and Jackson (1985) orthogonally manipulated identifiability and comparability, using a brainstorming task in which participants were asked to generate as many uses as possible for an object. Replicating previous loafing research, when outputs were identifiable, participants generated more uses than when their outputs were pooled. However, this difference emerged only when participants believed that their outputs could be compared to their coworkers' performances.

These findings suggest that identifiability alone does not motivate performance. Participants must feel that their outputs can be compared to those of others. Without this potential for evaluation, participants whose outputs were individually identifiable exerted as little effort as those whose outputs were pooled. These data suggest that people loaf when their outputs cannot be evaluated, and because evaluation is not possible when outputs are pooled, it is this aspect of "working together" that leads to loafing.

Paradigms Combined

Viewed in this way, the experimental conditions that have been included in loafing and facilitation research fall into three cells of a 2 (Alone vs. Coaction) × 2 (Evaluation vs. No Evaluation) factorial design. Coaction in this context is defined as more than one person working on the same task during the same period of time. The manner in which the individual scores are to be treated is left unspecified (e.g., individual evaluation, summed). In this 2 × 2 design, facilitation studies are characterized by the comparison of the performances of coactors whose outputs can be evaluated (Coaction/Evaluation) to the performances of single participants whose outputs can also be evaluated (Alone/Evaluation). In virtually all loafing research, the performances of participants in a Coaction/Evaluation cell have been compared to the performances of coacting participants whose outputs were pooled

(Coaction/No Evaluation). The fourth cell, Alone/No Evaluation, has been run in *no* extant coaction study using either the facilitation or loafing paradigms. We propose that this combined design incorporates the processes that account for both facilitation and loafing effects, and addresses weaknesses present in each paradigm taken alone.

Social facilitation. Markus (1981) argued that those studies in which the mere presence hypothesis has not been confirmed "are studies in which there has not been a clear 'alone' condition as a comparison baseline" (p. 259). Consistent with the notion that experimenters have not been sufficiently aware of this problem, Bond and Titus (1983), in a review of social facilitation research, wrote: "In 96 of 241 studies, the experimenter was in the room with the 'alone' subject, and in 52 of these studies this 'alone' subject could see the experimenter!" (p. 271). Guerin (1986) reviewed 287 social facilitation studies and found only 11 published experiments that met his criteria for a test of the mere presence hypothesis. However, it could be argued that even Guerin's criteria, which included removing the experimenter from the room, were not strict enough for a reasonable test. Markus (1978) noted: "In virtually all experiments with humans, the subject in the alone condition is not 'phenomenologically' alone even when the experimenter is physically removed and out of sight. That is, he is quite aware of the experimenter and knows that his performance is being recorded, presumably for some present or future evaluation" (p. 391). What difference does it make whether the experimenter is out of the room, if that person has immediate access to a record of the participants' performances?

In all but one of the 11 published studies that Guerin cited as representing the best tests of the mere presence hypothesis, the experimenter had access to the participants' scores immediately after completion of the task. The sole exception was the Markus (1978) study in which the mere presence manipulation consisted of an attentive or inattentive audience that was present when the participants donned and doffed familiar and unfamiliar clothing. Apparently, there are no human coaction studies that incorporate appropriate tests of the mere presence hypothesis.

In the combined design we have described, the abilities of potential sources of evaluation, including the experimenter, to evaluate individual performances are minimized in the No Evaluation conditions. Thus, the addition of the conditions suggested by loafing research may offer a closer approximation to the conditions necessary for a test of the effects of mere presence on coaction, using tasks like those commonly employed in facilitation research.

Social loafing. In the loafing studies that we have described, the number of people present has been held constant. In only one loafing experiment has the performance of a person actually working alone been compared to the performances of people working together (Kerr & Bruun, 1981), and in this experiment, the number of people present and the manipulation of evaluation were confounded. That is, in the alone condition, a single person's outputs could be evaluated by the experimenter through comparison of that person's performance with the performances of the preceding and subsequent participants, while in the together conditions, there were at least two participants whose outputs were pooled and, therefore, could not be evaluated. Did participants in the alone condition put out more effort than the pooled participants because they were working alone or because their outputs could be evaluated? The description of the loafing effect points to the former possibility (e.g., Latané et al., 1979); however, the latter possibility is supported by the findings of Williams et al. (1981) and Harkins and Jackson (1985). The unified design clarifies the relationship between number and evaluation by orthogonally manipulating these variables.

Unified Paradigm Tested

To test this unified paradigm, the 2 × 2 design was run in two experiments (Harkins, 1987). In the first experiment, participants, tested alone or in pairs, were asked to generate as many uses for an object as they could. Crossed with the number manipulation, one-half of the participants were told that everyone in the experiment was generating uses for the same object (Evaluation), while the other half were told that each of the participants would be generating uses for a different object (No Evaluation).

In making the case that loafing and facilitation effects can be understood in the same framework, we have argued that pooling the participants' outputs leads them to reduce their efforts because it minimizes the possibility of evaluation. To provide additional support for this notion, a Coaction/Pooled Output condition was added to the design of the first experiment. To replicate the findings of previous loafing work, Coaction/Evaluation participants should generate more uses than Coaction/Pooled Output participants, who should perform at the same level as Coaction/No Evaluation participants, and this outcome is exactly what occurred. Ancillary measures were also supportive of this analysis. Participants in the loafing replication condition felt that their performances could not be evaluated because their outputs were pooled. The different object manipulation was intended to achieve the same end, and, consistent with this expectation, participants in the Coaction/No Evaluation condition reported that their outputs could not be evaluated to the same extent as participants in the Coaction/Pooled Output condition. The participants in each of these conditions reported that their outputs could be evaluated reliably less than participants in the Coaction/Evaluation condition.

In the basic 2×2 design, two main effects were obtained: Coactors outperformed singles, and participants whose outputs could be evaluated outperformed participants whose outputs could not. To assess the reliability and generality of these findings, the effects of number and evaluation potential were examined in a second experiment, using a different method of manipulating evaluation potential and a different task. Participants took part as singles or pairs in a vigilance task that required them to report signals presented on a TV screen. Evaluation was manipulated by leading the participants to believe either that the computer that kept track of their performances was functioning properly (Evaluation) or had malfunctioned (No Evaluation). As in the first experiment, two main effects and no interaction were obtained.

This analysis suggests that there is no discrepancy between the findings of loafing and facilitation research. In fact, the findings from these paradigms are complementary. In social facilitation research, when participants coact, their outputs can be compared and they work harder than participants working alone. In social loafing research, when participants coact, their outputs cannot be evaluated and they put out less effort than participants whose outputs can be compared. In both cases, evaluation is central. In social facilitation, working together enhances evaluation potential; in social loafing, working together reduces it. The findings from these experiments also refine our understanding of both facilitation and loafing effects.

Social facilitation. The two main effects are consistent with the argument that both mere presence and evaluation play a role in motivating performance. Of course, it is probably not possible to eliminate all concerns about the possibility of evaluation when participants know that they are in an experiment. However, by minimizing the apparent opportunities for evaluation by the experimenter, these experiments approached this goal more closely than previous coaction experiments in which no attempt was made to eliminate this source of evaluation. Though mere presence and evaluation apprehension have often been considered to be competing explanations, Markus (1981) pointed out that both processes can contribute to facilitation effects. In these experiments, both did, and in an additive fashion. These experiments suggest that to provide a complete account of facilitation effects, a theory must explain both number and evaluation effects.

Social loafing. Originally, Latané et al. (1979) described social loafing as the finding that participants working together put out less effort than participants working alone. Subsequent research (Harkins & Jackson, 1985; Williams et al., 1981) suggests that a particular aspect of "working together" was responsible for the loafing effect: When outputs are pooled, evaluation is not possible, leading the participants to reduce their efforts. This argument led us to suggest that facilitation and loafing paradigms could be unified. In our tests of this unified design, coactors outperformed participants working alone, not the reverse, as was suggested by the *description* of the loafing effect (e.g., Latané et al., 1979). Consistent with the *findings* of previous loafing research (e.g., Harkins & Jackson, 1985; Latané et al., 1979; Williams et al., 1981), participants whose outputs could be evaluated outperformed participants whose outputs could not.

Latané et al.'s original definition of loafing could be taken to be generic. That is, any motivation loss in groups could be called social loafing. For example, Kerr (1983) found evidence of reduced effort that he termed "free rider" and "sucker" effects when disjunctive and conjunctive scoring schemes were used in groups. These findings would appear to fall under the rubric "social loafing," because participants working together put out less effort than those working individually. However, these participants' individual outputs were always identifiable. Hence, it is quite unlikely that these findings can be attributed to the effects of evaluation. The current analysis argues in favor of a restricted definition of loafing that focuses on the fact that "working together" leads to reduced effort because there is no opportunity for evaluation. When we refer to social loafing, we will be using the term in this restricted sense.

Simple Versus Complex Tasks

Our analysis has focused on the simple, well-learned tasks that have been used in most loafing research. On tasks like rope-pulling, shouting, pumping air, and vigilance, greater effort leads to better performance. However, when *complex* tasks are used in facilitation research (e.g., Martens & Landers, 1972; Seta, Paulus, & Schkade, 1976), greater effort leads to poorer performance. This interpretation suggests that if, instead of the simple tasks typically used in loafing research, complex tasks were used, participants in the Coaction/No Evaluation (loafing) condition should perform *better* than participants in the Coaction/Evaluation condition, and this outcome is exactly what was found by Jackson and Williams (1985). Participants in a Coaction/Evaluation condition performed better on simple mazes than participants whose outcomes were pooled (Coaction/No Evaluation), a loafing effect. But when the mazes were complex, the pattern was reversed; participants whose outputs were pooled performed better than participants whose individual outputs could be compared. Thus it appears that this approach can account for performance on both simple and complex tasks.

EVALUATION REEVALUATED

The potential for evaluation plays a central role in this analysis of loafing and facilitation effects, but evaluation by whom? There are three potential sources of evaluation in these paradigms: the experimenter, the coactor(s), and the participant.

Sources of Evaluation in Social Facilitation

Social facilitation researchers have referred to each of these potential sources in their accounts of coaction effects (e.g., coactor evaluation, Klinger, 1969; self-evaluation, Sanders, Baron & Moore, 1978; experimenter evaluation, Seta et al., 1976). Thus, the coaction effect may occur because the participant can evaluate his or her own output by comparing it against the coactor's; or the experimenter can evaluate the participant's output by comparing it against the coactor's. Of course, in the "experimenter" account, the experimenter can also evaluate the outputs of the participants in the "alone" condition, but it is apparently assumed that the prospect of having the experimenter compare one's score against the score of a coactor who is physically present is more arousing than the more remote comparison of one's performance against the performances of the preceding participants.

Despite the fact that each of these sources has been incorporated into accounts of coaction effects, there is no compelling evidence that these accounts have captured the motivational structure of the experiments they were meant to describe. For example, though Sanders et al. (1978) alluded to self-evaluation in their interpretation, when the participant could evaluate himself or herself, the coactor could also evaluate the participant, and the evaluation potential of the experimenter was likely to have been particularly salient at that time. In many of these facilitation experiments, it is not clear what the participants were told or what they inferred about evaluation potential.

Cottrell (1972) defined the independent variable in coaction research as "the presence of others who work simultaneously and independently on the same task on which the subject is working" (p. 185). Presumably, it is the effects that these other workers have on the subject that are of interest. However, in these studies, self and coactor evaluation must have had their effects over and above the effect of experimenter evaluation, because, as noted in our discussion of mere presence effects, the experimenter had access to individual scores and could evaluate performances either during or after task performance.

Sources of Evaluation in Social Loafing

In loafing research, the role of the experimenter as evaluator has been emphasized. For example, Harkins et al. (1980) wrote: "The results (social loafing) are easily explained by a minimizing strategy where participants are motivated to work only as hard as necessary to gain credit for a good performance or to avoid blame for a bad one. When the experimenter was unable to monitor individual outputs directly, performers sloughed off" (p. 464). When the success of the pooling manipulation has been assessed (e.g., Harkins & Jackson, 1985; Harkins & Petty, 1982; Jackson & Williams, 1985), it has only been the participants' perception of the experimenter's ability to evaluate individual performance that has been checked. There has been no attempt to ascertain the motivational role, if any, of the other sources. However, when outputs are pooled, it is not only the case that the experimenter cannot evaluate individual output, neither can the co-actor(s) nor the participant. For example, during the performance trials in the shouting paradigm no evaluation is possible because the masking noise eliminates the possibility that the participants can hear or be heard. After the session, if the participants have access to the scores, it is possible for them to compare (evaluate) individual performances, but they are as unable to decompose "group" shouts as the experimenter. A review of other loafing research reveals similar features of the pooling manipulations. Thus, when outputs are pooled, participants may feel that they cannot evaluate their own outputs, nor can these outputs be evaluated by their fellow participants.

Evaluation, But By Whom?

So, in both loafing and facilitation research, it appears that the potential for evaluation plays a central role in motivating performance. Beyond this, we know very little about the motivational structures of these paradigms. Based on a meta-analysis of the facilitation literature, Bond and Titus (1983) argued that evaluation has minimal, if any, systematic effects on facilitation. It is quite likely that the haphazard manipulation of evaluation accounts for the unimpressive effects of what should be a powerful manipulation. Almost 90 years after Triplett's initial experiment, we are left with considerable ambiguity about the working of a variable central to our understanding of this "rudimentary social arrangement" (Cottrell, 1972).

Cottrell (1972) argued that understanding these simple social arrangements is of fundamental importance to social psychology because they are included in almost all social relationships. To achieve this understanding will require a systematic analysis of the role played by each of the potential sources in motivating performance. This analysis must begin with a consideration of what is necessary for evaluation.

Requirements for Evaluation

For evaluation by any source to be possible, two pieces of information must be known: the participant's output and a standard against which this output can be compared. This need for a standard can be satisfied in several ways. If a participant has had extensive experience with a given task, it is possible that she or he could have some notion concerning how the current level of performance compares to these earlier levels. In this case, the standard would be provided by the participant's own previous performances.

In most loafing and facilitation research, this sort of standard is not likely to be available, because the tasks are unfamiliar to the participants. In the absence of a personal standard, the need for a standard could also be satisfied by an objective criterion or by a social one. Depending on the task, one or both of these criteria may be available. On optimizing tasks (Steiner, 1972), which require the participant to achieve some criterion performance, both are available. That is, the participant's output could be compared against both an objective standard (e.g., the number of signals presented in a vigilance task), and a social one (e.g., the number of signals detected by other participants).

On maximizing tasks (Steiner, 1972), which require the participant to put out as much effort as possible, only a social standard is available; there is no objective criterion of success. For example, on shouting or brainstorming tasks, the only criterion of success is how well a given participant did vis-à-vis other participants. There is no "correct" performance. In facilitation research, of course, the typical criterion is social, that is, whether a given participant surpassed or fell short of the performance level of the coactors. In any case, by manipulating to whom this information is made available, it is possible to determine how the potential for evaluation by these different sources function independently and in concert to motivate performance.

As we have noted, in previous research the potential for evaluation by the experimenter could have mediated both facilitation and loafing effects. Of course, the effects of the potential for evaluation by this source may be of interest, if one is concerned with the role played by an expert audience. However, certainly in facilitation research interest has ostensibly been focused on the effects of the presence of coworkers. Viewed in this way, the experimenter appears to be an interloper in this setting. The effects of the potential for evaluation by the coactor are certainly part of this "pristine" coaction setting, but these effects are likely to be similar to those of the experimenter, another external source of evaluation. Tasks like those used in facilitation and loafing research have been described as "noncompetitive, boring, tiring" (Harkins et al., 1980) and "unlikely to be personally involving for students, providing intrinsic importance, personal meaning or significant consequences for one's life" (Brickner et al., 1986). Given these descriptions of the tasks, it is not unreasonable to think that surveillance by some external source, like the experimenter, would be necessary to motivate performance. In the research to be described, we tested the intriguing possibility that the potential for self-evaluation alone was sufficient to motivate performance even on these uninteresting tasks.

Self-Evaluation

In this experiment (Szymanski & Harkins, in press), the potential for evaluation by the experimenter was crossed with a manipulation of the potential for self-evaluation. To manipulate the potential for self-evaluation, it is necessary to take into account what participants think they know about the task. Because participants in loafing and facilitation research are unlikely to have had any prior experience with the tasks, we made the assumption that no standard was available unless it was provided by us. However, we did not make a similar assumption about the participants' knowledge of their own output. That is, after completion of a particular task, participants may feel that they know what their output was, while after completing another, they may feel they do not know. For example, pilot work has shown that after participants have generated as many uses for an object as they can (brainstorming), they think they know how many uses they have generated. This suggested that the potential for self-evaluation could be manipulated on this task simply by providing or withholding a standard. Because this was a maximizing task, a social criterion was required.

Participants were tested in pairs, and were asked to generate as many uses as they could for an ordinary object, a box. The participants were asked to write each use on a separate slip of paper, to fold the slip, and to slide it down a tube that extended into a box. For one half of the pairs, the box was divided so that the person's output could be counted (Experimenter Evaluation). For the other half, there was no divider, so that the two participants' uses were pooled (No Experimenter Evaluation). Crossed with this manipulation, one-third of the pairs were given a social standard; that is, they were told that this was a replication of another experiment and that at the end of the session they would be told the average number of uses from this previous experiment, but they should hold this information in confidence (Standard). One-third of the pairs were told that they could not be given this information since it could affect the performance of later participants (No Standard). The final third of the pairs were told nothing about the previous experiment and served as a control (Social Loafing Control).

Manipulation checks were administered to assess the role played by the potential for evaluation by each of the possible sources (experimenter, coactor, and self), and these were analyzed in 2 (Experimenter Evaluation vs. No Experimenter Evaluation) $\times$ 3 (Standard, No Standard, Control) ANOVAs. When the participants' outputs fell into separate compartments (Experimenter Evaluation), participants acknowledged that the possibility of experimenter evaluation was greater ($M = 8.4$ on an 11-point scale) than when these outputs were pooled ($M = 4.8$, $p < .001$). There were no reliable differences on the coactor evaluation measure (Overall M = 3.2). On the self-evaluation measure, there was an Instruction main effect. Participants in the Standard condition reported that they could evaluate their own performances to a greater extent (M = 7.7) than participants in either the No Standard (M = 4.5) or Control conditions (M = 4.8, ps < .05). These latter conditions did not differ (p > .20).

Analysis of the number of uses revealed a reliable interaction (p < .001). In the Control cell, replicating previous loafing research, participants whose outputs could be evaluated by the experimenter generated more uses (M = 28.4) than participants whose outputs were pooled (M = 20.0, p < .05). Likewise, in the No Standard condition, Experimenter Evaluation participants generated more uses (M = 25.4) than Pooled participants (M = 18.2, p < .05). In these conditions, the participants had not anticipated the possibility of self-evaluation. In the Standard condition, in which this possibility was anticipated, participants in the pooled condition generated as many uses (M = 27.3) as participants whose outputs could be evaluated by the experimenter (M = 25.9, p > .20).

This experiment suggests that the potential for self-evaluation is sufficient to motivate performance, even when experimenter evaluation is not possible. In this experiment we used a social criterion. To test the motivational properties of an objective standard, we also conducted an experiment in which we used an optimizing task, vigilance. In the crucial condition of the experiment, in which there was no possibility of evaluation by the experimenter but the participants could self-evaluate by comparing the number of signals they detected to the total number presented (the objective criterion), there was no loafing. Thus, both on a maximizing task, brainstorming, for which a social standard was used, and on an optimizing task, vigilance, for which an objective standard was used, participants whose only source of motivation was the opportunity to compare their outputs to these standards worked as hard as participants whose performances could be evaluated by the experimenter.

Social facilitation. When participants coact, there is the opportunity for self-evaluation through the comparison of one's performance to that of the coactor's. This source of evaluation has been alluded to by previous social facilitation researchers (e.g., Sanders et. al., 1978), but its independent effects on performance have yet to be demonstrated, because, in previous work, the effects of the potential for evaluation by the two other sources, coactor and experimenter, were confounded with the potential for self-evaluation. Our studies suggest that the potential for self-evaluation has motivational effects independent of those resulting from other sources. In addition to demonstrating the potential contribution of self-evaluation to coaction effects, these experiments represent tests of various aspects of the explanations for facilitation effects. For example, Bond's (1982) self-presentational view "attributes social facilitation to the performer's active regulation of a public image" (p. 1042). In the self-evaluation conditions of the current experiments, there was no external audience to whom an image could be presented, yet these participants worked as hard as participants whose outputs would be known to the experimenter.

Social loafing. Previous research (e.g., Harkins et al., 1980) has accorded the experimenter a central role in motivating performance in the loafing paradigm. For example, Harkins et al. (1980) wrote: "Our data suggest that to the extent that participants cannot be rewarded or punished for their individual performances, people will loaf" (p. 463). This interpretation suggests a rather pessimistic view of individual motivation in its emphasis on the role of external agents in motivating behavior. Without the intervention of ever-watchful observers, it appears that participants loaf. The current research suggests, however, that this pessimistic view is not warranted; the potential for self-evaluation alone is sufficient to eliminate the loafing effect.

Theories of self-evaluation. Of course, many social psychological theories have incorporated the notion that the potential for self-evaluation motivates performance (e.g., Bandura's 1986 theory of self-efficacy; Deci & Ryan's 1985 theory of intrinsic motivation and self-determination; Festinger's 1954 theory of social comparison; Greenwald and Breckler's 1985 ego-task analysis). The findings of these experiments are relevant for these accounts of self-evaluation. For example, Greenwald and Breckler's ego-task analysis specifies three facets of the self that are relevant for evaluation concerns: the public self, the private self, and the collective self. At the heart of this typology is the notion that people's behavior is motivated by concern about evaluation by these sources. As Greenwald and Breckler argued: "The prevalent assumption heretofore has been that self-presentations are targeted at audiences of others. We have reviewed evidence that there is also an important inner audience, oneself" (p. 141). The current findings are consistent with Greenwald and Breckler's notion of the motivational efficacy of the private self. Not only does the current work bring these various approaches to self-evaluation into contact with "group" research, it also suggests ways of testing these approaches that minimize the effects of evaluation pressures from other sources, so that the effects of self-evaluation can be seen in isolation.

CONCLUSIONS

To represent the ways in which the presence of others could affect an individual's task performance on one dimension, one could imagine one extreme anchored by the performance of a person working "alone" and the other anchored by the performance of a person embedded in an interacting, cohesive group with a prior history of encounters. On this dimension, social facilitation falls next to the "presocial" setting represented by a person working alone, because it represents the effect of the "sheer presence" (Zajonc, 1965) of others. Social loafing has been seen as occupying a position on the "groupier" end of the dimension. The current analysis suggests that, at the least, loafing falls immediately adjacent to facilitation, and, more than this, it appears to be facilitation's complement.

Though it is clear that evaluation plays a central role in producing each of these phenomena, there is much left to be learned about exactly how the various sources of evaluation available in these settings operate singly and in concert to produce these effects. The research on self-evaluation reported here demonstrates at least one way to attack problems posed by previous research in which the effects of these sources have been confounded.

In this chapter, we have focused on the role that evaluation plays in producing facilitation and loafing effects. We are not proposing that effects stemming from manipulations of evaluation potential account for all, or even most, motivation losses in groups. Any number of other variables may affect performance in group settings (e.g., dispensability of member effort, Kerr, 1983). Rather, we are arguing that evaluation potential plays a central role in producing the reduction in effort that has been termed social loafing, and the enhancement in effort that has been termed social facilitation. Even when our attention is limited to the loafing paradigm, it is clear that other factors motivate performance, regardless of the potential for evaluation. For example, creativity (Bartis, Szymanski, & Harkins, in press), personal involvement (Brickner et al., 1986), partner effort (Jackson & Harkins, 1985), and group cohesion (Williams, 1981) have all been shown to eliminate the loafing effect, even though the potential for evaluation by each of the sources was minimized. In future work, it will be necessary to determine how these other factors interact with the potential for evaluation to motivate performance in these settings.

REFERENCES

Allport, F. (1920). The influence of the group upon association and thought. *Journal of Experimental Psychology, 3,* 159-182.

Asch, S. (1952). *Social psychology.* New York: Holt, Rinehart & Winston.

Bandura, A. (1986). *Social foundations of thought and action: A social cognitive theory.* Englewood Cliffs, NJ: Prentice-Hall.

Baron, R. (1986). Distraction-conflict theory: Progress and problems. In L. Berkowitz (Ed.), *Advances in experimental social psychology* (Vol. 19, pp. 1-40). New York: Academic Press.

Bartis, S., Szymanski, K., & Harkins, S. (in press). *Evaluation of performance: A two-edged knife. Personality and Social Psychology Bulletin.*

Bond, C. (1982). Social facilitation: A self-presentational view. *Journal of Personality and Social Psychology, 42,* 1042-1050.

Bond, C., & Titus, L. (1983). Social facilitation: A meta-analysis of 241 studies. *Psychology Bulletin, 94,* 265-292.

Brickner, M., Harkins, S., & Ostrom, T. (1986). Personal involvement: Thought provoking implications for social loafing. *Journal of Personality and Social Psychology, 51,* 763-769.

Carver, C., & Scheier, M. (1981). The self-attention-induced feedback loop and social facilitation. *Journal of Experimental Social Psychology, 17,* 545-568.

Cottrell, N. (1972). Social facilitation. In C. McClintock (Ed.) , *Experimental social psychology.* (pp. 185-236). New York: Holt, Rinehart & Winston.

Dashiell, J. (1935). Experimental studies of the influence of social situations on the behavior of individual human adults. In C. Murchison (Ed.), *Handbook of social psychology* (pp. 1097-1158). Worcester, MA: Clark University.

Davis, J. (1969). *Group performance.* Reading, MA: Addison-Wesley.

Deci, E., & Ryan, R. (1985). *Intrinsic motivation and self-determination in human behavior.* New York: Plenum.

Festinger, L. (1954). A theory of social comparison processes. *Human Relations, 7,* 117-140.

Forsyth, D. (1983). *An introduction to group dynamics.* Monterey, CA: Brooks/Cole.

Geen, R. (in press). Alternative conceptions of social facilitation. In P. Paulus (Ed.), *Psychology of group influence.* Hillsdale, NJ: Lawrence Erlbaum.

Geen, R., & Gange, J. (1977). Drive theory of social facilitation: Twelve years of theory and research. *Psychological Bulletin, 84,* 1267-1288.

Greenwald, A., & Breckler, S. (1985). To whom is the self presented? In B. Schlenker (Ed.), *The self and social life.* (pp. 126-145). New York: McGraw-Hill.

Guerin, B. (1986). Mere presence effects in humans: A review. *Journal of Experimental Social Psychology, 22,* 38-77.

Guerin, B., & Innes, J. (1982). Social facilitation and social monitoring: A new look at Zajonc's mere presence hypothesis. *British Journal of Social Psychology, 7*, 81-90.

Harkins, S. (1987). Social loafing and social facilitation. *Journal of Experimental Social Psychology 23*, 1-18.

Harkins, S., & Jackson, J. (1985). The role of evaluation in eliminating social loafing. *Personality and Social Psychology Bulletin, 11*, 457-465.

Harkins, S., Latané, B., & Williams, K. (1980). Social loafing: Allocating effort or taking it easy? *Journal of Experimental Social Psychology, 16*, 457-465.

Harkins, S., & Petty, R. (1982). Effects of task difficulty and task uniqueness on social loafing. *Journal of Personality and Social Psychology, 43*, 1214-1229.

Ingham, A., Levinger, G., Graves, J., & Peckham, V. (1974). The Ringelmann effect: Studies of group size and group performance. *Journal of Experimental Social Psychology, 10*, 371-384.

Jackson, J., & Harkins, S. (1985). Equity in effort: An explanation of the social loafing effect. *Journal of Personality and Social Psychology, 49*, 1199-1206.

Jackson, J., & Williams, K. (1985). Social loafing on difficult tasks: Working collectively can improve performance. *Journal of Personality and Social Psychology, 49*, 937-942.

Kerr, N. (1983). Motivation losses in small groups: A social dilemma analysis. *Journal of Personality and Social Psychology, 45*, 819-828.

Kerr, N., & Bruun, S. (1981). Ringelmann revisited: Alternative explanations for the social loafing effect. *Personality and Social Psychology Bulletin, 7*, 224-231.

Klinger, E. (1969). Feedback effects and social facilitation of vigilance performance: Mere coaction versus potential evaluation. *Psychonomic Science, 14*, 161-162.

Kravitz, D., & Martin, B. (1986). Ringelmann rediscovered: The original article. *Journal of Personality and Social Psychology, 50*, 936-941.

Latané, B., Williams, K., & Harkins, S. (1979). Many hands make light the work: The causes and consequences of social loafing. *Journal of Personality and Social Psychology, 37*, 823-832.

Markus, H. (1978). The effect of mere presence on social facilitation: An unobtrusive test. *Journal of Experimental Social Psychology, 14*, 389-397.

Markus, H. (1981). The drive for integration: Some comments. *Journal of Experimental Social Psychology, 17*, 257-261.

Martens, R., & Landers, D. (1972). Evaluation potential as a determinant of coaction effects. *Journal of Experimental Social Psychology, 8*, 347-359.

Petty, R., Harkins, S., Williams, K., & Latané, B. (1977). The effects of group size on cognitive effort and evaluation. *Personality and Social Psychology Bulletin, 3*, 579-582.

Ringelmann, M. (1913). Recherches sur les moteurs animes: Travail de l'homme. *Annales de l'Institut National Agronomique*, 2e serie—tome XII, 1-40.

Sanders, G., Baron, R., & Moore, D. (1978). Distraction and social comparison as mediators of social facilitation effects. *Journal of Experimental Social Psychology, 14*, 291-303.

Seta, J., Paulus, P., & Schkade, J. (1976). Effects of group size and proximity under cooperative and competitive conditions. *Journal of Personality and Social Psychology, 34*, 47-53.

Steiner, I. (1972). *Group process and productivity.* New York: Academic Press.

Szymanski, K., & Harkins, S. (in press). Social Loafing and self-evaluation with a social standard. *Journal of Personality and Social Psycholology.*

Triplett, N. (1898). The dynamogenic factors in pacemaking and competition. *American Journal of Psychology, 9,* 507-533.

Williams, K. (1981, May). *The effects of group cohesiveness on social loafing.* Paper presented at the annual meeting of the Midwestern Psychological Association, Detroit, MI.

Williams, K., Harkins, S., & Latané, B. (1981). Identifiability as a deterrent to social loafing: Two cheering experiments. *Journal of Experimental Social Psychology, 40,* 303-311.

Zajonc, R. (1965). Social facilitation. *Science, 149,* 269-274.

Zajonc, R. (1966). *Social psychology: An experimental approach.* Belmont, CA: Wadsworth.

Zajonc, R. (1980). Compresence. In P. Paulus (Ed.), *Psychology of group influence* (pp. 35-60). Hillsdale, NJ: Lawrence Erlbaum.

8

Group Effects on
Self-Attention and Performance
SOCIAL LOAFING, SOCIAL FACILITATION, AND SOCIAL IMPAIRMENT

BRIAN MULLEN
ROY F. BAUMEISTER

Brian Mullen is an Assistant Professor at Syracuse University. His research interests include group composition effects from a self-attention theory perspective. He has edited a book in collaboration with George R. Goethals, *Theories of Group Behavior* (Springer-Verlag, 1987). Other interests include social projection phenomena, and meta-analytic statistics, for example, Mullen & Rosenthal, *BASIC Meta-Analysis: Procedures and Programs* (Lawrence Erlbaum, 1985).

Roy F. Baumeister is an Associate Professor at Case Western Reserve University. He received his Ph.D. in social psychology from Princeton in 1978. His research interests include performance under pressure, public and private aspects of the self, personality structure, and interdisciplinary work. His first two books, *Identity: Cultural Change and the Struggle for Self* (Oxford), and *Public Self and Private Self* (Springer-Verlag) appeared in 1986.

Many scholars have long recognized that the effect of the group on the individual is a double-edged sword. Sometimes becoming lost in the crowd has been viewed as the greatest stumbling block to human progress. For example, Charles Horton Cooley once said that "to lose the sense of a separate, productive, resisting self, would be to melt and merge and cease to be" (1902, p. 164). At other times, being the center of attention has been viewed as the most severe impediment. For example, Tsengtse said, "What ten eyes are beholding and what ten hands are pointing to—isn't it frightening?" (Yutang, 1938, p. 144).

Becoming lost in the crowd or being the center of attention: Either extreme can have both detrimental and beneficial effects on the

AUTHORS' NOTE: The authors would like to thank Sidney Arenson, Marilynn Brewer, George R. Goethals, Li-tze Hu, and Phil Shaver for comments on an earlier draft of this chapter.

individual (see Anderson, 1978; Buys, 1978). In this chapter, we will develop a framework that attempts to integrate previous research on group composition effects, self-attention processes, and performance. We identify three general classes of group effects on performance: social loafing, social facilitation, and social impairment. Three particular species of social impairment are described: diving, withdrawing, and choking. We review the results of previous research that lends support to this theoretical integration. We conclude by considering the practical, social engineering implications of this approach to group effects on performance.

GROUP COMPOSITION EFFECTS ON SELF-ATTENTION PROCESSES

Self-attention theory (Carver, 1979, 1984; Carver & Scheier, 1981; Duval & Wicklund, 1972; Wicklund, 1980, 1982) is concerned with the self-regulation processes that occur when one is the figure of one's attentional focus. According to self-attention theory, self-awareness makes people concerned about matching their present behavior to salient standards. Becoming focally aware of one's self makes one more likely to recognize discrepancies between present states (e.g., current performance) and salient standards of behavior (e.g., excellence in performance). Carver and Scheier (1981) described a variety of intentional behaviors in terms of attempts to match present states to salient behavioral standards. Self-regulation was conceptualized as intentional attempts to reduce discrepancies between salient behavioral standards and present behavioral states.

Much recent research has examined the effect of the group on the individual from the perspective of self-attention theory (Diener, 1980; Duval & Siegal, 1978; Mullen, 1983, 1987; Wegner & Guiliano, 1982; Wicklund, 1980, 1982). This work reveals that members of a heterogeneous group become more self-attentive as the relative size of their own subgroup decreases. In a picture, the small central object that captures attention emerges as the perceptual figure or object of attention; everything else fades back into the ground (Coran, Porac, & Ward, 1979; Koffka, 1935; Riley, 1958). In an analogous way, the smaller subgroup in a group tends to emerge as the perceptual figure of the people in the group. And the more distinct that smaller subgroup, the more it stands out (Campbell, 1958; Diener, 1980; Duval & Siegal, 1978; Gerard & Hoyt, 1974; McGuire & McGuire, 1982; Taylor, Fiske,

Etcoff, & Ruderman, 1978; Wegner & Schaefer, 1978; Wicklund, 1980; Ziller, 1964).

Other-Total Ratio

A simple algorithm called the Other-Total Ratio has been proposed as a means of characterizing the effects of group composition on self-attention. The Other-Total Ratio is defined as the number of people in the other subgroup divided by the total number of people in the group. As one's own subgroup becomes proportionally smaller, the Other-Total Ratio becomes proportionally larger. Thus members of the smaller subgroup are more likely to become the center of their own attentional focus, and to become more concerned with matching their performance to salient standards of behavior. Conversely, members of the larger subgroup are more likely to become lost in the crowd or deindividuated (Diener, 1980; Festinger, Pepitone, & Newcomb, 1952; Simmel, 1950; Zimbardo, 1970), to focus upon the other subgroup (and not themselves), and to become less concerned with matching their performance to behavioral standards.

Research has demonstrated the utility of the Other-Total Ratio for characterizing the effects of group composition in a variety of settings. For example, the mediating mechanism of self-attention has been demonstrated to vary as a function of the Other-Total Ratio is a variety of laboratory settings (Mullen, 1983, Studies 1 and 2), in the context of classroom discussions (Mullen, 1985a), and even in the discussions of Nixon, Haldeman, and Ehrlichman in the Watergate transcripts (Mullen & Peaugh, 1986). Further, the Other-Total Ratio has been demonstrated to be a useful predictor of such diverse social behaviors as conformity, prosocial behavior, social loafing, and antisocial behavior (Mullen, 1983, Studies 3-6, respectively), participation in religious groups (Mullen, 1984; Mullen & Hu, 1986), participation in discussions (Mullen, 1985a; Mullen & Peaugh, 1986), verbal disfluencies among stutterers (Mullen, 1985b, 1986b), atrocities committed by lynch mobs (Mullen, 1986a), resource use in the commons dilemma (Mullen & Chapman, 1987), and organizational productivity (Mullen, Johnson, & Drake, in press).

Thus group contexts affect the extent to which the individual becomes concerned with matching to standards of excellence in performance by affecting the extent to which the individual becomes self-aware. When individuals are lost in the crowd, or deindividuated, they are less likely to assess what they are currently doing against what they should be doing. This can lead to a failure to self-regulate. On the other hand, when individuals become the center of attention (and therefore self-attentive) they are more likely to notice differences between what they are currently doing and what they should be doing. Under some conditions, such self-attention leads to successful self-regulation, but under other conditions it leads to unsuccessful self-regulation. We will now consider a framework that predicts how these various types of effects will occur.

GENERAL CLASSES OF GROUP EFFECTS ON PERFORMANCE: SOCIAL LOAFING, SOCIAL FACILITATION, AND SOCIAL IMPAIRMENT

These three broad categories of group performance effects can be explained in terms of the interaction between self-attention due to group composition and a family of moderator variables. This interaction and the three classes of group effects on performance are presented in Figure 8.1.

Social Loafing

Low self-awareness caused by group settings can lead to poor performance. Social loafing can be viewed as an unintentional decrement in performance that occurs under conditions of a low Other-Total Ratio. The moderator variables that influence social facilitation and social impairment do not influence social loafing, because the self-regulation process never even begins. In social loafing, the individual is lost in the crowd (i.e., non-self aware, or deindividuated) and does not consider levels of performance and salient standards of excellence. Examples of social loafing can be found in Campbell (1952); Egarbladh (1976); Harkins, Latané, and Williams (1980); Williams, Harkins, and Latané, (1981); Ingham, Levinger, Graves, & Peckham (1974); Kerr and Bruun (1981); Kravitz and Martin (1986); and Mullen, Johnson, and Drake (in press). In each case, people performing while lost in the crowd (i.e., immersed in some proportionately larger performing subgroup) exhibited performance decrements. The repeated finding that increasing the performer's identifiability reduces social loafing is consistent with this rationale: Making the individual's performance contribution more identifiable vitiates the perceptual sense of "being lost in the crowd,"

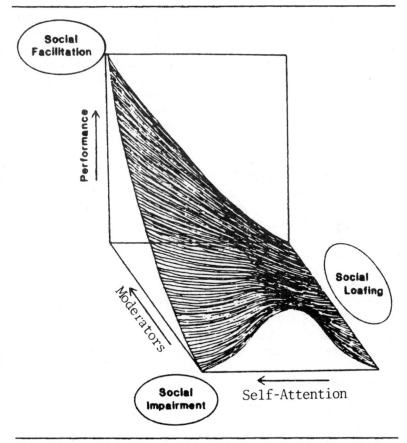

Figure 8.1 Three General Classes of Group Effects on Performance, Resulting from the Interaction Between Self-Attention and Moderator Variables

which would otherwise occur in the large group of performers (e.g., Gear, Marsh, & Sergent, 1985; Nida & Majanovich, 1986; Sweeney, 1973; Williams, Harkins, & Latané, 1981). Social loafing represents what Carver and Scheier (1981) describe as the absence of regulation.

Social Facilitation

High self-awareness caused by group settings can improve performance. Social facilitation can be viewed as an enhancement in performance that occurs under conditions of a high Other-Total Ratio, and under favorable conditions of various moderator variables. In such settings, the individual is not lost in the crowd, but is instead the center of attention. The individual is therefore quite concerned with discrepancies between present levels of performance and salient standards of excellence in performance. Moreover, there is nothing about the group, the individual, or the task that can interfere with or subvert efforts to match one's performance to standards of excellence.

Examples of such social facilitation effects can be found in Bergum and Lehr (1963); Carver and Scheier (1981); Markus (1978); Sasfy and Okun (1974); Strube, Miles, and French (1981); Travis (1925); and Worringham and Messick (1983). In each case, people performing while being the center of attention (i.e., performing in front of some proportionately larger observing subgroup) exhibited better performance. The group made people self-attentive, leading to self-regulation that in turn benefited performance. Social facilitation represents what Carver and Scheier (1981) have described as self-regulation.

Taken together, social facilitation and social loafing seem to suggest that performance is good when groups cause high self-attention (indexed by a high Other-Total Ratio) and poor when groups cause low self-attention (indexed by a low Other-Total Ratio). Such a generalization is oversimplified, however. Under certain circumstances, performance can be poor when groups engender high self-attention.

Social Impairment

Social impairment refers to a class of performance decrements that occurs under conditions of a high Other-Total Ratio and under unfavorable conditions of the various moderator variables. In this type of performance setting, the individual is the center of attention and is concerned with discrepancies between present performance and standards of excellence. However, certain moderator variables pertaining to the group, the individual, or the task interfere with efforts to perform well. Social impairment represents what Carver and Scheier (1981) described as misregulation.

SPECIES OF SOCIAL IMPAIRMENT: DIVING, WITHDRAWING, AND CHOKING

Table 8.1 presents three general categories of moderator variables and the associated three species of social impairment. The three types of social impairment are likely to occur under the same group composition

TABLE 8.1
Species of Social Impairment

Type	Source	Moderators
Diving	Group	Group defines standards of excellence as inappropriate for all group members Group defines standards of excellence as inappropriate for particular performing individual
Withdrawing	Individual	Individual developes poor outcome expectancy Individual perceives low performance–outcome instrumentality Individual perceives personal inequity
Choking	Task	Task involves a large skill component Task involves incompatible standards of excellence

conditions and may appear to be identical because each refers to a performance decrement. However, the three species of social impairment involve the influences of different moderators.

DIVING

Diving, or taking a dive, refers to an intentional decision not to perform well, caused by the group's devaluation of a salient standard of excellence. One may recognize a discrepancy between current performance and excellence in performance, but also recognize that excellence is deemed inappropriate by the group. Williams (1984) observed that the influence of a cohesive primary group could either support or oppose the norms of some higher authority. Diving occurs when the influence of the primary group is in opposition to the norms of some higher authority.

There are actually two types of diving. On the one hand, the group may deem excellence to be inappropriate for anyone in the group. For example, in Roethlisberger and Dickson's (1939) discussion of the Hawthorne studies, the work group easily established the maximum level of performance that group members could attain (despite management's efforts to increase output). Anyone who performed above this level was accused of rate busting and was subjected to sanctions. Rommetveit (1955) coined the term "norm sending" to refer to the process whereby the group legitimizes or delegitimizes particular standards of behavior. Berkowitz and Levy (1956) described how members of B29 flight crews performed in accordance with their group's norm, regardless of the broader goals of the military command. In another example drawn from organizational psychology, Kelly and Nicholson (1980) referred to this type of social diving production slow-down as a form of "unorganized conflict." Kett (1977) described how student populations have sometimes developed norms of anti-intellec-tuality, making it less likely that a student would engage in intellectual classroom behavior.

The second type of diving can occur when the standard of excellence is deemed inappropriate for a specific individual. For example, the group may express expectations of poorer performance from the token representative of a lower-status group. For example, a lone female in an otherwise all-male group might exhibit this type of diving (Garland & Price, 1977; Izraeli, 1984; Kanter, 1977; Laws, 1975; Lord & Saenz, 1985; Mamola, 1979; Mullen, 1983). Diving is also likely to occur as a result of the delegitimization of standards of excellence for individuals of minority ethnic background (Dutton, 1976; Hall & Hall, 1976; Katz, 1964; Lefcourt & Ladwig, 1965; Webster & Driskell, 1978). Grush's (1978) study is consistent with this notion of diving. Subjects previously identified as competitive engaged in competition in front of an audience of previous winners, but refrained from competition in front of an audience of "human relations people." Finally, Baumeister, Cooper, and Skib (1979) found that subjects were willing to "take a dive to make a point." That is, subjects performed poorly if they expected that poor performances demonstrated some other socially desirable attribute.

WITHDRAWING

Withdrawing refers to a self-attention-based performance decrement caused by intentional reduction of effort by an individual. Withdrawing differs from social loafing in that withdrawing is an intentional product of self-regulation under conditions of high self-attention, whereas social loafing is an unintentional product of the absence of self-regulation under conditions of low self-attention. One important cause of with-drawing is a poor outcome expectancy, that is, a low subjective probability of success. A poor outcome expectancy can result from failure experiences or from experiences with difficult and complicated tasks (Carver & Blaney, 1977; Carver, Blaney, & Scheier, 1979, 1980; Carver & Scheier, 1981; Good, 1973; Steenbarger & Aderman, 1979) or from feedback that highlights the lack of contingency between effort and success (Feinberg, Miller, Mathews, & Denig, 1979). Withdrawing may also result from low performance-outcome instrumentality (Ban-dura, 1977; Lawler & Porter, 1967), perceived personal inequity regarding further effort on a difficult task that is unlikely to pay off (Seta & Seta, 1982; see also Tomie's 1976 discussion of the learned laziness phenomenon). Despite the many differences between these various intraindividual moderators, in each case withdrawing can be viewed as a rational, cost-effective cessation of effort on the part of a self-attentive performer in situations where performance is perceived as futile or valueless.

CHOKING

Choking refers to a self-attention based performance decrement that can be attributed to something about the task. Groups can engender audience pressure in two ways. First, the mere presence of other people as spectators constitutes pressure (Baumeister, 1984; Baumeister & Showers, in press; Tice, Buder, & Baumeister, 1985). Second, audience expectations for success can further contribute to audience pressure (Baumeister, Hamilton, & Tice, 1985; Baumeister & Steinhilber, 1984). Audience pressure creates self-attention that impairs performance on complicated, difficult, or skillful tasks.

In choking, the self-regulation efforts oriented toward performing well backfire and produce poor performance. For this reason, choking has been regarded as a paradoxical effect. Increases in self-attention can generate continual or exaggerated comparisons of performance to behavioral standards (e.g., Carver & Scheier, 1981). Normally, increased attention to one's performance and task feedback may provide valuable information regarding the accuracy of motor responses, the imminence of successful task completion, and so on. However, increased attention to performance and task feedback on complicated, well-learned, or highly skillful tasks may interfere with their smooth execution (Baumeister, 1984; Baumeister & Steinhilber, 1984; Berger, Carli, Garcia, & Brady, 1982; Carver & Scheier, 1981; Kimble & Perlmuter, 1970; Langer & Imber, 1979; Baumeister & Showers, in press).

Choking would be more likely to occur on tasks involving a large skill component (e.g., classical piano, playing baseball) than on tasks based more directly on sheer effort (e.g., letter copying tasks, vigilance tasks). Paulus (e.g., Paulus & Cornelius, 1974; Paulus, Shannon, Wilson, & Boone, 1972) has demonstrated that audiences produce less performance decrement in the performance of beginning gymnasts than in the performance of skilled gymnasts. Also, Forgas, Brennan, Howe, Kane, and Sweet (1980) have similarly observed exaggerated choking effects among skilled squash players, relative to unskilled players.

For some complicated tasks, standards of excellence may be incompatible. For example, on simple letter copying tasks, speed of performance will be inversely related to accuracy. If performance is measured on only one standard, the self-attentive performer might appear to exhibit a performance decrement relative to a non-self-attentive performer, because the self-attentive performer may be increasing performance along one dimension (e.g., accuracy of copying) at the cost of performance along the other, more critical dimension (e.g., speed) (see Carver & Scheier's 1981 discussion of Leibling & Shaver's 1973 work from this perspective). This possibility suggests an intriguing view of mastery that is consistent with some recent conceptualizations (e.g., Dreyfus & Dreyfus, 1986): Mastery may involve the ability to recognize which elements of task performance are critical and to increase performance along these dimensions at the cost of other, less critical elements.

Thus the group can lead to enhanced or imparied performance, depending upon attributes of the group, the individual, and the task. When the individual is lost in the crowd, the self-regulation processes necessary for successful task performance never even begins, and performance is impaired (social loafing). When the individual is the center of attention, low levels of performance may still occur (social impairment) if the group defines successful task performance as inappropriate (diving), the individual believes performance attempts to be futile or valueless (withdrawing), or, self-awareness interferes with the skillful performance of the task (choking). If the individual is the center of attention, and if none of these limiting conditions is present to interfere with successful task performance, then the individual will be likely to engage in the normal self-regulation process leading to successful task performance (social facilitation).

CONCLUSION

Self-attention theory's integration of group effects on performance is consistent with previous research on the effect of the group on the individual. It should be recognized that alternative theoretical perspectives can be brought to bear upon group effects on performance. For example, the drive-arousal hypothesis (Baron, 1986; Zajonc, 1965) or the notion of concern with evaluation (Harkins & Szymanski, this volume) might also be invoked to account for social facilitation, social impairment, and social loafing effects. Our concern in the present chapter has been to develop a general model from the perspective of self-attention theory. Future research might be more effectively directed toward critical tests between such competing or complementary models.

Consider the implications of this perspective from a social engineering standpoint. If one is concerned with improving poor performance in a group setting, a number of different recommendations can be proffered, depending upon the type of poor performance being considered. If one is interested in decreasing social loafing, the first step would be to somehow increase the performing individuals' levels of self-attention. As noted earlier, such increases have been accomplished experimentally by making the performing individual identifiable and linking the individual to his or her own performance. This eliminates the sense of being lost in the crowd and makes it more likely that the individual will begin the self-regulation processes necessary for successful performance.

If the poorly performing individual is not lost in the crowd, the first step would be to determine whether the social impairment represents diving, withdrawing, or choking. Once the species of social impairment has been identified, one knows whether to concentrate one's effort on the group, the individual, or the task. For diving, one might persuade the observing group that excellence in performance is a legitimate behavioral standard for the performing individual. Diving is probably the most difficult type of impairment to counteract. It requires coordinated change of attitude among members of a group that may be based on a pervasive, shared, motivated set of beliefs (e.g., antagonism toward a manipulative company management; prejudice regarding members of an out-group). Research on the contact hypothesis (see Miller & Brewer, 1984; Stephan, this volume) reveals that changing this type of belief is difficult and time-consuming at best.

For withdrawing, one might have to persuade the performing individual that he or she can perform the task successfully and/or that successful performance will be worth the effort. Applied social technologists (coaches, priests, parents) have long appreciated the potential value of prearranged success experiences, pep talks, and bribes. However, it is important to recognize that these overused tactics are likely to be effective only for the withdrawing species of social impairment. A pep talk would be a misguided strategy if the social impairment under consideration is diving on the part of a token black member of a group otherwise composed of prejudiced whites.

For choking, it would often be difficult to modify the task itself. Many real world tasks require some integration of multiple, conflicting standards into a skillful performance on a task that cannot be modified in its basic structure. An alternative strategy would be to reduce the performer's self-attention. Manipulating group composition by increasing the number of performers and/or decreasing the number of observers is likely to be effective in reducing choking. For example, verbal disfluencies among stutterers can to be alleviated by having the stutters speak in unison with other speakers (Mullen, 1985b). Similarly, a parlor entertainment popular in England during the 1920s and 1930's was "choral speaking." Gullan (1931) argued that choral speaking could reduce a disruptive self-consciousness, leading to an improvement in speech and tone.

Just as it may be difficult to change the nature of the task, it may often be difficult to change the composition of the group. In such instances, it would be desirable to teach the performing individual how to cope and perform effectively despite high self-attention. For example, advice sometimes given to the stage-frightened concert pianist is to "remember, there is only you and the piano." There is evidence that individuals who are chronically in a state of high self-attention are less prone to choking than others (Baumeister, 1984). Probably, their long-term experience with self-attention has allowed them to learn how to cope with its disruptive effects. Other potential therapeutic interventions for choking are noted by Baumeister and Showers (in press).

It should be recognized that the integration developed in this chapter is not necessarily limited in application to performance settings. Presumably, any type of social behavior that involves these basic self-regulation processes could be analyzed in the same way. For example, consider the recent research interest in the commons dilemma: Individuals harvest points from a common pool that is only slowly replenished. When lost in the crowd of other harvesting subjects, the individual inevitably harvests more than when alone, eventually leading to the depletion of the pool (Hardin, 1968; Olson, 1965). This squanderous use of resources represents one form of "social loafing" in the commons dilemma (Allison & Messick, 1984; Brewer & Kramer, 1985; Mullen & Chapman, 1987). The more conservative use of resources on the part of the subject confronted with many experimenters represents a form of "social facilitation" in the commons dilemma (Mullen & Chapman, 1987). A form of "social impairment" in the commons dilemma has yet to be demonstrated. However, it is easy to imagine the lone, self-focused subject, confronted with a group of observing experimenters, who still squanderously overharvests in belief that cautious and conservative use of the resource pool is deemed inappropriate by the observing experimenters (diving), or that attempts to maintain the pool through conservative harvesting will be futile (withdrawing), or who inadequately balances the two incompatible standards of "harvest large amounts now to maximize immediate individual gain" versus "harvest small amounts now to maintain the resource pool for as long as possible" (choking). The present framework should apply equally well to an understanding of self-regulation processes in such diverse social phenomena as persuasion, prosocial behavior, and transgressive behavior. While it remains for future efforts to pursue such extensions, present applications of self-attention theory are encouraging.

REFERENCES

Allison, S. T., & Messick, D. M. (1985). Effects of experience on performance in a replenishable resource trap. *Journal of Personality and Social Psychology, 49,* 943-948.

Anderson, L. R. (1978). Groups would do better without humans. *Personality and Social Psychology Bulletin, 4,* 557-558.

Bandura, A. (1977). Self-efficacy: Toward a unifying theory of behavioral change. *Psychological Review, 84,* 191-215.

Baron, R. S. (1985). Distraction-Conflict Theory: Progress and problems. In L. Berkowitz (Ed.), *Advances in experimental social psychology* (Vol. 19, pp. 1-40). New York: Academic Press.

Baumeister, R. F. (1984). Choking under pressure: Self-consciousness and paradoxical effects of incentives on skillful performance. *Journal of Personality and Social Psychology, 46,* 610-620.

Baumeister, R. F., Cooper, J., & Skib, B. A. (1979). Inferior performance as a selective response to expectancy: Taking a dive to make a point. *Journal of Personality and Social Psychology, 37,* 424-432.

Baumeister, R. F., Hamilton, J. C., & Tice, D. (1985). Public vs. private expectancy of success: Confidence booster or performance pressure? *Journal of Personality and Social Psychology, 48,* 1447-1457.

Baumeister, R. F., & Showers, C. J. (in press). A review of paradoxical performance effects: Choking under pressure in sports and mental tests. *European Journal of Social Psychology.*

Baumeister, R. F., & Steinhilber, A. (1984). Paradoxical effects of supportive audiences on performance under pressure: The home killer choke effect in sports championships. *Journal of Personality and Social Psychology, 47,* 85-93.

Berger, S. M., Carli, L. C., Garcia, R., & Brady, J. J. (1982). Audience effects in anticipatory learning: A comparison of drive and practice-inhibition analyses. *Journal of Personality and Social Psychology, 42,* 478-486.

Bergum, B. O., & Lehr, D. (1963). Effects of authoritarianism on vigilance performance. *Journal of Applied Psychology, 47,* 75-77.

Berkowitz, L., & Levy, B. I. (1956). Pride in group performance and group-task motivation. *Journal of Abnormal and Social Psychology, 53,* 300-306.

Brewer, M. B., & Kramer, R. (1985). *Choice behavior in social dilemmas: Effects of social identity, group size, and decision framing.* Unpublished manuscript, University of California at Los Angeles.

Buys, C. J. (1978). Humans would do better without groups. *Personality and Social Psychology Bulletin, 4,* 123-125.

Campbell, D. T. (1958). Common fate, similarity, and other indices of the status of aggregates of persons as social entities. *Behavioral Science, 3,* 14-25.

Campbell, H. (1952). Group incentive payment schemes: The effects of a lack of understanding and group size. *Occupational Psychology, 26,* 15-21.

Carver, C. S. (1979). A cybernetic model of self-attention processes. *Journal of Personality and Social Psychology, 37,* 1251-1281.

Carver, C. S. (1984). *Cybernetics: Meta-theoretical implications for social psychology.* Paper presented at the annual meeting of the Society of Southeastern Social Psychologists.

Carver, C. S., & Blaney, P. H. (1977). Perceived arousal, focus of attention and avoidance behavior. *Journal of Abnormal Psychology, 86,* 154-162.

Carver, C. S., Blaney, P. H., & Scheier, M. F. (1979). Focus of attention, chronic expectancy and responses to a feared stimulus. *Journal of Personality and Social Psychology, 37,* 1185-1195.

Carver, C. S., Blaney, P. H., & Scheier, M. F. (1980). Reassertion and giving up: The interactive role of self-attention and outcome expectancy. *Journal of Personality and Social Psychology, 37,* 1859-1870.

Carver, C. S., & Scheier, M. F. (1981). *Attention and self-regulation: A control theory approach to human behavior.* New York: Springer-Verlag.

Cooley, C. H. (1902). *Human nature and the social order.* New York: Scribner.

Coren, S., Porac, C., & Ward, L. M. (1979). *Sensation and perception.* New York: Academic Press.

Diener, E. (1980). Deindividuation: The absence of self-awareness and self-regulation in group members. In P. B. Paulus (Ed.), *Psychology of group influence* (pp. 209-242). Hillsdale, NJ: Lawrence Erlbaum.

Dreyfus, H., & Dreyfus, S. (1986). *Mind over machine.* New York: Free Press.

Dutton, D. G. (1976). Tokenism, reverse discrimination, and egalitarianism in interracial behavior. *Journal of Social Issues, 32,* 93-107.

Duval, S., & Siegal, K. (1978). *Some determinants of objective self-awareness: Quantitative novelty.* Paper presented at the annual meeting of the American Psychological Association, Toronto, Ontario.

Duval, S., & Wicklund, R. A. (1972). *A theory of objective self-awareness.* New York: Academic Press.

Egarbladh, T. (1976). The function of group size and ability level on solving a multidimensional complementary task. *Journal of Personality and Social Psychology, 34,* 805-808.

Feinberg, R. A., Miller, F. G., Mathews, G., & Denig, G. (1979). *The social facilitation of learned helplessness.* Paper presented at the annual meeting of the Midwestern Psychological Association, Chicago, IL.

Festinger, L., Pepitone, A., & Newcomb, T. (1952). Some consequences of deindividuation in a group. *Journal of Abnormal and Social Psychology, 47,* 382-389.

Forgas, J. P., Brennan, G., Howe, S., Kane, J. F., & Sweet, S. (1980). Audience effects on squash players' performance. *Journal of Social Psychology, 111,* 41-47.

Garland, H., & Price, K. H. (1977). Attitudes toward women in management and attributions for their success and failure in managerial positions. *Journal of Applied Psychology, 62,* 29-33.

Gear, T. E., Marsh, N. R., & Sergent, P. (1985). Semi-automated feedback and team behavior. *Human Relations, 38,* 707-721.

Gerard, H. B., & Hoyt, M. F. (1974). Distinctiveness of social categorization and attitude toward ingroup members. *Journal of Personality and Social Psychology, 29,* 836-842.

Good, K. J. (1973. Social facilitation effects of performance anticipation, evaluation, and response competition on free associations. *Journal of Personality and Social Psychology, 28,* 270-275.

Grush, J.E . (1978). Audiences can inhibit or facilitate competitive behavior. *Personality and Social Psychology Bulletin, 4,* 119-122.

Gullan, M. (1931). *Choral speaking.* Boston, MA: Expression.

Hall, S. F., & Hall, D. T. (1976). Effects of job incumbents' race and sex on evaluation of managerial performance. *Academy of Management Journal, 19,* 476-481.

Hardin, G. (1968). The tragedy of the commons. *Science, 162,* 1243-1248.

Harkins, S., Latané, B., & Williams, K. (1980). Social loafing: Allocating effort or taking it easy? *Journal of Experimental Social Psychology, 16,* 457-465.

Ingham, A. G., Levinger, G., Graves, J., & Peckham, V. (1974). The Ringelmann effect: Studies of group size and group performance. *Journal of Experimental Social Psychology, 10,* 371-384.

Izraeli, D. N. (1984). The attitudinal effects of gender mix in union committees. *Industrial and Labor Relations Review, 37,* 212-221.

Kanter, R. M. (1977). Some effects of proportions on group life: Skewed sex ratios and responses to token women. *American Journal of Sociology, 82,* 465-490.

Katz, I. (1964). Review of evidence relating to the effects of desegregation on the intellectual performance of Negroes. *American Psychologist, 19,* 381-399.

Kelly, J., & Nicholson, N. (1980). Strikes and other forms of industrial action. *Industrial Relations Journal, 11,* 20-31.

Kerr, N. L., & Braun, S. E. (1981). Ringelmann revisited: Alternative explanations for the social loafing effect. *Personality and Social Psychology Bulletin, 7,* 224-231.

Kett, J. F. (1977). *Rites of passage: Adolescence in America 1790 to the present.* New York: Basic Books.

Kimble, G., & Perlmuter, L. (1970). The problem of volition. *Psychological Review, 77,* 361-384.

Koffka, K. (1935). *Principles of gestalt psychology.* New York: Harcourt, Brace.

Kravitz, D. A., & Martin, B. (1986). Ringelmann rediscovered: The original article. *Journal of Personality and Social Psychology, 50,* 936-941.

Langer, E., & Imber, L. G. (1979). When practice makes imperfect: Debilitating effects of overlearning. *Journal of Personality and Social Psychology, 37,* 2014-2024.

Lawler, E. E., & Porter, L. W. (1967). The effect of performance on job satisfaction. *Industrial Relations, 7,* 20-28.

Laws, J. L. (1975). The psychology of tokenism: An analysis. *Sex Roles, 1,* 51-67.

Lefcourt. H., & Ladwig, G. (1965). The effect of reference group upon Negroes' task persistence in a biracial competitive game. *Journal of Personality and Social Psychology, 1*, 668-671.

Liebling, B. A., & Shaver. P. (1973). Evaluation, self-awareness, and task performance. *Journal of Experimental Social Psychology, 9,* 298-306.

Lord, C. G., & Saenz, D. S. (1985). Memory deficits and memory surfeits: Differential cognitive consequences of tokenism for tokens and observers. *Journal of Personality and Social Psychology, 49,* 918-926.

Mamola, C. (1979). Women in mixed groups: Some research findings. *Small Group Behavior: 10,* 431-440.

Markus, H. (1978). The effect of mere presence on social facilitation. *Journal of Experimental Social Psychology, 14,* 389-397.

McGuire, W. J., & McGuire, C. V. (1982). Significant others in self space: Sex differences and developmental trends in the social self. In J. Suls (Ed.). *Psychological perspectives on the self* (Vol. 1, pp. 71-96). Hillsdale, NJ: Lawrence Erlbaum.

Miller, N., & Brewer, M. B. (Eds.). (1984). *Groups in contact: The psychology of desegregation.* New York: Academic Press.

Mullen, B. (1983). Operationalizing the effect of the group on the individual: A self-attention perspective. *Journal of Experimental Social Psychology, 19,* 295-322.

Mullen, B. (1984). Participation in religious groups as a function of group composition: A self-attention perspective. *Journal of Applied Social Psychology, 14,* 509-518.

Mullen, B. (1985a). *Participation in class discussions: A self-attention perspective.* Paper presented at the annual meeting of the American Educational Research Association, Chicago, IL.

Mullen, B. (1985b). *The effects of multiple subgroups on the individual: A self-attention perspective.* Paper presented at the 56th annual meeting of the Eastern Psychological Association, Boston, MA.

Mullen, B. (1986a). Atrocity as a function of lynch mob composition: A self-attention perspective. *Personality and Social Psychology Bulletin, 12,* 187-197.

Mullen, B. (1986b). Stuttering, audience size, and the Other-Total Ratio: A self-attention perspective. *Journal of Applied Social Psychology, 16,* 141-151.

Mullen, B. (1987). Self-attention theory. In B. Mullen & G. R. Goethals (Eds.), *Theories of group behavior* (pp. 125-146). New York: Springer-Verlag.

Mullen, B., & Chapman, J. (1987). *Resource use in the commons dilemma as a function of group composition: A self-attention perspective.* Paper presented at the 58th annual meeting of the Eastern Psychological Association, Arlington, VA.

Mullen, B., & Hu, L. (1986). *Group composition, the self, and religious experience: East and West.* Paper presented at the British Psychological Society's International Conference on Eastern Approaches to Self and Mind, Cardiff, Wales.

Mullen, B., Johnson, D. A., & Drake, S. D. (in press). Organizational productivity as a function of group composition: A self-attention perspective. *Journal of Social Psychology.*

Mullen, B., & Peaugh, S. (1986). *Focus of attention in group settings: A self-attention perspective.* Unpublished manuscript, Syracuse University, Syracuse, NY.

Nida, S. A., & Majanovich, M. (1986). *The effects of group size and identifiability on cognitive effort.* Paper presented at the annual meeting of the Midwestern Psychological Society, Chicago, IL.

Olson, M. (1965). *The logic of collective action.* Cambridge, MA: Harvard University Press.

Paulus, P. B., & Cornelius, W. L. (1974). An analysis of gymnastic performance under conditions of practice and spectator observation. *Research Quarterly, 45,* 56-63.

Paulus, P., Shannon, J. C., Wilson, D. L., & Boone, T. D. (1972). The effect of spectator presence on gymnastic performance in a field situation. *Psychonomic Science, 29,* 88-90.

Riley, D. A. (1958). The nature of the effective stimulus in animal discrimination learning. *Psychological Review, 65,* 1-7.

Roethlisberger, F. J., & Dickson, W. J. (1939). *Management and the worker.* Cambridge, MA: Harvard University Press.

Rommetveit, R. (1955). *Social norms and roles: explorations in the psychology of enduring social pressures.* Minneapolis, MN: University of Minnestota Press.

Sasfy, J., & Okun, M. (1974). Form of evaluation and audience expertness as joint determinants of audience effects. *Journal of Experimental Social Psychology, 10,* 461-467.

Seta, J. J., & Seta, C. E. (1982). Personal equity: An intrapersonal comparator system analysis of reward value. *Journal of Personality and Social Psychology, 43,* 222-235.

Simmel, G. (1950). *The sociology of Georg Simmel* (K. Wolff, trans.). New York: Free Press.

Steenbarger, B. N., & Aderman, D. (1979). Objective self-awareness as a nonaversive state: Effect of anticipatory discrepancy reduction. *Journal of Personality, 47,* 330-339.

Strube, M. J., Miles, M. E., & Finch, W. H. (1981). The social facilitation of a simple task: Field tests of alternative explanations. *Personality and Social Psychology Bulletin, 7,* 701-707.

Sweeney, J. (1973). An experimental investigation of the free-rider problem. *Social Science Research, 2,* 277-292.

Taylor, S. E., Fiske, S. T. Etcoff, N. L., & Rudermanm A. J. (1978). Categorical and contextual bases of person memory and stereotyping. *Journal of Personality and Social Psychology, 36,* 778-793.

Tice, D., Buder, J., & Baumeister, R. F. (1985). Development of self-consciousness: At what age does audience pressure disrupt performance? *Adolescence, 20,* 301-305.

Tomie, A. (1976). Retardation of autoshaping control by contextual stimuli. *Science, 192,* 1244-1246.

Travis, L. E. (1925). The effect of a small audience upon eye-hand coordination. *Journal of Abnormal and Social Psychology, 20,* 142-146.

Webster, M., & Driskell, J. E. (1978). Status generalization: A review and some new data. *American Sociological Review, 43,* 220-236.

Wegner, D. M., & Guiliano, T. (1982). The forms of social awareness. In W. Ickes & E. S. Knowles (Eds.), *Personality, roles, and social behavior* (pp. 165-198). New York: Springer-Verlag.

Wegner, D. M., & Schaefer, D. (1978). The concentration of responsibility: An objective self-awareness analysis of group size effects in helping situations. *Journal of Personality and Social Psychology, 36,* 147-155.

Wicklund, R. A. (1980). Group contact and self-focused attention. In P. B. Paulus (Ed.), *Psychology of group influence* (pp. 189-208). Hillsdale, NJ: Lawrence Erlbaum.

Wicklund, R. A. (1982). How society uses self-awareness. In J. Suls (Ed.), *Psychological perspectives on the self* (Vol. 1, pp. 209-230). Hillsdale, NJ: Lawrence Erlbaum.

Williams, K., Harkins, S., & Latané, B. (1981). Identifiability as a deterrent to social loafing: Two cheering experiments. *Journal of Personality and Social Psychology, 40,* 303-311.

Williams, R. (1984). Field observations and surveys in combat zones. *Social Psychology Quarterly, 47,* 186-192.

Worringham, C. J., & Messick, D. M. (1983). Social facilitation of running: An unobtrusive study. *Journal of Social Psychology, 121,* 23-29.

Yutang, L. (1938). *The wisdom of Confuscius.* New York: Modern Library.

Zajonc, R. B. (1965). Social facilitation. *Science, 149,* 269-274.

Ziller, R. C. (1964). Individuation and socialization: A theory of assimilation in large organizations. *Human Relations, 17,* 341-360.

Zimbardo, P. (1970). The human choice: Individuation, reason and order versus deindividuation, impulse, and chaos. In W. J. Arnold & D. Levine (Eds.), *Nebraska symposium of motivation* (Vol. 18, pp. 237-308). Lincoln, NE: University of Nebraska Press.

9

Groups in Organizations
EXTENDING LABORATORY MODELS

DEBORAH GLADSTEIN ANCONA

Deborah Gladstein Ancona received her Ph.D. from Columbia University in 1982 and is Assistant Professor of Organization Studies at the Sloan School, M.I.T. Her research interests include group decision making, group effectiveness, and new product team performance.

This article focuses on task groups in organizations, while much of the research on small groups focuses on the individual. In the individual approach, the group is seen as a setting that shapes individual attitudes, attributions, and decisions. A recent chapter on intergroup relations (Stephan, 1984, p. 599) exemplifies this approach: "First, the level of analysis of a social psychological inquiry into intergroup relations is the individual and his or her relationship with social groups. The primary justification for focusing on the individual level of analysis is that it is the individual's perception of social reality and the processing of this information that influence individual behavior." Missing from this perspective is the study of groups qua groups and how a group interacts with its context.

An alternative focus for small group research is to look from the group boundary outward. An external perspective shifts the focus of research so that (1) the group is the level of analysis, (2) the social context of groups is examined to explain behavior, and (3) the group has an existence and purpose apart from serving as a setting and apart from the individuals who compose it (Pfeffer, 1986).

The external perspective requires a different set of research questions. Rather than "How does the group influence individuals?" the question is "How does the organization influence the group?" The question is not

AUTHOR'S NOTE: The author would like to thank Jeanne Brett, Connie Gersick, Clyde Hendrick, Jane Salk, Edgar Schein and the anonymous reviewers for their help in this paper.

"How do individuals attend to the group and model it?" but "How does the group model and reach out to the organization?" Most significantly, the focus is not solely on intragroup decision making and the impact of roles on group members, but on examining the internal and boundary-spanning roles and decisions that are most appropriate in a particular environment.

This perspective is not new. At the organizational level of analysis, resource dependence, population ecology, and interorganizational theorists have refocused research toward organizations functioning in their environments, rather than merely as settings for managerial functioning (see Aldrich & Pfeffer, 1976; McKelvey, 1982; Whetten, 1983). At the group level, group-environment interactions have played a primary role in several research streams, the Hawthorne studies and studies of intergroup competition, for example (see Homans, 1950; Sherif, 1966). More recent research also reflects an increased interest in the impact of organizational variables on group process and performance (see Goodman, 1986; Hackman, 1983).

Although the perspective is not new, this sort of research has not reached beyond the organizational behavior research community. It may be quite new to the readers of this volume. By pulling together the findings of researchers who are using parts of this perspective, possibly without knowing it, I have tried to see what new insights arise. Also, borrowing from the organizational level of analysis allows new ideas for group theory to emerge. Finally, summarizing and applying the outward-focusing perspective to key group research areas provides a means of integrating prior perspectives with this one.

This paper focuses on how groups function in a setting of external constraints and opportunities. More specifically, it examines ways of analyzing and describing the organization and external task environment, ways in which that environment constrains group behavior, and ways in which the group proactively tries to adapt to, and control, that environment. These new variables have application for old theories of group development and group decision making. They suggest new directions for group research.

Some Limitations and Definitions

To bound the inquiry into the relationship between the group and its environment, we need some definitions. First, we are interested primarily in groups within organizations. A group is a set of interdependent individuals who view themselves as a group, and who have the common goal of producing something (Alderfer, 1976; Goodman, 1986). The "something" could be a new product, service, a policy decision, or a marketing plan.

Group effectiveness is the major output of small-group behavior. Effectiveness has three components: group performance, satisfaction of group-member needs, and the ability of the group to exist over time (Hackman & Morris, 1975). Group effectiveness is judged by the people who use or buy the group's product or service (say, the task assigner or the customer), as well as by the group members themselves.

Group process includes the intragroup and intergroup actions that transform resources into a product. Process includes both the way in which group members interact with one another, and the way in which they interact with those outside the group boundaries. Although many group researchers have emphasized group member interaction, boundary-spanning behaviors are important in the case of organizational task groups that depend on organizational members outside the group for resources, information, or support. Support for this contention comes from a study of a hundred sales teams (Gladstein, 1984) whose members conceptualized process as both internal and external interaction.

The environment of the group is a combination of the organization in which the group is situated and its external task environment. The external task environment consists of entities outside the organizational boundaries that either provide input or receive output from the group. It could include customers, suppliers, competitors, or government agencies that regulate the product the group is working on.

THE EXTERNAL PERSPECTIVE: BORROWING FROM ORGANIZATION THEORISTS

Organization theorists from a variety of theoretical orientations—resource dependence, strategic management, adaptation, and population ecology—have explored the relationship between an organization and its environment. Although their work has a different emphasis from work at the group level, it seems appropriate to review briefly their theories with the aim of borrowing some concepts. Given the limitations of space, the goal of this section is not to describe these orientations fully (see Astley & Van de Ven, 1983, for a thorough review) but to draw out salient contributions to the external perspective.

Resource Dependence

The resource dependence perspective asserts that interdependence with, and uncertainty about, actions of those outside the organization creates uncertainty as to the survival of the organization. Organizations therefore try to manage these external dependencies. They are never completely successful, however, which gives rise to new patterns of dependence and interdependence requiring further management (Pfeffer, 1986). These patterns are a source of intergroup power, because those groups that have resources that are needed and scarce are more powerful (Brett & Rognes, 1986).

From the resource dependence perspective, the most critical determinant of organizational viability is the ability to obtain critical resources (Pfeffer & Salancik, 1978). A quest for control over resources, and a decrease in dependence, is seen as an imperative for all organizations (Ancona & Salk, 1986). Common mechanisms by which organizations deal with their dependence include interlocking directorates, mergers and acquisitions, and joint ventures (see Pennings, 1980; Pfeffer, 1972; Van de Ven & Walker, 1984). These structures serve to co-opt, absorb, or partially absorb interdependence. As an example, a company that depends heavily on a supplier who is consistently late on delivery and poor on quality can acquire the supplier, hence gaining more control over delivery and quality.

Strategic Management

Strategic management theorists, like the resource dependence theorists, posit an environment that is not fixed and immutable; it can be changed and manipulated through reorganization and negotiation to fit the needs of top management (Lorange, 1980). In contrast to the resource dependence perspective that stresses environmental constraints on organizational action, however, the strategic management view stresses the choices and autonomy of individuals in organizations. According to the resource dependence perspective, an organization is constrained in that it must establish and stabilize negotiations with more powerful entities. In contrast, the strategic management school does not view the environment as an objective reality but as an entity that can be enacted to embody the meanings of individuals—particularly those in power (Astley & Van de Ven, 1983). For example, revolutionary factions can be portrayed as traitors or as freedom fighters. This perspective stresses that organizations do not necessarily have to be seen as reactive to the environment; they can be proactive. In fact, they partially create the environment they face.

Adaptation

In contrast to the proactive view of the previous orientations is the adaptation, or system-structural view, which argues that the manager's role is reactive and adaptive. "The manager must perceive, process, and respond to a changing environment and adapt by rearranging internal organizational structure to ensure survival or effectiveness" (Astley & Van de Ven, 1983, p. 248).

For example, managers must match the information-processing capacity of their units with the information-processing requirements of the unit's task. Organizations operating in an expanding or high-growth market have more information-processing requirements than those operating in a stable market. To increase their information-processing capacity, the organizations facing an expanding market have to add employees and hence form new organizational structures (Greiner, 1972). These organizations can adapt to their environment by having more periods of revolutionary, as opposed to evolutionary, change in structures, processes, and people (Romanelli & Tushman, 1986).

Population Ecology

Another organizational perspective is the population ecology model, which ascribes little power to the manager to either act or react. This view stresses the limits of strategic choice and to adaptation. It describes environmental resources as structured in the form of "niches" beyond organizational manipulation. Organizations are at the mercy of their environments—they either fit into a niche or are "selected out" and fail. For example, even if management sees a decline in demand for a particular product and a higher demand for another product, historical precedent and resistance to change limit its ability to adapt (Astley & Van de Ven, 1983). Firms producing this product may differ from one another in various ways. Some may offer high quality, while others offer low price. According to population ecologists, some firms will flourish more in a given environment than others. "Successful" firms are selected by the environment in the sense that some of their ways of organizing and operating will work better in a given environment than another. Here the focus of analysis is not on the organization but on the population of organizations within a given niche.

One of the major things that group theorists can borrow from the population ecology model is the description of the environment. This model argues that certain types of environments exist that reward organizations selectively; some survive, others fail. Aldrich (1979) defines six characteristics of the environment. Environments can be categorized by the degree to which they are rich or lean, homogeneous or heterogeneous, stable or unstable, concentrated or dispersed, there is consensus or dissension, and turbulence or lack thereof. Each characteristic rewards particular ways of behavior. For example, organizations in a lean environment have little access to resources, and hence efficiency in the use of resources is rewarded.

Applying Organization Theory to Groups

I do not intend to argue for the correctness of one organization-environment model over another. In any case, each model represents a "pure" type. In reality, research has tended to show that aspects of several models may operate at once. Taking a middle of the road stance, we will posit that organizations, and groups, neither totally subjectively define (strategic adaptation) nor totally react to their environments (system-structural view). I assume that management has some leeway in creating and defining the group context; it does not simply engineer the correct response to organizational parameters. Similarly, groups operate by certain rules within objective environmental conditions. Managers who want to succeed have choices, but complete disregard for the rules cannot serve their interests. One can claim that one's group is doing wonderful work, daring anyone to prove otherwise, sometimes for long periods of time, but when sales figures slide, reality is quite influential.

The middle-of-the-road stance applies to the role of the environment as well. Here we do not assume either that organization or group survival is determined completely by natural selection procedures (population ecology), or that there is complete voluntary choice of how to proceed (strategic adaptation). Rather, managers choose how to configure resources and approach their environment within the constraints imposed by that environment. Thus we will assume that groups, like organizations, need to (1) manage their dependence on other parts of the organization and task environment, (2) mold or enact parts of their environment, (3) adapt to environmental demands, and (4) watch for being "selected out." While it might be dangerous to move directly from the organization to the group, borrowing some concepts may prove useful. Several implications stand out in applying these new orientations to groups.

First and foremost is the notion that groups, like organizations, can be productive vis-à-vis their environment. In contrast to the standard input-process-output model, which views a group as a function of environmental inputs, a new view emerges: A group often can alter and control the inputs. Rather than the view that the organization endows a group with resources and information that determine group power and productivity is the notion that the group can be a more active player in determining the distribution of resources. Second, in contrast to many group leader and member schema that view the primary determinant of group success to be changes in internal processes (Gladstein, 1984), this model provides a new framework, where the management of external dependence and adaptation to external demands allows success.

Third, the external perspective offers a different set of dimensions by which to categorize the group environment. Some group researchers to date have concentrated on defining the characteristics of a "supportive" environment, one that facilitates group effectiveness (McCormick, 1985). Hackman (1983) postulates that the organization context contributes to effectiveness with rewards and objectives for good performance, availability of task-relevant training and technical consultation, and clear and complete data about performance requirements, constraints, and consequences. Bushe (1986) argues that a supportive environment consists of (1) recognition, (2) responsiveness to the group's requests for information, resources, and action, (3) legitimization of the group's task and process, and (4) expectation of group success. In a study of planned change projects, McCormick (1985) added openness of group influence and consistency in messages sent to the group. From an external point of view, these researchers suggest that an environment can be set up that reduces the group's external dependence and task uncertainty.

The population ecology perspective, on the other hand, provides a very different approach. Its emphasis is not simply on how the environment can provide resources, but also on what aspects of group functioning might be supported and reinforced in environments with a particular configuration of resources. More fundamentally, this perspective does not attempt to reduce uncertainty and dependence but to provide a means of looking at the nature of that dependence and uncertainty. It does not assume that the organization should provide the resources a group needs, but it evaluates the degree of richness in the environment and suggests what that type of environment rewards. Together the two perspectives complement one another. One addresses ways of allocating resources to groups to enhance effectiveness while the other assumes the current array of resources will remain and the group must have the appropriate structure to survive.

To the remaining questions—How actually do groups manage their dependence? What types of organizational environments reward which group structures? What is the relationship of external activity to internal group processes?—organization and group theorists provide some responses.

GROUP-ORGANIZATION INTERACTION

Central to the external perspective is the assumption that groups cannot maintain isolation from the rest of the organization and the task environment, because they depend upon the environment for resources. They must adapt to, model, or be influenced by changing environmental conditions. Therefore, a central activity of groups in context must be reaching out, directing activity outward. One new set of variables introduced by this perspective is the group's external activities. Different theoretical orientations predict different types of external linkages including negotiation, information exchange and scanning, profile management, and buffering.

Dealing with Dependence—Negotiating

We have said that the resource dependence perspective asserts that dependence on, and uncertainty about, actions of those outside the group creates uncertainty as to the survival of the group. Groups must manage these external dependencies. In organizational studies, researchers have described how organizations attempt to deal with their dependence using structures such as interlocking directorates, mergers, and joint ventures (see Pennings, 1980; Pfeffer, 1972; Van de Ven & Walker, 1984). At the group level, there are no perfect correlates to such structures, but researchers may find these ideas helpful in the design of groups. The structures attempt to co-opt or absorb interdependence by changing organizational boundaries. Groups can change their boundaries by exerting control over who is assigned to be in the group, how open or closed group membership will be, and whether group members also spend time in other parts of the organization or task environment (Gladstein & Caldwell, 1985).

As an example, let us examine a new product team that is dependent upon other groups in the organization to get the product designed and produced, say, marketing, manufacturing, and sales. Much as an organization might, the group can try to have its leader serve on important committees in these other functional areas. It can invite marketing or manufacturing personnel to become group members during key periods of interdependence, or it can permanently include in the group all the people it needs from these other areas.

Besides structural mechanisms that lessen external dependence, group researchers have identified process behaviors that groups use to manage that dependence. Brett and Rognes (1986) argue that within the organizational context intergroup conflict is the main interface issue. They assert that conflict occurs when groups that are linked in a power-dependency relationship disagree about the terms of that relationship. This conflict is endemic to organizations that function by transferring resources among specialized, differentiated groups (McCann & Galbraith, 1983). Brett and Rognes go on to say that although the causes of conflict are structural, intergroup negotiation can compensate for structure. The conflict is never resolved, because it is inherent in the system, but negotiation can result in exchange agreements that endure until changes in the environment make them obsolete.

It is important to note that an intergroup transaction is not the same as an interpersonal one, although both take place between individuals. A group member involved in intergroup transactions acts as a representative of the group, in accordance with the group's expectations. The member is not acting solely on an individual agenda (Brett & Rognes, 1986; Pfeffer, 1986).

Structural co-optation or negotiating are necessary for groups to acquire resources under conditions where those possessing the resources have a different preference ordering. The greater the dependence on external entities, the greater the need to absorb the dependence through shifting group boundaries or negotiating a settlement.

Adapting to the External Environment— Information Exchange and Scanning

A second aspect of dealing with the organization and task environment is adapting internal group functioning to meet external demands.

In other words, the group must be able to reach out and adapt to its particular environment by tailoring its responses to the demands of others. The information processing approach is an adaptation model that has been applied at the group, as well as at the organization, level of analysis. It argues that to be effective groups have to deal with work-related uncertainty. Uncertainty creates information processing requirements that the group adapts to by changing its information processing capability. Information collection and exchange is one means to accomplish this adaptation (Allen, 1970; Katz, 1982; Mintzberg, 1973).

At the group level, information collection and exchange have been studied extensively in communication studies in development teams. Research results have demonstrated a strong association between project performance and a high degree of technical communication with sources outside the group but within the organization (Allen, 1970; Farris, 1969). These results did not hold for sources outside the organization, ostensibly because of the difficulty of accurately communicating across organizational boundaries (Allen, 1984). It was discovered, however, that a group could effectively channel external information into the group by means of a gatekeeper. Communication is a two-step process: The gatekeeper first gathers external information, then translates it into useful terms that can be understood by other project members (Allen & Cohen, 1969; Katz & Tushman, 1981).

The information processing approach suggests that groups have to match their information collection and exchange to the level of uncertainty in the environment. An example of matching is the case of development projects communicating outside the organization through a technological gatekeeper, while research project members have direct contact with outside sources. The critical difference between these kinds of projects is that development projects are more difficult for outsiders to understand since they are defined in organizational terms, not universal scientific terms (Allen, Tushman, & Lee, 1979).

While these studies have focused on research and development teams needing to import technical information, organizational researchers have studied a broader set of information flows. Adams (1980) predicted that two types of external information appear to be important to organizational and group functioning. One type is operating information needed for current decision making and coordinating, and it requires focused search. The other form of information is more unpredictable: It is about events that might occur, or that might have relevance to the organization or group if they did occur. To obtain this form of information, scanning the environment is required in addition to focused information exchange. Scanning allows groups to map their environment and note changing demands.

In a study of project group longevity, Katz (1982) found that over time groups tend to have less and less communication outside their borders, leading to isolation from critical sources of new ideas, information, and feedback, resulting in lower performance over time. If, indeed, groups work to develop stable linking mechanisms, and negotiate settlements to deal with external uncertainty and dependence, these may become patterned and routine forms of interaction in which precedent plays a large part (Katz, 1982; Weick, 1969). Over time, as external contingencies change, such reliance on habit and old models of dependence results in poor adaptation. Hence, the scanning process— that is, collection of unpredictable as well as operating information— appears critical for group performance (Adams, 1980).

Strategic Management—Profile Management

The emphasis of the last section was on the input of information from the environment in order to adapt. A group also has the option of exporting information in order to shape external demands and constraints. Adams (1980) spoke of representation as a key boundary process. Representation involves developing and maintaining channels of communication with powerful outsiders in order to shape their beliefs and behaviors. Representation allows a group to take a more proactive approach. A related behavior that has been observed in groups is profile management. Here group members plan and manage the information that they send out to the external world in order to project the image they want others to have of them. Weick (1980) argued that managing eloquence is crucial in shaping how others interpret the behavior that they see. "If leaders can influence what people say to themselves, then they can influence what those same people are thinking" (p. 18). By providing meanings to those outside the group, the group controls their interpretation of what the group is doing.

For example, in *The Soul of a New Machine* (Kidder, 1981), Tom West, the leader of a team designing a computer, presented his computer differently to various groups. By presenting it as insurance (we will have it in case the other one doesn't work) to top management, he is allowed to set up a team that competes with another team in the company. By presenting it as a technical challenge to engineers, he is able to attract the best of them. By not saying anything at all to external competitors, he protects his company. Profile management lets the group influence its environment by shaping the image of itself it wants to present.

How can this need for importing and exporting information be balanced with the group's need to buffer itself from external interference?

Balancing Internal and External Demands—Buffering

The previous sections argued that the group must reach out to adapt to, monitor, and change the organizational environment. Included in deciding when and how to reach out is deciding when not to. Thus, when Adams (1980) defined classes of boundary activities, he included buffering: protecting the organization from external threat and pressure. While externally oriented activity such as negotiating and scanning helps the group to deal with demands, constraints, and opportunities from the outside, the external activity may hinder internal functions of coordinating group member effort and building a group culture that supports individual needs and fosters commitment to the group task (Parsons, 1960; Lyden, 1975).

Buffering may be adaptive or maladaptive. It is adaptive to the extent that it is used as a short-term tactic to prevent overload and/or to buy time for the group to get its internal functions running more efficiently (Adams, 1980). It is maladaptive if it is a long-term and sole response to external threat (Janis, 1972; Staw, Sandelands, & Dutton, 1981). Long-term isolation, for example, can lead groups to become more and more out of touch with new environmental contingencies. That isolation may allow the group to move more quickly and efficiently, but in the wrong direction. Groups have to find ways of both identifying and adapting to external constraints and attending to internal functioning.

A recent study of new product teams in high technology companies found that groups cope with these disparate demands using the specialized roles of scout, ambassador, sentry, and guard (Gladstein & Caldwell, 1985). The scout scans the environment and brings information into the group, while the ambassador represents the group to outsiders and carries on the negotiation needed to obtain more resources. The sentry and guard protect the team by buffering the group from excess input, political pressure, and attempts to take resources. The sentry and guard roles allow the group to focus on internal innovation, while the scout and ambassador deal with external relations.

Over time effective groups will shift their emphasis on these roles to deal with shifts in internal and external priorities.

Population Ecology—
Does the Group Have Control?

While there are means by which the group deals with dependence, adaptation, and strategy, the population ecology perspective argues that natural selection governs group success. That is, the environment selects for survival those most fitted to the niche. Certain environments may reward more proactive behavior while others reward adaptation. At the same time inertia and resistance to change limit a group's ability to shift its process and structure. It is not known whether natural selection operates in groups in organizations. Nonetheless, some preliminary hypotheses have been made using organizational level environmental dimensions and group process variables (Ancona & Salk, 1986). For example, it is predicted that organizations characterized by scarcity, decentralized distribution of resources, and heterogeneity will select for survival those groups that engage in more negotiating, information exchange, and scanning.

The hypotheses set forth by the organization theorists also might be tested at the group level. In a homogeneous environment there is similarity between the elements of the environment that the organization has to deal with, and this type of environment rewards standardized ways of dealing with the environment. Environmental stability is the degree to which there is turnover in the elements of the environment. A stable environment rewards formalized structures and tends to select organizations by age, because older organizations are farther along in the learning curve. Established organizations, however, have more difficulty adapting to change because they have few established procedures for responding. Environmental concentration refers to the degree to which resources are spread throughout the environment or concentrated in particular locations. In concentrated environments, strategies for getting resources can be more easily learned, and position in the environment determines selection. Consensus refers to the extent to which an organization's claim to a domain is disputed. Selection here is governed not only by defining a niche and acquiring resources, but also by obtaining legitimacy from other actors in the domain (Aldrich, 1979).

The new set of variables and perspectives that I have identified focuses attention from variables that influence group member attitudes and behaviors to those that the group must adopt to influence group performance in the organizational context. New categories for describing a group's environment and new processes to deal with that environment have been identified. It is left to address how to apply these variables profitably to classical areas of small group research, namely, group development and group decision making.

GROUP DEVELOPMENT

Hundreds of studies of group development have been done (see Hare, 1973; Heinen & Jacobson, 1976; Tuckman, 1965), but it is not clear that these group dynamics studies adequately address developmental issues in task groups within organizations. Most of these studies accord with Bennis and Shepard (1956) in postulating that group development requires the resolution of two major issues: authority and intimacy (how will leadership emerge, and how close will members become?). Their focus is on interaction among group members.

This section summarizes some of the findings in the group development literature and shows some examples of what studies using the external perspective can provide to development theory.

Group Dynamics Literature

Group dynamics models of development typically describe the sequential stages through which therapy groups, self-growth groups, laboratory groups, or natural groups mature (see Dunphy, 1964; Mann, 1967; Mills, 1964; Tuckman & Jensen, 1977). Generally, during the initial stage, the individual group member is concerned with his or her personal role within the group, as well as with becoming familiar with other group members. Following this orientation period, some degree of conflict develops, as group members confront issues about which members exert power and who will subsequently have control. As these issues of power and control are resolved, members become able to agree on group norms and rules that define the operational structure that the group can use to achieve its goals and/or complete its task. Heinen and Jacobson (1976), in a review of the group development models, concluded that the initial and final stages (orientation and work) are similar among the models, but that the number and nature of the middle stages can vary.

Researchers have also focused on the problem-solving phases and recursive models. Bales and Strodtbeck (1951) observed phases of orientation, evaluation, and control. Recursive models describe groups as not following a distinct set of stages, but rather as repeatedly returning to particular themes over time. In a review of recursive models, Shambaugh (1978) postulated that groups alternate between patterns showing closeness and separateness. During periods of closeness, the group culture is established, while during periods of separateness group members carry on work-related tasks. Similarly Bion (1961) observed that groups go back and forth between work and three emotional states: dependency, fight-flight, and pairing.

It is important to note that an external perspective has been introduced in group development research. For example, in the Tavistock School the trainer in a training group represents external authority so group-trainer relations represent group-environmental relations. In his work on the development of group and organizational culture, Schein (1985) pointed out that groups develop models about how to interact both internally and externally. Nonetheless, many group dynamics studies call for observing a laboratory or training group, then coding interpersonal behavior according to a prespecified scheme (e.g., shows agreement, active, dominant, talks a lot; see Bales, 1958). A stage is considered ended when the dominant type of behavior changes. The study of development changes when the external perspective is applied more explicitly.

Applying the External Perspective to Group Development

From the external perspective, much has been left out of the study of group development. The question of how does the group adapt to the organizational environment gets added to the question of how individuals come to know their role in the group. If group process is viewed as task and maintenance behavior, it is quite interesting to see that certain maintenance functions precede task functioning. What happens if process is viewed as intragroup and intergroup behavior? What set of processes appears first? Are they taken on sequentially? Are there different rates of adaptation that can be matched to different early developmental sequences? Do different types of environments cause, or reward, different developmental sequences?

The external perspective poses questions of earlier findings as well. Are there differences in the development of authority and intimacy when external relations are also being developed? Are there issues of authority and intimacy between the group and its external resource allocators as there are between the leader and group members? Is there an external interaction leader who emerges as the task and maintenance leaders emerge? How do groups develop when the time frame shifts from several hours or several weeks to several months or years? Fortunately, new group research has started to answer some of these questions.

In a study of eight temporary task forces in six different organizations, Gersick (1983) found that groups did not develop according to a series of universal stages as traditional group development models predict. Instead, teams progressed in two main phases bisected by a major transition. Each team developed a unique framework of behavior patterns and approaches to work that formed almost immediately at the first meeting and remained through the first half of the group's existence. The midpoint between the group's first meeting and its deadline was seen as a transition point in all groups; at this time groups dropped old frameworks and searched for new ones. The new frameworks carried the group through a second period of momentum to a final burst of activity prior to the deadline.

Rather than a developmental model of distinct, identifiable, behavioral stages, we see a model of punctuated equilibrium (see Romanelli & Tushman, 1986, for the organizational counterpart) or a shift from inertia to revolution in framework and behavior. More interesting from the external perspective is the group's shift in openness to input from the external environment. It appears that the external environment has a major influence on the group only at certain periods of time: at the first meeting when basic approaches to work are set up, and at the transition point when groups are looking for feedback from the context to reformulate their understanding of how to meet external demands. In contrast, the two major phases of activity are closed periods when the group takes a more internal focus (Gersick, 1983; Hackman & Walton, 1986).

In a second developmental study taking an external perspective, five consulting teams in a matrix structure were observed during the first five months of their existence (Ancona, 1986). Team leaders were interviewed before formation of the groups to determine their plans and expectations for operation of the teams. Three different types of plans existed: (1) internal passive, where the leader planned to have little interaction with the external environment, to model the environment and come up with a strategy based on team member knowledge, and to present the strategy to the external world once it was developed; (2) internal actives; leaders planned to model the environment based on existing team member knowledge but wanted to maintain their visibility to those who would use and evaluate their services; and (3) external actives; leaders assumed that old models of the environment were not useful and that a lot of external interaction would be needed to revise their old models and to develop a strategy that matched external demands. External actives engaged in more diagnosis and discussion of possible strategies with those who would use and evaluate their services than other groups.

The teams actually developed in a manner similar to leader plans. In the short term, the internal passive team had trouble between the leader and members, and the external actives had some coordination problems. The internal actives were the most satisfied and cohesive. Evaluating performance a year later, however, the head of the organization and the head of human resources rated the external actives as the two highest performing teams. These two teams had done the best job of satisfying external demands and communicating their accomplishments to top management.

Thus, while there appears to be long-term benefits to a style of early mapping of the external environment, there may be short-run costs in terms of satisfaction and cohesion. As in the Gersick (1983) study, this research supports the need to examine both intragroup and external behaviors over time to get a full view of group development. Just as individuals must learn to adapt to being group members by satisfying individual and group goals, groups must learn to adapt to organizational contexts by satisfying both internal demands and external constraints. The group development literature would do well to focus as much on the latter as on the former and to examine the impact of different developmental sequences in various environmental contexts.

GROUP DECISION MAKING

Much of the research on group decision making accepts a normative model of the decision-making process and examines how groups deviate from that process or proposes structures a group can use to maintain that process. Again, this orientation assumes an internal or local perspective. If we apply an external perspective, the whole definition of normative comes into question.

The normative model of group decision making posits a process-performance relationship. Authors argue that the outcomes for the organization will improve, if a group follows the normative model: (1) thoroughly canvasses a wide range of policy alternatives, (2) takes account of the full range of objectives to be fulfilled and the values implicated by the choice, (3) carefully weighs negative and positive consequences, (4) intensively searches for new information relevant for further evaluation, (5) accounts for new information, (6) reexamines positive and negative consequences of all known alternatives, and (7) provides detailed provisions for implementation (Janis & Mann, 1977).

Unfortunately, groups do not often follow the normative model, and researchers have documented deviations from it. Groups have been known to suffer from group polarization (Moscovici & Zavalloni, 1969), groupthink (Janis, 1972), decision biases (Tversky & Sattath, 1979), unconscious mechanisms that cause a group to stray from work behavior (Bion, 1961), solution-mindedness (Hoffman & Maier, 1964), and dominance of verbal, but not necessarily accurate, group members (Hoffman & Clark, 1979). Many structural and process mechanisms have been suggested to correct for these problems. Examples include more active discussion of performance strategies (Hackman, 1983), and the use of the nominal group technique and the Delphi method (Delbecq, Van de Ven, & Gustafson, 1975). All these methods are aimed at getting the best decision.

Returning to an external perspective, however, we see that the group not only has to come up with a decision, but also must adapt to an external environment. External constituencies need to be convinced that the decision is a good one and often have to be cajoled into playing a part in the implementation of that decision. A new project team might design a state-of-the-art product, for example, but if manufacturing cannot produce it, the effort is for naught. An external perspective can suggest alternative views of what is normative.

Some researchers who have taken this external perspective into account propose that, while the normative model operates under decision rationality, "action rationality" may be more appropriate when commitment and motivation are primary outcomes of interest (Brunsson, 1982). Here the objective is not arriving at the "best" decision in some abstract sense, but rather involving people in the decision-making process in order to gain their input in molding the decision and their cooperation in implementing it. The emphasis changes to one of efficiency—how can decisions best be carried out (Pfeffer & Salancik, 1978).

Under action rationality, the group may be involved in symbolic management, establishing acceptability for the group and its activities. It does this by providing explanation, rationalization, and argument for chosen courses of action both within the group and externally. Myths, symbols, and images—even if they are stereotyped images—are used to legitimize behavior in the larger context (Gladstein & Quinn, 1985). Rationalization, stereotyping, and the illusion of unanimity are important tools in building commitment both within and outside the group, even though these are symptoms of groupthink.

Note that processes that are often labelled ineffective under conditions of decision rationality can be useful. These include (1) seeking information that solely bolsters particular alternatives, (2) viewing group decisions as more favorable than is warranted objectively, (3) making suboptimal decisions to avoid conflict or to maintain cohesion, and (4) considering implementation throughout the process (Brunsson, 1982). The consideration of multiple alternatives could evoke dysfunctional uncertainty while consideration of all positive and negative consequences of alternatives also may increase uncertainty and conflict. At some point, bolstering of a few alternatives is needed to move the group along (Brunsson, 1982).

Both decision and action rationality may be appropriate under different conditions. Action rationality may be optimal for groups making decisions where a serious threat requires rapid cohesive action, when continuing unity is more important than other consequences, or when the group has as much information as it believes it can effectively obtain. In a top management group, the spiraling incremental development of a company strategy requires that a group alternate between formulation and implementation and, therefore, the decision making process may have to shift over time from decision to action rationality and back again. The balance may vary depending on the stage of organizational development and organizational mode (Gladstein & Quinn, 1985; Romanelli & Tushman, 1986). Here again, the external perspective suggests alternative group processes as well as alternative ways of evaluating those processes. A process that is normative in an isolated setting may be inappropriate in certain environmental contexts where commitment to the decision both inside and outside the group is most important. An external perspective sheds light on many other questions: What other kinds of decision processes that were thought of as negative are adaptive in the organizational context? Under which environmental conditions are these processes adaptive and maladaptive? Are group members able to correctly assess environmental conditions and change their mode of decision making?

DISCUSSION

Researchers have often viewed groups as settings that shape individual preferences, attitudes, and decisions. This approach toward the group takes the internal perspective. The research lens is on the group boundary focusing inward. I have advocated an external perspective. That is to say, group process is not simply what goes on inside the group—it also encompasses how the group reaches out to the external environment. The level of analysis is not the individual but the group and its ability to adapt to environmental constraints. The group context includes not only those resources that the group receives at the onset but also the configuration of resources and information in the group's environment that impose constraints and selectively reward particular group responses.

The external perspective borrows heavily from researchers at the organizational level of analysis, specifically those studying resource dependence, adaptation, and population ecology. These researchers offer a view of the group that complements the laboratory view. The group is not only an aggregation of individual preferences, but an entity whose activities are to some extent determined and rewarded by the pattern of dependence the group has with other parts of the organization. The group is also able to exert control over its environment by shaping external preferences.

While it is dangerous to assume that phenomena at one level of analysis can be translated to another level, empirical testing will be the final judge of the applicability of these concepts to the group level. Nonetheless, it is clear that groups, like organizations, are open systems with a layer of ties to other parts of the organization and external task environment, so the concepts may well apply.

This external perspective provides new directions in the area of group development and group decision making. The group must not only evolve in ways that allow individuals to develop positions of authority and intimacy, but it must also find ways to balance internal needs of coordination with external adaptation. Furthermore, individuals within the group assume positions not solely due to verbal acumen or charisma (individual characteristics), but also of their ability to deal with critical external contingencies that the group faces (Pfeffer, 1986). The group must come up with appropriate decisions, but it needs also to find ways to get outsiders to commit to those decisions.

Such a perspective forces us to rethink our traditional models, and methods. An organizational task group operates not in isolation, but it reaches out to, or buffers itself from the organization. As the organization reacts to the group's behavior, a new cycle of activity begins. Researchers need to find ways to monitor and evaluate that group-context interaction. An orientation that specializes in the individual's perception of social reality, added to an external organization perspective, gives us expanded laboratory models.

REFERENCES

Ackoff, R. L. (1971). Frontiers of management science. *TIMS: The Bulletin, 1,* 19-24.

Adams, J. S. (1980). Interorganizational processes and organization boundary activities. In B. Staw & L. Cummings (Eds.), *Research in organizational behavior* (Vol. 2, pp. 321-355). Greenwich, CT: JAI Press.

Alderfer, C. P. (1976). Boundary relations and organizational diagnosis. In M. Meltzer & F. R. Wickert (Eds.), *Humanizing organizational behavior* (pp. 109-133). Springfield, IL: Charles Thomas.

Aldrich, H. E. (1979). *Organizations and environments.* Englewood Cliffs, NJ: Prentice-Hall.

Aldrich, H. E., & Pfeffer, J. (1976). Environments of organizations. In A. Inkeles, J. Coleman, & N. Smelser (Eds.), *Annual review of sociology* (Vol. 2, pp. 79-105). Palo Alto, CA: Annual Reviews.

Allen, T. J. (1970). Communication networks in R&D labs. *R&D Management, 1,* 14-21.

Allen, T. J. (1984). *Managing the flow of technology: Technology transfer and the dissemination of technological information within the R&D organization.* Cambridge, MA: M.I.T. Press.

Allen, T. J., & Cohen, S. (1969). Information flow in R&D laboratories. *Administrative Science Quarterly, 14,* 12-19.

Allen, T. J., Tushman, M. L., & Lee, D.M.S. (1979). Technology transfer as a function of position in the spectrum from research through development to technical services. *Academy of Management Journal, 22,* 694-708.

Ancona, D. (1986). *Group development in organizations: From the outside in.* M.I.T. Sloan School of Management Working Paper.

Ancona, D., & Salk, J. (1986). *Group behavior from an organizational perspective.* M.I.T. Sloan School of Management Working Paper.

Astley, W. G., & Van de Ven, A. H. (1983). Central perspectives and debates in organization theory. *Administrative Science Quarterly, 28,* 245-273.

Bales, R. F. (1958). Task roles and social roles in problem-solving groups. In E. Maccoby, T. M. Newcomb, & E. L. Hartley (Eds.), *Readings in social psychology* (3rd ed., pp. 437-447). New York: Holt, Rinehart & Winston.

Bales, R. F. & Strodtbeck, F. L. (1951). Phases in group problem solving. *Journal of Abnormal and Social Psychology, 46,* 485-495.

Bass, B. M. (1970). When planning for others. *Journal of Applied Behavioral Science, 6,* 151-171.

Bennis, W. G., & Shepard, H. H. (1956). A theory of group development. *Human Relations, 9,* 415-457.

Bion, W. R. (1961). *Experiences in groups.* London: Tavistock.

Brett, J. M. & Rognes, J. K. (1986). Intergroup relations in organizations: A negotiations perspective. In P. Goodman (Ed.), *Designing effective work groups* (pp. 202-236). San Francisco, CA: Jossey-Bass.

Brunsson, N. (1982). The irrationality of action and action rationality: Decisions, ideologies, and organizational actions. *Journal of Management Studies, 19,* 29-44.

Bushe, G. R. (1986). *Managing groups from the outside: A model of cognitive task-group types.* Paper presented at the Annual Meeting of the Western Academy.

Delbecq, A. L., Van de Ven, A. H., & Gustafson, D. H. (1975). *Group techniques for programming planning: A guide to nominal and delphi processes.* Glenview, IL: Scott, Foresman.

Dunphy, D. C. (1964). *Social change in self-analytic groups.* Unpublished doctoral dissertation, Harvard University.

Farrell, M. P. (1976). Patterns in the development of self-analytic groups. *Journal of Applied Behavioral Science, 12,* 523-542.

Farris, G. (1969). Organizational factors and individual performance. *Journal of Applied Psychology, 53,* 86-92.

Gersick, C.J.G. (1983). *Life cycles of ad hoc task groups.* T.R. No. 4, Group Effectiveness Research Project, School of Organization and Management, Yale University.

Gladstein, D. (1984). Groups in context: A model of task group effectiveness. *Administrative Science Quarterly, 29,* 499-517.

Gladstein, D., & Caldwell, D. (1985). Boundary management in new product teams. *Academy of Management Proceedings,* 161-165.

Gladstein, D. & Quinn, J. B. (1985). Making decisions and producing action: The two faces of strategy. In J. M. Pennings (Ed.), *Organizational strategy and change* (pp. 198-216). San Francisco: Jossey-Bass.

Goodman, P. (1986). The impact of task and technology on group performance. In P. Goodman (Ed.), *Designing effective work groups* (pp. 120-167). San Francisco, CA: Jossey-Bass.

Greiner, L. E. (1972, July-August). Evolution and revolution as organizations grow. *Harvard Business Review,* 37-46.

Hackman, J. R. (1983). The design of work teams. In J. W. Lorsch (Ed.), *Handbook of organizational behavior* (pp. 315-342). Englewood Cliffs, NJ: Prentice-Hall.

Hackman, J. R., & Morris, C. G. (1975). Group tasks, group interaction process and group performance effectiveness: A review and proposed integration. In L. Berkowitz (Ed.), *Advances in experimental social psychology* (Vol. 8, pp. 45-99). New York: Academic Press.

Hackman, J. R. & Walton, R. E. (1986). Leading groups in organizations. In P. Goodman (Ed.), *Designing effective work groups* (pp. 72-119). San Francisco, CA: Jossey-Bass.

Hare, A. P. (1973). Theories of group development and categories for interaction analysis. *Small Group Behavior, 4,* (3), 259-304.

Heinen, J. S., & Jacobson, E. (1976). A model of task group development in complex organizations and a strategy of implementation. *Academy of Management Review, 19,* 98-111.

Hoffman, L. R., & Clark, M. M. (1979). Participation and influence in problem solving groups. In L. R. Hoffman (Ed.), *The group problem solving process: Studies of a valence model* (pp. 82-97). New York: Praeger.

Hoffman, L. R., & Maier, M.R.F. (1964). Valence in the adoption of solutions by problem solving groups: Concept, method, and results. *Journal of Abnormal and Social Psychology, 69,* 264-271.

Homans, G. (1950). *The human group.* New York: Harcourt Brace Jovanovich.

Janis, I. L. (1972). *Victims of groupthink.* Boston, MA: Houghton Mifflin.

Janis, I. L., & Mann, L. (1977). *Decision making: A psychological analysis of conflict, choice and commitment.* New York: Free Press.

Katz, R. (1982). The effects of group longevity on project communication and performance. *Administrative Science Quarterly, 27,* 81-104.

Katz, R., & Tushman, M. (1981). An investigation into the managerial roles and career paths of gatekeepers and project supervisors in a major R&D facility. *R&D Management, 11,* 103-110.

Kidder, T. (1981). *The soul of a new machine.* Boston, MA: Little, Brown.

Lorange. P. (1980). *Corporate planning: An executive viewpoint.* Englewood Cliffs, NJ: Prentice-Hall.

Lyden, F. J. (1975). Using Parsons' functional analysis in the study of public organizations. *Administrative Science Quarterly, 20,* 59-69.

Mann, R. D. (1967). *Interpersonal styles and group development.* New York: John Wiley.

McCann, J., & Galbraith, J. R. (1983). Interdepartmental relations. In P. C. Nystrom & W. H. Starbuck (Eds.), *Handbook of organizational design* (pp. 60-84). New York: Oxford Press.

McCormick, D. W. (1985). *Environmental relations and group effectiveness in planned change projects.* Unpublished doctoral dissertation, Case Western Reserve University, Cleveland.

McGrath, J. E. (1984). *Groups: Interaction and performance.* Englewood Cliffs, NJ: Prentice-Hall.

McKelvey, B. (1982). *Organizational systemics: Taxonomy, evolution, and classification.* Berkeley, CA: University of California Press.

Mills, T. M. (1964). *Group transformation: An analysis of a learning group.* Englewood Cliffs, NJ: Prentice-Hall.

Mintzberg, H. (1973). *The nature of managerial work.* New York: Harper & Row.

Moscovici, S., & Zavalloni, M. (1969). The group as a polarizer of attitudes. *Journal of Personality and Social Psychology, 12,* 125-135.

Osborn, A. F. (1957). *Applied imagination* (rev. ed.). New York: Scribner.

Parsons, T. (1960). *Structure and process in modern society.* New York: Free Press.

Pennings, J. M. (1980). *Interlocking directorates.* San Francisco, CA: Jossey-Bass.

Pfeffer, J. (1972). Merger as a response to organizational interdependence. *Administrative Science Quarterly, 17,* 382-394.

Pfeffer, J. (1986). A resource dependence perspective on intercorporate relations. In M. S. Mizruchi & M. Schwartz (Eds.), *Structural analysis of business* (pp. 117-132). New York: Academic Press.

Pfeffer, J., & Salancik, G. R. (1978). *The external control of organizations: A resource dependence perspective.* New York: Harper & Row.

Phillip, H., & Dunphy, D. (1959). Developmental trends in small groups. *Sociometry, 22,* 162-174.

Quinn, J. B. (1982). Managing strategies incrementally. *Omega, 10,* 613-627.

Romanelli, E., & Tushman, M. (1986). Inertia, environments and strategic choice: A quasi-experimental design for comparative-longitudinal research. *Management Science, 32,* 608-621.

Schein, E. H. (1985). *Organizational culture and leadership.* San Francisco, CA: Jossey-Bass.

Shambaugh, P. W. (1978). The development of the small group. *Human Relations, 31* (3), 283-295.

Sherif, M. (1966). *In common predicament: Social psychology of intergroup conflict and cooperation.* Boston, MA: Hougton Mifflin.

Stephan, W. G. (1984). Intergroup relations. In G. Lindzey & E. Aronson (Eds.), *Handbook of social psychology: Special fields and applications* (Vol. 2, 3rd ed., pp. 599-658). New York: Random House.

Staw, B. M., Sandelands, L. E., & Dutton, J. E. (1981). Thread-rigidity effects in organizational behavior: Multi-level analysis. *Administrative Science Quarterly, 26,* pp. 501-524.

Tuckman, B. W. (1965). Developmental sequence in small group. *Psychological Bulletin, 63* (6), 384-399.

Tuckman, B. W., & Jensen, M. (1977). Stages of small group development. *Group and Organizational Studies, 2,* 419-427.

Tushman, M. (1977). Special boundary roles in the innovation process. *Administrative Science Quarterly, 22,* 587-605.

Tushman, M. (1979). Work characteristics and subunit communication structure: A contingency analysis. *Administrative Science Quarterly, 24,* 82-98.

Tversky, A., & Sattath, S. (1979). Preference trees. *Psychological Review, 86,* 542-573.

Van de Ven, A. H., & Walker, G. (1984). The dynamics of interorganizational coordination. *Administrative Science Quarterly, 29,* 598-621.

Weick, K. E. (1969). *The social psychology of organizing.* Reading, MA: Addison-Wesley.

Weick, K. E. (1980). The management of eloquence. *Executive, 6,* 18-21.

Whetten, D. A. (1983). Interorganizational relations. In J. Lorsch (Ed.), *Handbook of organizational behavior* (pp. 238-254). Englewood Cliffs, NJ: Prentice-Hall.

10

Social Psychology
of Terrorist Groups

CLARK R. McCAULEY
MARY E. SEGAL

Clark R. McCauley received his Ph.D. in social psychology from the University of Pennsylvania in 1970, and is Professor of Psychology at Bryn Mawr College. His current research interests include stereotyping, social ecology, lie detection, and quality of life after medical intervention. His interest in the dynamics of terrorist groups was stimulated by Dr. Jerrold Post at a conference on terrorism sponsored by the Harry Frank Guggenheim Foundation.

Mary E. Segal received her Ph.D. in social psychology at Bryn Mawr College in 1983 and teaches psychology at Villanova University. Her research focuses on effects of the environment on social networks, and on individual differences in person perception.

Every year, hundreds of terrorist incidents occur around the world. Some, like the 1985 Palestinian hijacking of a TWA jet airliner, create international crises as the television cameras roll. Others, the work of obscure groups with causes we perceive dimly or not at all, receive barely a squib in the morning newspaper. The tactics are now familiar: bombings, hijackings, seizure of embassies, kidnappings, and assassinations. Terrorist activity appears to be increasing steadily (Cordes et al., 1984, p. 46), and although governments have scored some important gains, terrorism has proved remarkably resistant to efforts to control it.

It is often said that one man's terrorist is another man's freedom fighter. For instance, do their gasoline "necklaces" make the African National Congress a terrorist organization? Schmid (1983, p. 6-158) has reviewed the complexities of distinguishing terrorism from violence, anarchism, guerrilla warfare, and crime; here we (somewhat arbitrarily) adopt the following definition: The use or threat of violence, by small groups against non-combatants of large groups, for avowed political goals (see Kellen, 1979, p. 9). We restrict our analysis to what Laqueur (1977, p. 7) has called terrorism "from below," that is, concerned with grievances or ideologies opposed to the existing state, as distinct from state-directed terrorism imposed on citizens from above. Although state-directed terrorism is certainly the larger contributor to human misery, its understanding calls for a psychology of bureaucracy substantially different from the social psychology of terrorism from below.

Our survey of the literature suggests that a central aspect of terrorist activity is often largely ignored: Terrorism is a *group* phenomenon. Terrorist organizations are not just collections of separate individuals; they are functioning units that exert strong pressures on their members and hold out powerful rewards. In this chapter, we examine data and theory from three areas of research relevant to the social psychology of terrorist groups: religious conversion to cults, extremity shift of group opinions, and individual extremity shift in obedience studies. First, we present an overview of what is known about terrorist groups and their members, and then demonstrate how a social psychological framework can be useful in the analysis of terrorist behavior.

Not surprisingly, most of the literature on terrorist groups and their members is recent, and Laqueur's (1977) already-classic work is one of the oldest in the field. This is because terrorism has emerged only during the last several years as a pressing issue among industrialized nations; a quantitative escalation of terrorist violence has been accompanied by increasingly more lethal and less discriminant choices of targets (Cordes et al., 1984, p. vi). In addition to its immaturity, the literature suffers from methodological constraints: Obvious hazards preclude original field studies; content analyses of terrorists' public declarations are more revealing of what terrorists wish us to think than of the reality of their experiences; and post hoc interviews with ex-terrorists are problematic in terms of subjects' selective and reconstructive recall. Nevertheless, the beginnings of a consensus appear to be emerging in the description of terrorist groups and their members.

TERRORISTS AS INDIVIDUALS

A few demographic generalizations can be made with confidence, among them the fact that terrorists are predominately male (Laqueur, 1977, p. 121; Russell & Miller, 1983). Exceptions include the nineteenth-century Russian terrorists, in which one-quarter of the membership was composed of women, and the Baader-Meinhof group, in which one-third of the operational personnel were women. Although a few other groups have included a woman in a position of leadership, these are isolated cases; in general, women have tended to occupy secondary support roles at the periphery of the organizations (for an interesting discussion of women as terrorists, see Georges-Abeyie, 1983).

Terrorists are also young, usually in their (often early) twenties, although leaders may be in their thirties and older (Russell & Miller, 1983; Laqueur, 1977, p. 120). Most terrorists come from middle-class or professional families. Many have at least some university education; indeed, nineteenth-century Russian, as well as contemporary West German, Italian, United States, Japanese, and Uruguayan terrorist movements have been direct outgrowths of student unrest (Crenshaw, 1981). Sixty-five percent of the Baader-Meinhof group has been estimated to be middle class; 80% had at least some university training (Russell & Miller, 1983). Similar profiles are characteristic of Japanese and U.S. terrorist groups, which have included a large number of university dropouts (Laqueur, 1977, p. 123). In Turkish, Iranian, and Palestinian terrorist groups, the great majority are middle- and upper-class students and professionals. South American terrorist groups follow a similar pattern: The Argentinian ERP and Montoneros were both middle class (with some working class in the latter); the urban terrorists active in Venezuela in the early 1960s were predominately students; and 90% of the Tupamaros in Uruguay were middle and upper-class students and young professionals. (See Table 10.1 for explication of ERP and later abbreviations of the names of terrorist groups.) Crenshaw (1985) notes that the leader of the Shining Path organization in Peru is a former philosophy professor, and that the entire movement was first a product of the university, and only later enlisted peasant support. The Italian Red Brigade appears to be an exception to the general rule, as it was at least initially composed mainly of working class members (Laqueur, 1977, p. 211).

Post (1985) has made an interesting distinction between two types of terrorists: the "anarchic-ideologues" and the "nationalist-separatists." The former are committed to the overthrow of the government and social order that are supported by their parents (examples are the German Red Army Faction and the Italian Red Brigade), while the latter attempt to redress grievances held against the prevailing order by their parents (e.g., the Basque ETA and the Armenian ASALA). In general, nationalist-separatist groups appear to draw more heavily on the working class for membership than do anarchic-ideologue groups. The FLN in Algeria were mostly of modest means from small towns and villages; many had been in the French army (Hutchinson, 1978, p. 7). Forty percent of the Basque ETA have some university training (Russell & Miller, 1983), but this figure is considerably lower than those reported for anarchic-ideologue groups such as the Baader-Meinhof (80%) or the

TABLE 10.1
Abbreviations of Names of Terrorist Groups

Armenian ASALA	Armenian Secret Army for the Liberation of Armenia
Argentinian ERP	People's Revolutionary Army
Basque ETA	Euzkadi Ta Askatasuna
Algerian FLN	National Liberation Front (Front de Liberation Nationale)
Canadian FLQ	Quebec Liberation Front (Front de Liberation du Quebec)
Irish IRA	Irish Republican Army
Palestinian PFLP	Popular Front for the Liberation of Palestine
German RAF	Red Army Faction

Tupamaros (75%). The IRA are predominantly members of the working and lower-middle classes (Laqueur, 1977, p. 119). As noted above, the Palestinians provide at least one exception to this generalization.

Thus, terrorists can be demographically characterized as male, young, and middle or professional class (with more working-class members represented in nationalist-separatist groups). Psychological generalizations are more elusive. Perhaps the best-documented generalization is negative: Terrorists do not show any striking psychopathology (Post, 1985). According to Crenshaw (1981, p. 390), "the outstanding common characteristic of terrorists is their normality." Potential recruits into terrorist organizations who seem to be merely seeking danger and excitement are not encouraged. Laqueur (1977, p. 121) notes that the nineteenth-century Russian terrorists were in general balanced, normal people. Hutchinson (1978, p. 142) points out that in the FLN in Algeria during the 1950s, "terrorism was basically a reasonable and considered political choice," and terrorists were, on the whole, normal people. Members of the IRA in Northern Ireland do not appear to be clinically disturbed by any measure (Heskin, 1984).

Further evidence of terrorists' lack of overt psychopathology is found in reports of their ambivalence toward the human suffering caused by their violent actions (Knutson, 1981). Burton (1978; quoted in Heskin, 1984) suggests that depression, self-doubt, and guilt are not uncommon among IRA activists. The Red Army Faction leader Ulrike Meinhof was terrified of guns (Demaris, 1977, p. 220). Crenshaw (1986) notes the PFLP terrorist Leila Khaled was able to deal with the presence of children on a plane she hijacked only by closing her mind to the possible consequences of the hijacking for them. These feelings are hardly consistent with our general notions of pathologically disturbed individuals.

Beyond suggesting an absence of pathology, attempts to delineate a "terrorist personality" have not been very fruitful. A suggestion worth further investigation has been made by Heskin (1984), who has noted that the single most likely characteristic of IRA members is authoritarianism. A generalization that has received some support across various terrorist groups was made by Laqueur (1977, p. 147), who suggested that terrorists possess a kind of "free-floating activism." Becker (1977) frequently refers to the Baader-Meinhof group's impatience with words and desire for action. Crenshaw (1986) notes that the Basque ETA came to place a premium on armed conflict as an end, rather than as a means toward obtaining other objectives, and mentions the South American terrorist theoretician Marighella's focus on revolutionary action as opposed to discussion.

If terrorists are in general rather normal individuals who are inclined toward direct action regarding some perceived grievance or ideological position, we still have not come very far in describing characteristics that might predispose them toward terrorist activity. Hoffman (1985a) reports on studies of terrorist prisoners in countries, including Italy, Germany, and Turkey, that suggest that an individual's decision to join a left-wing, as opposed to a right-wing, organization is often a matter of little more than chance. Something more powerful than ideology is at work. Bollinger (1981; quoted in Billig, 1985) has suggested that social deficits in West German terrorists' personal lives may have been key factors in their attraction to group membership in the RAF; Post (1985) believes that joining an extremist group represents above all an attempt to belong. As Crenshaw (1985, p. 471) explains, "The group, as selector and interpreter of ideology, is central." We focus next on the group context of terrorist activities.

TERRORIST GROUPS

The Increasingly Extreme Behavior of Members of Terrorist Groups

In understanding how normal and even idealistic people can become terrorists, it is important to recognize that their radical behavior is acquired gradually, progressing from the less to the more extreme. Often, an individual will join a succession of groups and causes, beginning with ones that advocate relatively pacifist goals (Crenshaw, 1985); in some cases, the commitment to terrorism may be made only when it appears to the individual that terrorist action is the only possible alternative in effecting social or political change. The German RAF leader Meinhof headed community efforts in the city of Munster opposing nuclear weapons during the 1950s; her increasing disillusionment with society occurred gradually throughout the following decade until she became a leader of the Baader-Meinhof group (Demaris, 1977, p. 218). Horst Mahler, another RAF leader, was a member of the moderate Social Democratic Party of Germany and the Socialist German Student Society, but left these organizations before helping to found the RAF (Billig, 1985). In a case study of a second-generation RAF terrorist referred to as "Rolfe," Billig (1984) notes that his subject joined radical groups and student Vietnam protests in late adolescence, and then went on to start a venture that printed literature for some radical organizations before actually being recruited into the RAF.

It is also possible that an individual member becomes more extreme as the whole group undergoes radical change. For example, the nineteenth-century Russian terrorist group known as "The People's Will" (Narodnaya Volya) broke off from a larger revolutionary movement because its leaders advocated terrorism. "The person who has become extremely dependent on the group will move with it to the new activity, without necessarily having made an independent choice" (Crenshaw, 1985, p. 477). Salvioni and Stephanson (1985; quoted in Crenshaw, 1986) note that early Red Brigade activity in Italy centered on issues such as the campaign in Milan for free mass transit, and later escalated to violence justified by the terrorists as retribution for working class injustice. The German RAF's declarations suggest that the group's mission changed from (an albeit) limited commitment to working inside the social structure toward purely illegal activities (see "The concept of the urban guerrilla," published in 1971; reprinted in Laqueur, 1978, p. 179). Bollinger (1982, p. 118) discusses a process of "double marginalization" among the members of the RAF, first in the leftist student movement, and then beyond the limits of that movement into a distinct subculture in which a separate system of norms gradually developed.

Furthermore, it should be recognized that there is specialization and hierarchy of violent behavior in terrorist groups; thus, depending upon their roles and status within the organization, terrorists vary in the extremity of their actual behavior. Division of labor has been documented in the Argentinian Montoneros, which included divisions for logistics, documents, planning, and psychological action (Crenshaw, 1985), and in the Algerian ALN, the military arm of the FLN, which included separate sections for bombings, attacks on police, logistics, and so forth. These divisions themselves were compartmentalized: The bomb section, for example, included laboratory work, transportation, storage, distribution, and placement (Hutchinson, 1978, p. 10). Thus, all terrorists are not required to hijack planes or plant bombs.

Once connected with an extreme group, a new recruit may gradually move from peripheral activities designed to support the group's terrorist tactics to the acts of violence that are central to the group's purpose. Thus the RAF member "Rolfe" mentioned above, who was eventually arrested in the kidnap-murder of the German industrialist Hans-Martin Schleyer in 1977, began his career with the RAF as a courier (Billig, 1984). Clark (1983) mentions a similar gradation in the recruitment phases of the Basque ETA membership.

Conflict in Terrorist Groups

In understanding the social psychological factors in terrorist organizations, it is important to recognize that all extreme groups, including anarchic-ideologues as well as nationalist-separatists, are at the apex of a much larger number of sympathizers and supporters. As Laqueur (1977, p. 110) points out, a measure of popular support is crucial for a terrorist organization. After RAF leader Meinhof's suicide in 1976, 4,000 mourners attended her funeral (Becker, 1977, p. 282). Crenshaw (1985, p. 467) notes that the IRA and the ETA are "components of broader organizational structures and possess a reservoir of support in society because the grievances of (their) communities . . . remain unsolved."

An important factor in the psychosocial reality of terrorist groups is constant and pervasive conflict. Obviously, terrorists are in conflict with the prevailing social and political order. A factor less often recognized is that extremist groups, particularly nationalist-separatist groups, must deal with their supporters—people in basic sympathy with their goals who nevertheless do not condone violent tactics beyond a certain limit— as another potential source of conflict. Thus the French Canadian community that supported the separatist goals of the FLQ was deeply disturbed by the group's 1970 kidnap-murder of Laporte (Laqueur, 1977, p. 196). The IRA is concerned about the organization's public image, and recognizes the importance of avoiding any backlash in the general population (Crenshaw, 1984). Thompson (1985) provides a vivid example: In 1977 the Provisional IRA murdered a woman, a part-time member of the Ulster Defence Regiment, while she slept in her home, and shot at her three-year-old daughter. The action was widely denounced by IRA supporters. Thompson notes that shared extra-political values operate in such situations as constraints against further escalation.

Intergroup conflict is also not unusual. Rivalry between the Provisional IRA and the official IRA (from which the Provos had split) resulted in outright assassination plots during the 1970s (Laqueur, 1977, p. 189). Often, rivalry between competing terrorist groups causes an escalation of violence against the commonly perceived enemy. Thus the IRA assassination of Lord Mountbatten in 1979 may have been in response to escalated attacks on the British by the Irish National Liberation Army (Crenshaw, 1984). Palestinian terrorist attacks are frequently aimed not only at the intimidation of Israel, but also at influence among competing Palestinian factions (Crenshaw, 1981). Hoffman (1985b) interprets both the 1985 TWA hijacking and the seizure of the luxury liner *Achille Lauro* as attempts by Palestinian terrorists to gain advantage over rival groups. Other nations with feuding terrorist groups include Italy, Armenia, and Argentina (Crenshaw, 1985).

Finally, and perhaps most important, intragroup conflict leads to constant and powerful tensions among group members (Post, 1985). Bollinger (1982, p. 118) suggests that in the RAF, there was a great deal of infighting and rivalry, "even rivalry about the topic who is the most leftist or the most determined." Demaris (1977, p. 232) mentions the frequent conflicts among the RAF leaders, notably between Baader and Meinhof; Billig (1985) maintains that relations were equally strained between Mahler and Meinhof. Laqueur (1977, p. 125) describes a grisly 1972 incident in which some 14 members of the Japanese United Red Army were slain by fellow terrorists. As Zawodny (1983) notes, an important function of external violence is to restore cohesion within the terrorist group. Without action and external threat, the group may destroy itself.

The conflict among group members may be especially threatening because individual survival depends on group solidarity. A member's defection is extremely upsetting to those who remain (Post, 1985). Thus strong group norms develop against any form of rebellion; indeed, any questioning of authority amounted to risking one's place in the Baader-Meinhof group (Post, 1985). Such sanctions can be powerful pressures toward conformity, particularly because members need the group as protection against an unfriendly outside world. Although it is possible for a member of an extreme group to leave the organization, it is generally difficult and dangerous to do so (Crenshaw, 1985). Ex-terrorists are pursued by both government forces and their former comrades.

However, members do in fact leave: Post (1985, p. 11) cites findings that as many as 23% of the RAF dropped out. In general, the dropouts were "ambivalent on joining, never fully resolved their doubts, and increasingly questioned the espoused goals of the group and whether the group's actions actually served those goals." On the average, they dropped out after only one year of active membership; 36% of the dropouts had lasted only six months in the organization. The numerous Italian Red Brigade defections in response to government promises of reduced sentences provide another example (Crenshaw, 1986). Sometimes a group of dissatisfied members will leave to form a separate splinter faction, as described above in the case of the Provisional IRA. Indeed, Crenshaw (1986) cites a high rate of attrition in terrorist organizations, which makes stable membership unlikely.

Rewards of Terrorist Group Membership

Even to a dissatisfied member, however, the group offers powerful incentives to remain. One class of reward for membership is material; terrorists support themselves through bank robberies and ransoms, and in some cases, funding from foreign states. Between June 1, 1970, and November 1, 1978, paid ransoms for terrorists' kidnap victims exceeded $145,000,000 (Miller & Russell, 1979).

Beyond the material rewards are emotional, cognitive, and social gains of group membership. The terrorist group is able to satisfy the emotional needs of members for action over words (discussed earlier), because of its greater command of resources than would be possible for any single individual. Vengeance against the enemy may be a strong emotional need shared by many terrorists (Crenshaw, 1984). As noted earlier, some terrorist recruits may need family substitutes (Billig, 1984). Cognitive rewards of group membership include reinforcement of the individual's sense of mission and self-righteousness (Crenshaw, 1981) in a social reality (Festinger, 1950) that can give especially the drifting or unsuccessful individual a new and significant self-image. Cordes et al. (1984, p. 49) note that terrorists live in a kind of "fantasy world" underground, cut off from most normal contacts with society, and that this kind of existence can produce disturbed perceptions of the real world. These are then further reinforced through reference to the group (see "group think"—Janis, 1972).

Finally, the group offers powerful social rewards. In the case of nationalist-separatist groups, the rewards may extend outside the group itself and result in increased status and admiration by family and peers (Crenshaw, 1985); the ETA and the IRA are clear examples. Within the group, terrorist organizations offer mutual solidarity and feelings of comradeship that are very important, given the illegal nature of terrorist actions. Above and beyond the solidarity necessary to cope with life underground, these kinds of rewards may be particularly relevant to individuals like the RAF member "Rolfe" described earlier; Billig (1984) characterizes him as engaged during much of his pre-RAF life in a constant struggle for recognition. According to Billig (1985, p. 46), the West German terrorists "became dependent on each other for support and considered the outside world an evil system to be eliminated." Clark (1983) notes that the principal sources of support among ETA members are fellow terrorists. Indeed, the ETA places primary emphasis on the importance of social support during its entire recruitment process: An already-active, often older, member will be the potential recruit's sole contact within the organization, and will offer him an ongoing supportive relationship from the first mention of the ETA in discussion, through minor involvements of increasing complexity and danger, to actually escorting him to his first cell meeting.

Terrorist Objectives

Terrorist objectives can be divided into two categories: ultimate objectives (i.e., the grievance the group claims to redress or the ideology it avows) and proximate objectives (well-being of the group, change of public opinion in terms of desirability of group membership, capture of public attention via publicity in the media, etc.). There seems to be a strong tendency for proximate objectives to take on a life of their own, such that terrorism becomes an end in itself (Cordes et al., 1984, p. 50) and group dynamics become more important than ideology (Post, 1985). For the RAF, any commitment to ideology seemed lost after imprisonment of its early leaders, and obtaining their release seemed to preempt any ideological motivations in the actions of the remaining members at large. If the most basic reason for terrorist activity is to gain recognition and attention (Crenshaw, 1981), the focus of the attention is the group, not necessarily the ideology. Historically, terrorist successes in terms of ultimate objectives may be limited to the overthrow of colonial governments (Crenshaw, 1983; Cordes et al., 1984). But in terms of more limited, proximate objectives of recognition and attention, the effects of the current wave of terrorist incidents seem obvious: heightened security measures at airports, an increase in internal security budgets, and in some countries, a general broadening of police powers (Wardlaw, 1982, p. 58). As Newhouse (1985) points out, diplomats now are advised to avoid routine patterns of behavior, and to carry guns—developments that represent major gains for terrorists seeking to threaten the people responsible for the functioning of our institutions. Crenshaw's comments (1986, p. 17) on millenarians seem appropriate here: "The full achievement of the organization's external goals is secondary. Any action in the service of the cause can be interpreted as success."

In the pursuit of recognition and attention, a major (sometimes only) aim of terrorist action is media coverage, with extent of coverage an important reinforcement of the terrorist's sense of power (Wardlaw, 1982, p. 77; Rubin & Friedland, 1986). The symbiotic relationship between terrorists and the media is a phenomenon that has received much attention (Cooper, 1977). Schmid and de Graaf (1982, p. 48) quote a West German terrorist: "Without journalistic reporting, we would find ourselves facing a certain vacuum. It is through the press that our cause is maintained in the just manner." Laqueur (1977, p. 109), noting that "the success of a terrorist operation depends almost entirely on the amount of publicity it receives," quotes an Algerian terrorist leader: "Is it better for our cause to kill ten of our enemies in a remote village where this will not cause comment, or to kill one man in Algeria where the American press will get hold of the story the next day?" Bassiouoni (1983, p. 181) quotes the Brazilian terrorist Marighella, author of the Minimanual of the Urban Guerrilla: "The war of nerves or psychological war is an aggressive technique, based on the direct or indirect use of mass means of communication and news transmitted orally in order to demoralize the government." The escalation of terrorist violence in the last two decades is correlated with technical innovations that have led to almost instantaneous reporting of information to mass audiences (Bassiouni, 1983).

With this broad outline of facts about terrorist groups and their members, we now turn to a discussion of some relevant social psychological research.

CULT CONVERSION AS A MODEL OF TERRORIST RECRUITMENT

Post (1984) appears to have been the first to recognize that cult recruiting can provide a useful model of terrorist recruiting. The analogy begins by noting that individuals who join either a cult or a

terrorist group are likely to be characterized as "crazy." This character-
ization conveys a judgment that circumstances and situation cannot
explain how anyone could be converted to such extremity without prior
personality defect. But a contrary judgment is embodied in sociological
theories of deviance (Traub & Little, 1980), which have in common a
reaction against explanations in terms of individual pathology and a
presumption in favor of explanations in terms of the structural
conditions of society. Insofar as cults and terrorist groups are seen as
deviant groups by the larger society, sociological theories of deviance
should be valuable in understanding both. Here we follow Post in
emphasizing a more social psychological analysis, although we acknowl-
edge that this analysis has much in common with the sociological theory
of "differential association" (Sutherland, 1955).

Much has been written on how to define a cult, especially on how to
distinguish a cult from other kinds of religious groups (Stark &
Bainbridge, 1979). As we noted earlier, a similar uncertainty exists
concerning the definition of a terrorist, especially on how to distinguish
terrorists from guerrillas and freedom fighters. These definitional
disputes need not be pursued here, since the greatest accumulation of
research on cults has focused on the Unification Church of the Reverend
Sun Myung Moon, and we are unaware of any definition of cult that
excludes this group.

Study of the Unification Church began soon after its first missionary
arrived in the United States from Korea. A report by Lofland and Stark
(1965) titled "Becoming a World Saver" chronicled the beginnings of the
UC in America, and its surprise value was its emphasis on the
importance of social networks in religious conversion. The first
missionary began her work in Eugene, Oregon, in 1961 and her first
convert contributed a social network that was exploited for additional
recruits. Indeed, "the great majority of converts in Eugene were linked
by long-standing relationships prior to any contact with Moon's
movement" (Stark & Bainbridge, 1980, p. 1379). The importance of this
social network was made plain to Lofland and Stark when the group left
Eugene for San Francisco—and stopped growing for lack of social ties
to potential recruits in the Bay Area. Recruiting efforts during the early
sixties in San Francisco were not the sophisticated and successful
techniques for which the group is known today. Rather, they were
"weak, haphazard, and bumbling" (Lofland, 1977). Improved techniques were evidently more the product of trial and error than of theory,
but did finally succeed by providing a means of reaching out to develop
personal relationships with newcomers to the Bay Area. Stark and

Bainbridge (1980) point out that this solution was satisficing rather than maximizing, since recruiting was slower than if new converts had provided local acquaintance networks within which to attract additional converts. Compared with geometric progression in Eugene, recruiting in the Bay Area was reduced to arithmetic progression.

The emphasis given by Lofland and Stark (1965) to social networks was a watershed in the study of cults. The established view (Clark, 1937; Linton, 1943; Smelser, 1963) pointed to the match between the needs of the individual and the ideology of the group to explain why some people and not others join a cult or sect. This view assumes that any deviant group will tend to attract individuals with a grievance or deprivation for which the group offers some interpretation and remedy. In retrospect, the deprivation explanation was always too broad, because most individuals who suffer a particular deprivation do not ever join a deviant group. Thus Lofland and Stark did not so much contradict the established view as complement it. Perceived deprivation establishes the pool of potential converts to a particular cult, but social networks determine who among the many in the pool are likely to be among the few actually recruited.

The interaction of deprivation and social networks in predicting cult recruitment is nowhere better represented than in some remarkable studies of the UC carried out by an investigator with the cooperation of church leaders. Galanter, Rabkin, Rabkin, and Deutsch (1979) obtained 237 completed questionnaires from a representative sample of UC members living in the church's residences in a large metropolitan area. Most were unmarried (91%), white (89%), and young (mean age 25 years). Consistent with the deprivation hypothesis, most (67%) had been at least moderately committed to their family's religion before the age of 15, but had lost this commitment: 90% reported at least some commitment to an Eastern or fundamentalist Christian sect before joining the UC. Half reported some previous commitment to a political party or movement. More than half had attended college, although only a quarter held degrees. Thirty percent had experienced emotional problems leading them to seek professional help and 6% had been hospitalized for such problems. This is a picture of individuals dissatisfied and seeking support, and indeed 91% seem to have found some help in the UC, as evidenced by recollection of more psychological distress before joining than after. The same study also shows the importance of interpersonal bonds during the conversion period. Sixty-seven percent reported having felt during this period much more than usual "a great deal of respect for another person," 48% felt more than usual "close or intimate with another person," and 43% felt more than usual "cheered up."

Another study by Galanter (1980) provides questionnaire and outcome data for 104 individuals who began the 21-day sequence of lectures and group activities that ends with a decision whether or not to join the UC. Most of these individuals had been invited by a UC member whom they had met in some public place. Demographic and background data indicated that the 104 who attended the first weekend at a rustic center outside a metropolitan area in Southern California were very similar to UC membership as surveyed in the questionnaire study described above. Despite this similarity, 74 guests left at the end of the first weekend. Those who left differed from those who stayed in reported feelings toward "the ten or so people from the workshop (from outside the workshop) you know best," with dropouts reporting both less feeling for insiders and more feelings for outsiders. Dropouts also reported less acceptance of UC religious beliefs. Of the 30 guests who stayed at the center past the first weekend, 21 dropped out between days 3 and 22, and 9 ultimately joined the Church on day 22. The late dropouts did not differ from joiners in positive feelings toward workshop members or in acceptance of UC beliefs, but did report more positive feelings toward those outside the church. Galanter concludes that an important factor in joining the UC is lack of interpersonal attachments outside the church, and pays special attention to the power of the relationship with the UC host who, after inviting a guest, stays with that guest through the weeks of the recruiting sequence.

And what keeps the recruits in the cult? As indicated above (Galanter et al. 1979), cult members feel themselves less stressed than they were before joining. In this sense the cult experience is not a fraud and does fulfill the promise held out to recruits. The importance of social bonds to cult members has already been emphasized. But here we want to underscore what Stark and Bainbridge (1980, p. 1393) called the "missing factor" in understanding cults: the very concrete and material rewards of membership. Groups that live communally, such as the UC and the Hare Krishnas, combine the security of a family with the opportunities of a corporation. Stark and Bainbridge point out that such groups clothe, feed, and shelter their members, and provide opportunities within the movement to achieve positions of status and power. In this connection it must be recognized that the cult members encountered in public fund-raising or proselytizing are the cream of the movement. A look in the lobby of the old New Yorker hotel in New York City, now owned by the UC, will reveal a considerable number of crippled, ugly, nonyoung members going about their chores. These, the unwanted of our society, find in the UC a home that gives them meaning, work, and affection as well as material security.

The importance of personal ties in UC recruitment appears to fit what is known about other cults as well. For instance, Bainbridge (1978) found that interpersonal bonds were critical in both the formation and expansion of a Satanic cult he studied from 1970 to 1976. A doomsday cult studied by Hardyck and Braden (1962) offers similar evidence. Though the original report is familiar to social psychologists as a test of dissonance theory predictions, Hardyck recently reviewed her field notes (see Stark & Bainbridge, 1980) and reported that 75% of adult members of the cult formed a single kinship network. These and other explanations are reviewed by Stark and Bainbridge to argue that developing interpersonal bonds, in combination with ideology responsive to perceived deprivation, are at the bottom of recruitment to both cults and more traditional religious groups.

Another aspect of the experience of cult groups worth noting is the constant flux in the members' identities and levels of commitment. At any given time, some individuals are beginning to find out about a particular group, others are becoming committed, others are firmly committed, others becoming less committed, and still others are in the process of leaving entirely. Bird and Reimer (1982) examine survey data from Montreal and from the Bay Area of California and conclude that about 20% of the adult population has participated to some extent in a nontraditional religious or quasireligious movement (including Charismatics, Buddhists, Scientologists, EST, and other groups of Western, Eastern, and "scientific" disciples). The typical participant establishes a not-very-strong relationship with one of these groups and then drops out. Three-quarters of the Montreal respondents who had ever participated in one of these groups had dropped out, and fewer than 10% of all respondents were current members of any group. This larger picture from survey data is entirely consistent with our description earlier of UC recruitment, during which the great majority of guests at the UC center dropped out, leaving only a few converts at the end of 21 days. Perhaps part of the success of the UC technique is the compression into only 21 days of the winnowing of potential converts that occurs in any religion.

Even this brief review indicates a number of obvious parallels with what is known about recruitment into terrorist groups. Both pull mostly from the ranks of middle-class, twenty-year-olds with some college. Both depend for recruits on a pool of seekers or sympathizers much larger than the numbers actually recruited. Both require a socialization period during which recruits are brought to full commitment, with a constant flux of dropouts from the path that leads to full commitment and from among those already committed. It does seem that commitment is faster and dropping out likewise faster for cults than for terrorist groups. But this quantitative difference is easily attributable to the greater barriers to both entrance and exit from terrorist groups—barriers that stem from their greater deviance from the norms of the larger society. In terms of group dynamics, both cults and terrorist groups offer a full array of reinforcements to members: affective, social, cognitive, and material. These rewards depend in both kinds of groups on powerful interpersonal bonds among group members, bonds that appear to be very important in explaining how only a few of the many seekers or sympathizers are actually recruited.

A big difference between cults and terrorist groups appears to be the relative lack of intragroup conflict in the cults in comparison with the high levels of conflict reported within terrorist groups. One possible explanation of the difference is the norm of interpersonal warmth and sharing that is part of cult ideology. In contrast, terrorist groups have in common only their enemy and their action. What Marxist ideology is to be found among members of terrorist groups does not include norms of interpersonal intimacy. Another way of putting this possibility is to say that cults are closer to experiential groups (Back, 1972) than terrorist groups are. A prediction from this view is that movement from one group or cell to another should be easier and more frequent within a cult than within a terrorist organization.

Another possibility is that the high level of conflict within terrorist groups is attributable to their cellular organization, where contact with other cells and terrorist leadership must be minimized for reasons of security. The kind of continuous and hierarchical communication required for one person to control many is difficult when the followers are underground, particularly for a charismatic leader who depends on personal contacts for his impact. Strong and centralized leadership is common in cults and relatively rare in terrorist groups, especially radical terrorist groups where the RAF appears to be a rare example of centralization. But the leadership difference is understandable in terms of situational differences that do not get in the way of the substantial parallels in recruitment and group dynamics.

Studies of cult formation and recruitment have been primarily sociological in emphasis, and Stark and Bainbridge (1979, p. 130) argue that cults can be valuable as models of the evolution of culture and institutions. Similarly, cults have potential as natural laboratories for the study of personality and social psychology. Issues of leadership, affiliation, compliance and internalization, affect and cognition, attitudes and behavior, in-group and out-group perceptions—these familiar issues are raised, and we believe likely to be illuminated, by research on cults. Similarly, a comparison of cult dropouts with terrorist dropouts, especially as their perceptions and evaluations of their groups change with time since dropping out, could provide data of interest for issues of self-justification and in-group/out-group perceptions. Social psychologists could profit by taking up an interest in cults that has languished since prophecy failed (Festinger, Riecken, & Schachter, 1956) and failed again (Hardyck & Braden, 1962) for dissonance theorists.

GROUP EXTREMITY SHIFT

An observation about terrorist groups is that they become more extreme only gradually over a period of time. This can be understood in terms of several different kinds of social psychological theory and research. First, the shift to extremity occurs as a function of change in the membership of the group. Festinger's (1950) theory of informal social communication specifies that strong differences of opinion on important issues in a group will lead to communication aimed at reducing opinion discrepancy. If this communication does not succeed in reducing difference of opinion to tolerable levels, the theory predicts rejection of the group members holding the most deviant opinions (Schachter, 1951). Thus activist groups do not turn one day to full blown terrorist activity, but develop slowly as an ever more like-minded nucleus is condensed from a cloud of less committed and less extreme opinions. The Baader-Meinhof gang condensed out of German antiwar activists, the Weathermen out of American student activists, and the IRA out of the long history of anti-English sentiment in Ireland.

Groups become more extreme in another and perhaps more impressive way: The same membership may become more extreme over time. In other words, the average of group members' opinions and behaviors becomes more extreme. Put in this fashion, the transition to terrorism is a case of what has been studied in social psychology as group extremity shift. The beginning of this literature was the observation that the average opinion of group members became more risky after group discussion of a series of decisions involving risk (Stoner, 1961). Then it was noted that group opinions sometimes became more risky and sometimes more cautious, depending on the issue discussed (Stoner, 1968). Moscovici and Zavalloni (1969) broadened the scope of the phenomenon when they showed analogous group shifts after discussion of issues of opinion and judgment having nothing to do with risk. The consistent pattern of group shifts, whether or not involving risk, was that average opinion became more extreme after discussion in the direction of the side of the issue favored by average opinion before discussion (Myers, 1978). Beyond the laboratory, natural examples of group polarization—for example, in group conflict and group counseling—have been cited (Myers, 1982) as supporting the significance and generalizability of group extremity shifts.

After a few false starts in the direction of leadership, diffusion of responsibility, and familiarization, research on group extremity shifts settled down to two competing explanations. The first, relevant arguments, asserts that the shift is caused by exposure to a biased set of arguments in the course of discussion, arguments reflecting the relative strength of the values invested in the sides of an issue (Burnstein & Vinokur, 1977). These values bias the initial group opinions in one direction or another and bias the production of arguments in discussion so as to push group members still further toward the favored side as they hear arguments that had not previously considered. This is a rationalist explanation of the group shift—a picture of members swayed by argument.

The competing explanation of the group shift is less rationalist. Called social comparison theory, this explanation holds that the group shift is caused by the desire of group members not to fall behind in their apparent recognition of and devotion to the side of an issue favored by the majority (Sanders & Baron, 1977). According to social comparison theory, group members tend to admire persons with positions more extreme than their own on the favored side and want to be at least as extreme as the average of their group. In other words, everyone wants to be above average in exemplifying group anchored values. Discussion reveals the distribution of others' opinions and those who are less-than-average extreme are moved to become more extreme.

It is now generally accepted that both relevant arguments and social comparison contribute to the group shift effect (Myers, 1983; Brown, 1986). Furthermore, these two explanations have been linked to familiar processes of group dynamics, in particular to the distinction between normative and informational social influence (Deutsch & Gerard, 1955). Sanders and Baron (1977) and Myers (1983) identify relevant arguments with informational social influence and social comparison with normative social influence.

There is some evidence to support this identification of group shift mechanisms with the familiar processes of group dynamics. Group shift experiments consistently found decreased variance of opinions after group discussion, and there has never been any doubt (Brown, 1965) that this effect of group discussion is to be explained in terms of group dynamics. But there is evidence (McCauley, 1972) that, for both risk and attitude issues, the decrease in variance is larger for groups showing the larger group extremity shift. If the variance decrease is clearly an effect of the usual group dynamics processes, then the group extremity shift associated with the variance decrease is plausibly an effect of these same processes.

The implication of the group shift research for terrorist extremity shifts, then, is that shifts can be understood as the product of normal group dynamics such as have been studied in thousands of groups of college student subjects. As groups shed less extreme opinions about how to solve political problems, the opinions of group members become more homogeneous. These more homogeneous opinions interact in group discussion to become even more homogeneous (variance decrease) and more extreme (group shift). At the bottom of the group shift to more extreme political action are processes of relevant arguments and social comparison that are expressions of normative and informational social influence.

A problem remains in this analysis. Terrorist groups move toward extremity not only in the sense that the average opinion of the group becomes more extreme, but in the sense that the average individual becomes more extreme. The latter sense was implied by Moscovici and Zavalloni (1969) in describing group shift as a phenomenon of polarization. But McCauley (1972) found that, for both risk and nonrisk issues, extremity shift can occur for the group average opinion but not for the average individual opinion. That is, the group average moves farther from neutrality on an opinion scale after discussion, but the average individual is not farther from neutrality. This can happen because some individuals start off on the opposite side of the scale neutral point from the group average and, after group discussion, move only to neutrality or to mildly favoring the side of the issue favored by the majority. Thus individual extremity shifts in terrorist groups should occur after the group has shed the deviate opinions that favored inaction or only legitimate action—that is, after all the members of the group are on the same side of neutrality on issues of political action (see Myers & Bishop, 1970). A testable prediction from this analysis is that laboratory group shifts should continue over multiple discussions of the same issue, if the issue is of sufficient interest that multiple and continuing discussions do not lead merely to boredom. After group members are all on the same side of the opinion scale, further discussion should produce both group and individual extremity shift. As far as we are aware, group shift research has been limited to studying the impact of a single group interaction involving only one discussion of a particular issue.

INDIVIDUAL EXTREMITY SHIFT AND MILGRAM'S STUDIES OF OBEDIENCE

Individual extremity shift in terrorist groups can also be understood by reference to Milgram's (1974) studies of obedience. The results of this paradigm are well known: Normal subjects given the role of teacher in a psychology experiment will give high levels of shock to a protesting "victim" in the role of learner. The strength of the situation is apparent in the high percentage of subjects who are completely obedient (over 60% in the strongest version of the situation), and the subtlety of this strength is apparent in the failure of psychiatrists, college students, and middle-class adults to predict that even one subject would be completely obedient. Complete obedience requires the subject to raise the level of shock administered from 15 to 450 volts, with an increase of 15 volts every time the learner makes a mistake. This escalation is a shift to increased extremity of behavior in the sense that the higher levels of shock are increasing violations of the norm against hurting an innocent other, and we are not the first (see Heskin, 1984) to see Milgram's obedience paradigm as a model relevant to understanding terrorists' escalation of violence.

Milgram theorized about the power of his situation in terms of the structure of authority and an "agentic shift" in which subjects moved from seeing themselves as responsible for their behavior to seeing themselves as responsible to the experimenter. Without detracting from the value of this analysis, we follow Gilbert (1981) in emphasizing an aspect of the paradigm that receives only one paragraph of attention in Milgram's book (p. 149): the gradual and sequential nature of the shock escalation. All subjects were given a "demonstration" 45-volt shock that most people perceive as little more than a tickle. Thus subjects have no reason not to give the first low level shocks, especially as they cannot know ahead of time how many mistakes the learner will make and the level of shocks they will be required to administer. Once started administering the shocks, a subject is on a slippery slope. To refuse to give the next shock is inconsistent with having given the previous shock and requires the subject to question what he has done to this point. A psychology of self-justification is set in motion that Milgram (1974, p. 149) recognized as consistent with the predictions of dissonance theory. Whether dissonance is understood, as in Festinger (1957), as pure cognitive inconsistency, or whether it is understood, as Aronson (1969) later suggested, as inconsistency between behavior and a positive self-image, there is clearly dissonance created for a subject who breaks off at the nth shock after having already administered n-1 shocks.

An extension of social comparison theory (Festinger, 1954) provides another way of thinking about the difficulty subjects experience in breaking off the escalation of shocks in Milgram's paradigm. In the same way that we need to compare ourselves with others, we need to compare ourselves with our previous selves. Albert (1977) has argued that the predictions of social comparison can be directly translated into predictions concerning when and about what we most need to compare our present selves with the series of past selves that stretches back in time. Thus a subject looking back at n-1 shocks administered is looking back at n-1 interpretations of the situation from a self who, on the basis of attractiveness, is a powerful influence toward a similar interpretation and a similar choice for the nth shock. We might say that the most credible and trustworthy source of persuasion on the nth trial is not the experimenter, but the subject himself or herself (see Bem, 1967).

Both the dissonance and the social comparison understandings of the power of Milgram's situation point to the importance of the small gradations in the escalation of shock. As Milgram (1974, p. 149) points out, the subject "is implicated into the destructive behavior in piecemeal fashion." Although theologians have long been concerned about the slippery slope from small sin to great evil, social psychologists have not much inclined to see the devil emerging piecemeal from behavior. There has been little research that builds on Milgram's paradigm, although, as Gilbert (1981) points out, the "foot in the door" effect (Freedman & Fraser, 1966) can be considered an example of the power of a graded behavior sequence with the gradations reduced to only two.

An example of more gradual escalation to extreme behavior—in this case self-destructive behavior—is provided by the form of funny business called a "jam joint" (McCauley & Handlesman, 1976). A jam joint is a store, usually working off the sidewalks or boardwalks of a resort area, where a special sales technique is used to sell poor quality merchandise for inflated prices. The technique is complex, but depends notably on harnessing group pressure, greed, and small gifts to shape a slow escalation of two behaviors: saying "yes" and passing forward increasing sums of money to the jammers. The pressure for self-justification is so strong that victims seldom come back to the jam joint to complain.

This analysis of Milgram's situation leads to a testable prediction (Gilbert, 1981): Less gradual steps of escalation should lead to reduced obedience. As far as we know, neither Milgram nor any later investigator has examined the effect of manipulating the number and gradualness of steps in the escalation of extreme behavior. Harrison and Pepitone (1972) came close to the kind of study needed in their examination of contrast effects in the use of punishment. They showed that adding a high but "forbidden" shock level to the control panel increased the amount of moderate shock subjects would administer to a "learner" rat. Though a manipulation of the range of alternatives, this study does not provide evidence concerning the effect of manipulating the gradations within a given range. Even in the absence of direct evidence, however, we feel confident that the extreme form of an ungraduated shock series—15 volts to 450 volts as the only shock levels available—would produce much less obedience than Milgram observed with the same range divided into 30 steps. To the extent that this analysis focuses on internal pressures to escalation, it points to the desirability of going beyond obedience and disobedience to determine the level at which the subject first demurs, that is, the level at which subjects would break off in the absence of external pressure ("prods") from the experimenter. In retrospect, it is curious that Milgram provided only impressionistic data on the timing and level of the experimenter's prods.

The above analysis of Milgram's model of obedience can inform our understanding of shift to extremity in the terrorist group. To the extent that social influence in the group involves the individual in behavior more extreme than would be preferred alone, the pressure of self-justification will erode inhibitions against violence and conduce to another and even more extreme step. The escalation seen in many terrorist groups, from violence against property to violence against armed representatives of the state, from violence against unarmed representatives or supporters of the state to violence against random members of the society represented in the state—the kind of escalation reported with special clarity in Thompson's (1985) account of IRA activities in Ireland—this escalation is promoted and supported by individual self-justification.

CONCLUSION

We began by reviewing what is known about terrorists as individuals and as groups. The conclusion was that terrorism is not understandable in terms of individual psychopathology; rather it appears to be a phenomenon of group dynamics and normal psychology. We went on to analyze research on cult recruiting, group extremity shift, and obedience in order to illustrate several aspects of terrorist behavior. Our analysis is barely as long as our description and obviously amounts only to a beginning. Understanding of terrorism could be enlarged by consideration of many other areas of research, including research on minority influence, moral development, and leadership. But we hope our description is detailed enough to stimulate and support further contributions to the social psychology of terrorism.

REFERENCES

Albert, S. (1977). Temporal comparison theory. *Psychological Review, 84,* 485-503.

Aronson, E. (1969). The theory of cognitive dissonance: A current perspective. In L. Berkowitz (Ed.), *Advances in experimental social psychology* (Vol. 4, pp. 1-34). New York: Academic Press.

Back, K. W. (1972). *Beyond words.* New York: Russell Sage.

Bainbridge, W. S. (1978). *Satan's power.* Berkeley: University of California Press.

Bassiouni, M. C. (1983). Problems in media coverage of nonstate-sponsored terror-violence incidents. In L. Z. Freedman & Y. Alexander (Eds.), *Perspectives on terrorism* (pp. 177-200). Wilmington, DE: Scholarly Resources.

Becker, J. (1977). *Hitler's children: The story of the Baader-Meinhof terrorist gang.* New York: Lippincott.

Bem, D. J. (1967). Self-perception: An alternative interpretation of cognitive dissonance phenomena. *Psychological Review, 74,* 183-200.

Billig, O. (1984). Case history of a German terrorist. *Terrorism: An International Journal, 7,* 1-10.

Billig, O. (1985). The lawyer terrorist and his comrades. *Political Psychology, 6,* 29-46.

Bird, F., & Reimer, B. (1982). Participation rates in new religious and para-religious movements. *Journal for the Scientific Study of Religion, 21,* 1-14.

Bollinger, L. (1981). The development of terrorist actions as psychosocial process. In H. Jager & G. Schmidten (Eds.), *Analysen sum terrorism* (Vol. 4, pp. 175-231). Opladen: West Deutscher Verlag.

Bollinger, L. (1982). Remarks made in "Psychology of the followers." Symposium sponsored by the International Scientific Conference on Terror and Terrorism. Published in the *International Journal of Group Tensions, 12,* 105-121.

Brown, R. (1965). *Social psychology.* New York: Free Press.

Brown, R. (1986). *Social psychology* (2nd ed.). New York: Free Press.

Burnstein, E., & Vinokur, A. (1977). Persuasive argumentation and social comparison as determinants of attitude polarization. *Journal of Experimental Social Psychology, 13,* 315-332.

Clark, E. T. (1937). *The small sects in America.* Nashville, TN: Harper.

Clark, R. P. (1983). Patterns in the lives of ETA members. *Terrorism: An International Journal, 6,* 423-454.

Cooper, H.H.A. (1977). Terrorism and the media. In Y. Alexander & S. M. Finger (Eds.), *Terrorism: Interdisciplinary perspectives* (pp. 141-156). New York: John Jay Press.

Cordes, B., Hoffman, B., Jenkins, B., Kellen, K., Moran, S., & Sater, W. (1984). *Trends in international terrorism, 1982 and 1983.* Santa Monica, CA: Rand.

Crenshaw, M. (1981). The causes of terrorism. *Comparative Politics, 13,* 379-399.

Crenshaw, M. (1983). Reflections on the effects of terrorism. In M. Crenshaw (Ed.), *Terrorism, legitimacy, and power* (pp. 1-37). Middleton, CT: Wesleyan University Press.

Crenshaw, M. (1984). The persistence of IRA terrorists. In Y. Alexander & A. O'Day (Eds.) *Terrorism in Ireland* (pp. 246-271). New York: St. Martin's Press.

Crenshaw, M. (1985). An organizational approach to the analysis of political terrorism. *Orbis, 29,* 465-489.

Crenshaw, M. (1986). The subjective reality of the terrorist: Ideological and psychological factors in terrorism. In R. O. Slater & M. Stohl (Eds.), *Current perspectives on international terrorism.* New York: St. Martin's Press.

Demaris, O. (1977). *Brothers in blood.* New York: Scribner.

Deutsch, M., & Gerard, H. (1955). A study of the normative and informational social influence on individual judgment. *Journal of Abnormal and Social Psychology, 51,* 629-636.

Festinger, L. (1950). Informal social communication. *Psychological Review, 57,* 271-282.

Festinger, L. (1954). A theory of social comparison processes. *Human Relations, 7,* 117-140.

Festinger, L. (1957). *A theory of cognitive dissonance.* Evanston, IL: Row, Peterson.

Festinger, L., Riecken, H. W., & Schachter, S. (1956). *When prophecy fails.* Minneapolis: University of Minnesota Press.

Freedman, J. L., & Fraser, S. C. (1966). Compliance without pressure: The foot-in-the-door technique. *Journal of Personality and Social Psychology, 4,* 195-202.

Galanter, M. (1980). Psychological induction into the large group: Findings from a modern religious sect. *American Journal of Psychiatry, 137,* 1574-1579.

Galanter, M., Rabkin, R., Rabkin, J., & Deutsch, A. (1979). The "Moonies": A psychological study of conversion and membership in a contemporary religious sect. *American Journal of Psychiatry, 136,* 165-170.

Georges-Abeyie, D. E. (1983). Women as terrorists. In L. Z. Freedman & Y. Alexander (Eds.), *Perspectives on terrorism* (pp. 45-60). Wilmington, DE: Scholarly Resources.

Gilbert, S. J. (1981). Another look at the Milgram obedience studies: The role of the graduated series of shocks. *Personality and Social Psychology Bulletin, 7,* 690-695.

Hardyck, J. A., & Braden, M. (1962). Prophecy fails again: A report of a failure to replicate. *Journal of Abnormal and Social Psychology, 65,* 136-141.

Harrison, M., & Pepitone, A. (1972). Contrast effect in the use of punishment. *Journal of Personality and Social Psychology, 23,* 398-404.

Heskin, K. (1984). The psychology of terrorism in Ireland. In Y. Alexander & A. O'Day (Eds.), *Terrorism in Ireland* (pp. 88-105). New York: St. Martin's Press.

Hoffman, B. R. (1985a). *The prevention of terrorism and rehabilitation of terrorists: Some preliminary thoughts*: Santa Monica, CA: Rand.

Hoffman, B. R. (1985b). *More than meets the eye: The seizure of the* Achille Lauro. Santa Monica, CA: Rand.

Hutchinson, M. C. (1978). *Revolutionary terrorism: The FLN in Algeria, 1954-1962.* Stanford, CA: Hoover Institution Press.

Janis, I. (1972). *Victims of group think.* Boston: Houghton-Mifflin.

Kellen, K. (1979). *Terrorists—what are they like.* Santa Monica, CA: Rand.

Knutson, J. N. (1981). Social and psychodynamic pressures toward a negative identity: The case of an American revolutionary terrorist. In Y. Alexander & J. M. Gleason (Eds.), *Behavioral and quantitative perspectives on terrorism* (pp. 105-150). New York: Pergamon.

Laqueur, W. (1977). *Terrorism.* Boston: Little, Brown.

Laqueur, W. (Ed.). (1978). *The terrorism reader: A historical anthology.* Philadelphia: Temple University Press.

Linton, R. (1943). Nativistic movements. *American Anthropologist, 45,* 230-240.

Lofland, J. (1977). "Becoming a world-saver" revisited. *American Behavioral Scientist, 20,* 805-818.

Lofland, J., & Stark, R. (1965). Becoming a world-saver: A theory of conversion to a deviant perspective. *American Sociological Review, 30,* 862-875.

McCauley, C. (1972). Extremity shifts, risk shifts, and attitude shifts after group discussion. *European Journal of Social Psychology, 2,* 417-436.

McCauley, C., & Handelsman, M. (1976, December). Sales tricks of a con artist. *Psychology Today, 9* (12), 78 ff.

Milgram, S. (1974). *Obedience to authority.* New York: Harper.

Miller, B. H., & Russell, C. A. (1979). The evolution of revolutionary warfare: From Mao to Marighella and Meinhof. In R. H. Kupperman & D. M. Trent (Eds.), *Terrorism: Threat, reality, response* (pp. 185-199). Stanford, CA: Hoover Institution Press.

Moscovici, S., & Zavalloni, M. (1969). The group as a polarizer of attitudes. *Journal of Personality and Social Psychology, 12,* 124-135.

Myers, D. (1978). Polarizing effects of social comparison. *Journal of Experimental Social Psychology, 14,* 554-563.

Myers, D. G. (1982). Polarizing effects of social interaction. In H. Brandstattler, J. H. Davis, & G. Stocker-Kreichganer (Eds.), *Group decision making* (pp. 125-161). New York: Academic Press.

Myers, D. (1983). *Social psychology.* New York: McGraw-Hill.

Myers, D. G., & Bishop, G. D. (1970). Discussion effects on racial attitudes. *Science, 169,* 778-789.

Newhouse, J. (1985, July 8). The diplomatic round: A freemasonry of terrorism. *The New Yorker,* pp. 46, 63.

Post, J. M. (1984). Notes on a psychodynamic theory of terrorist behavior. *Terrorism: An International Journal, 7,* 241-256.

Post, J. M. (1985). Hostilite, conformite, fraternite: The group dynamics of terrorist behavior. *International Journal of Group Psychotherapy, 36,* 211-224.

Rubin, J. Z., & Friedland, N. (1986, March). Theater of terror. *Psychology Today, 20,* 18-28.

Russell, C. A., & Miller, B. H. (1983). Profile of a terrorist. In L. Z. Freedman & Y. Alexander (Eds.), *Perspectives on terrorism* (pp. 45-60). Wilmington, DE: Scholarly Resources.

Salvioni, D., & Stephanson, A. (1985). Reflections on the Red Brigades. *Orbis, 29*, 489-506.

Sanders, G. S., & Baron, R. S. (1977). Is social comparison irrelevant for producing choice shifts? *Journal of Experimental Social Psychology, 13*, 303-314.

Schachter, S. (1951). Deviation, rejection and communication. *Journal of Abnormal and Social Psychology, 46*, 190-207.

Schmid, A. P. (1983). *Political terrorism: A research guide to concepts, theories, data bases and literature.* Amsterdam: North-Holland.

Schmid, A. P., & de Graaf, J. (1982). *Violence as communication.* Newbury Park, CA: Sage Publications.

Smelser, N. J. (1963). *Theory of collective behavior.* New York: Free Press.

Stark, R., & Bainbridge, W. S. (1979). Of churches, sects, and cults: Preliminary concepts for a theory of religious movements. *Journal for the Scientific Study of Religion, 18*, 117-133.

Stark, R., & Bainbridge, W. S. (1980). Networks of faith: Interpersonal bonds and recruitment to cults and sects. *American Journal of Sociology, 85*, 1376-1395.

Stoner, J.A.F. (1961). *A comparison of individual and group decision including risk.* Unpublished master's thesis, School of Industrial Management, Massachusetts Institute of Technology.

Stoner, J.A.F. (1968). Risky and cautious shifts in group decisions: The influence of widely help values. *Journal of Experimental Social Psychology, 4*, 442-459.

Sutherland, E. H. (1955). *Principles of criminology* (rev. by D. R. Cressey). Chicago: Lippencott.

Thompson, J.L.P. (1985). *Crime, social control, and political killing.* Paper presented at the Annual Conference of the Sociological Association of Ireland, Belfast, Northern Ireland.

Traub, S. H. & Little, C. B. (1980). *Theories of deviance* (2nd ed.). Itasca, IL: Peacock.

Wardlaw, G. (1982). *Political terrorism: Theory, tactics and counter-measures.* New York: Cambridge University Press.

Zawodny, J. K. (1983). Infrastructures of terrorist organizations. In L. Z. Freedman & Y. Alexander (Eds.), *Perspectives on terrorism* (pp. 61-70). Wilmington, DE: Scholarly Resources.